Bibliometrics - An Essential Methodological Tool for Research Projects

Edited by Otávio José de Oliveira

Published in London, United Kingdom

Bibliometrics - An Essential Methodological Tool for Research Projects
http://dx.doi.org/10.5772/intechopen.1001662
Edited by Otávio José de Oliveira

Contributors
Aglaé Baptista Torres da Rocha, Aitor Martinez-Garcia, Alex Doboli, Alois Matorevhu, Ana Carolina Ferreira Costa, Berta Ferrer-Rosell, Carles Mulet-Forteza, Christian-Daniel Curiac, Daniel-Ioan Curiac, Humaira Farid, Imtiaz Ali, Konstantinos Karampelas, Kumbirai Takawira, Maximilian Espuny, Mihai Micea, Muhammad Asif Khan, Muzamil Mushtaq, Nyarai M. Mujuru, Otávio José de Oliveira, Patricia Horrach-Rosselló, Simona Doboli, Suhaib Ali, Traian-Radu Plosca

First published in London, United Kingdom, 2024 by IntechOpen
IntechOpen is the global imprint of INTECHOPEN LIMITED, registered in England and Wales, registration number: 11086078, 167-169 Great Portland Street, London, W1W 5PF, United Kingdom

For EU product safety concerns: IN TECH d.o.o., Prolaz Marije Krucifikse Kozulić 3, 51000 Rijeka, Croatia, info@intechopen.com or visit our website at intechopen.com.

British Library Cataloguing-in-Publication Data
A catalogue record for this book is available from the British Library

Bibliometrics - An Essential Methodological Tool for Research Projects
Edited by Otávio José de Oliveira
p. cm.
Print ISBN 978-0-85466-803-8
Online ISBN 978-0-85466-802-1
eBook (PDF) ISBN 978-0-85466-804-5

Meet the editor

Otávio José de Oliveira is a full professor of the Production Department at the Faculty of Engineering and Sciences at São Paulo State University (UNESP). He is a senior professor in integrated management systems (2012), with a post-doctorate (2006) and Ph.D. (2005) in civil engineering, and an MBA (2001) and degree in civil engineering (1997). He works mainly in integrated management systems, sustainability; and industry 4.0. He was head of the Production Department, has served two terms as coordinator of the Stricto Sensu Postgraduate Program, and was coordinator and vice-coordinator of the Undergraduate Course in Production Engineering. He has more than 200 articles published in journals and conferences, more than 10 books and book chapters, and more than 100 post-doctoral, doctoral, masters, MBA/specialization, scientific initiation, and course completion work supervisions.

Contents

Preface

The development of high-level scientific research requires in-depth prior knowledge of the subject to be studied. This is the only way to guarantee novelty, relevance, and a real scientific and applied need for the intended object of study. Bibliometrics is the methodological tool that enables this condition to be achieved, and it goes further by also being able to be used, in many cases, as an end-research method.

This book aims to support researchers at various scientific research and production stages. It is a guide to using bibliometrics to identify and confirm relevant topics for scientific research projects (scientific gaps). It also presents bibliometric solutions for mapping scientific scenarios to provide researchers with valuable information on the state of the art on the topic being researched and on the leading players involved in producing this knowledge. Finally, it goes beyond the academic world and presents combined tools for identifying contributions to research projects from governments, companies, nongovernmental organizations, and so forth.

This book is made up of chapters by authors from different parts of the world, which gives it a cosmopolitan character that provides plural views on a topic that is deeply relevant to the scientific world: bibliometrics. The first part of the book contains chapters on the basics of understanding and implementing bibliometrics. The second part contains chapters with examples of how to apply this tool.

Among the many important bibliometrics-related topics dealt with in this book, one of extreme relevance to the scientific world stands out: scientific retractions due to errors in articles, ethical issues, plagiarism, and so forth. This analysis sheds light on a universe unknown to most researchers but that is recurrent and that needs to be strongly avoided.

Another new subject related to bibliometrics covered in this book is the mapping of technical–scientific scenarios. This tool makes it possible to add applied elements from patents, business and government actions, start-up initiatives, technical information from secondary databases, and other sources to the already consolidated bibliometric methods. These features will give the projects an applied character, which can make them more successful when their results are used in practice.

Finally, we hope that this book will be an important motivational and informational tool for carrying out quality bibliometrics on a wide variety of subjects. We wish you all a good read.

Otávio José de Oliveira
Full Professor,
Production Department,
São Paulo State University (UNESP),
Guaratinguetá, Brazil

Section 1

Foundation of Bibliometrics

Chapter 1

Bibliometrics: Application Opportunities and Limitations

Alois Matorevhu

Abstract

With the advent of information and communication technology, research is increasingly being published; hence, keeping abreast with current research in any field is challenging. Bibliometric analysis has the capabilities to deal with this issue, since it can be used as a rigorous method of accessing and understanding massive scientific data that is continuously created. Using various indicators, bibliometric analysis enables the impact of scholarly publications and research out of institutions and countries to be assessed. Through the assessment of dynamics in research, bibliometrics provides opportunities for managing massive research data and knowledge and identification of gaps. Despite these advantages, bibliometric analysis has limitations; hence, to successfully apply bibliometric analysis, one has to be aware of both opportunities and limitations. This book chapter seeks to enable bibliometric analysis users to make informed, balanced decisions between the opportunities bibliometric analysis provides and the accompanying limitations. Information that will assist bibliometric analysis will be generated in this chapter through analysis of bibliometric literature.

Keywords: bibliometrics, bibliometrics analysis, opportunities and limitations, scholarly publications, citations trends

1. Introduction

First, defined by [1], bibliometric analysis is useful in identifying essential information for various purposes like prospective research opportunities. Based on citations, biliometric analysis enables the identification and analysis of the performance of research articles, journals, institutions and countries. Bibliometric analysis provides a means to give direction in the development of research projects [2]. The publication pattern in the world has been impacted positively by the advancements in information and communication technology (ICT). The ease with which people acquire and share information rapidly and efficiently has been enhanced through the extensive availability of digital media [3]. ICT has increased the range and depth of any topic, the number of scholars working on any topic and the number of publications that describe findings in the same field [4]. Competitiveness has led many countries to increasingly invest in scientific and technological development, which is essential for a sustainable economy [5]. Among other things, this development has led to the publication of many research articles daily, which are available in international databases for dissemination as research output from researchers in various universities and countries [6].

In this context, bibliometric analysis is an important way of measuring, monitoring and studying research outputs. Biliometric analysis enables mapping and expansion of knowledge in a particular area of research, as well as showing connections between publications, authors and institutions [7, 8]. As a tool for evaluation bibliometric analysis is used to justify decisions on research policies, funds, job offers, promotions and support for research projects [9]. With knowledge continuously evolving, bibliometric analysis is crucial in revealing research gaps [2]. Continuously increasing research publications in any field are progressively making it challenging for researchers to keep abreast with knowledge that is being created. As [10] stated, bibliometric analysis has the potential to mitigate this challenge. As the research landscape continues to expand rapidly, it is important to apply efficient methods for identifying research opportunities. Within interdisciplinary research framework, bibliometric analysis proves to be able to discover promising research areas. Bibliometric analysis is important in locating research opportunities, as well as enabling productivity in science to be understood by evaluating parameters like the number of studies, citations, and h-index [11]. Bibliometric analysis assists in exploring literature for relationships between scientific culture and social science issues in publications indexed by Scopus Database [12].

Due to its rigour in gaining access to and making sense of massive data, bibliometric analysis is widely used [13]. The rigour of bibliometric analysis is hinged on its use of quantitative and statistical approaches to analyse written material and explain behaviours [1]. Dissemination and impact of scholarly publications can be assessed using a variety of indicators and measures through bibliometric analysis [14]. Productivity, quality of research within a field or discipline, influence of specific publications and ability to identify publishing and citation trends can be determined by bibliometric analysis [15]. It is also important to note that bibliometic analysis promotes understanding of the structure and dynamics of study topics, which helps to identify developments in research areas, key players and knowledge gaps, hence areas for further research [10].

Methodological foundations of bibliometrics are quantitative production, growth, maturation and consumption of scientific publications. In this sense, the term bibliometrics was originally coined by [1], replacing statistical bibliographies. Currently, massive amount of data published in academic journals, books, patents, proceedings, etc., are organised and stored in bibliometric databases. These platforms, that is, citations, keywords, titles, journals, authors, institutions, etc., provide valuable sources for performing evaluation of research output using bibliometric techniques [16]. Bibliometric analysis has become important for assessing a researcher's output [17], collaboration between institutions [18], impact of scientific investment in national R&D productivity [19]. Indicators that are used in bibliometrics analysis include number of publications, number of citations, number of non-cited publications, research field classification and normalised citations. Scientific maps which represent relationships among different actors like authors, institutions and countries, can enhance bibliometrics analysis. Small (1999) in [20] defines a scientific map as a spatial representation of how disciplines, fields, individual papers of authors are related to each other by their relative locations. Having introduced the chapter through preceding paragraphs, the next paragraph explains the methodology used to develop this chapter.

Any knowledge has opportunities as well as limitations it offers to users. In this context, this book chapter seeks to enable bibliometric analysis users to make informed, balanced decisions between the opportunities bibliometric analysis provides and the accompanying limitations. The methodology used to develop this chapter involved the critical selection of publications, mostly from journals. Analysis of selected literature was done with the view of establishing themes that were logically aligned with the purpose and title of the book chapter. Analysis done under these themes subsequently led to the conclusion that highlights key issues in bibliometric analysis.

2. Bibliometrics databases and software

Gathering and assessing bibliometric data is possible through the availability of various databases and software applications. Bibliometric databases are discussed in Section 2.1 and bibliometric software in Section 2.2.

2.1 Biliometric databases

2.1.1 Web of Science and Scopus

When a researcher has defined the research area, the next crucial step is selecting robust databases from which to source data for bibliometric analysis. Currently two major databases available internationally are provided by Thompson Reuters Scientific as Web of Science (WoS) (www.webofknowledge.com) and Scopus (www.scopus.com). Various academic journals [10], conference proceedings and books are indexed on these databases, hence many scholars locate relevant publications as well as evaluating their impact and citation trends [21]. The Thompson Reuters Scientific database (WoS) covers 9000 of the most important journal titles selected mostly on the basis of their citation impact [22]. Web of Science (WoS) website provides access through subscription to multiple databases and citation data for 256 disciplines (science, social science, arts, humanities). The original producer of WoS was the Institute for Scientific Information (ISI). Later the intellectual property of WoS was given to Thomson Reuters, and currently maintenance is the responsibility of Clarivate Analytics. Various formats such as full-text articles, reviews, editorials, chronologies, abstracts, proceedings (journals and book-based) and technical papers are covered by WoS [20]. This (WoS) database can be used to analyse the occurrence of publications by year, publication by source information and authors, journals, countries, institutions, thematic maps, and current trends in a particular research field [10]. Scopus website offers access to databases and citation data on life sciences, social sciences, physical sciences and health sciences. It covers 15,400 journal titles across natural and social sciences, art and literature [21]. Elsevier provides through subscription, access to Scopus, for three types of biliometic analysis data sources namely, book series, journals and trade journals [20]. Bibliometric analysis can be used to explore research or publication trends indexed by Scopus database. For instance, the authors [22] posit that relevant literature between scientific literacy and socio-scientific issues can be explored through bibliometric analysis. Scopus can also be used to determine the number of publications, citations and h-indexes for researchers [11] such as extensive multidisciplinary databases Scopus and WoS are sources of publications. These databases provide data that is used to compare the performance of research articles according to each platform and then corroborate, complement or refute the results [2].

Integration of research data provided by these platforms makes it possible to obtain robust results from bibliometric analysis. Using search strategies which reflect the research topic, study objectives and the limits of the research field, high-quality data mining is made possible. Specific terms to the research field, publication period, document type, language and area of knowledge are the main criteria used in bibliometric analysis. Before data analysis, articles that do not belong to the field of study should be eliminated from the search results [2]. As is common with administration journals, some publications do not use keywords, so the researcher needs to review titles and even abstracts in the case of inaccurate titles to identify terms or expressions that identify the main topics covered [23, 24]. Titles of articles are bibliometric data which expose the most cited articles through the number of citations received. Classification of articles according to the number of citations reveals those that are among the most researched literature. Generating a chart with the most cited articles helps to reveal the evolution of citations for articles over the years, hence clarifying articles which increased in importance in the scientific world [2].

2.1.2 Google Scholar and Microsoft Academic

While Scopus and WoS are the most popular databases, it is important to note that other databases like Google Scholar may be suitable for particular research fields or subjects. Google Scholar was launched in 2004 as a freely available website. Full text or metadata of scientific literature from peer-reviewed online academic journals, books, conference papers, theses, preprints, abstracts, technical reports, court opinions and patents are indexed on this website [20]. While there is an acknowledgement of Google Scholar's convenience, its extensiveness and precision have been questioned [10]. Previously known as Microsoft Academic Search, Microsoft Academic (MA) was relaunched in 2016. Currently, it has over 230 million publications, of which 88 million are journal articles.

2.2 Bibliometric software

Bibliometric software assists researchers in analyses of bibliometric data to identify research trends, collaboration networks and citation patterns. Some prevalent bibliometric software includes VOSviewer, ScientoPy, Bibliometrics and SciMAT. It is important for researchers to bear in mind that while strengths of bibliometric software are applauded, each software has weaknesses such that it is important to decide when it is appropriate to use each software. There is also Python package ScientoPy which provides many tools for bibliometric analysis which include data extraction, cleaning and visualisation. In addition, it can analyse citation networks, co-authorship networks and keyword co-occurrence [25]. An R package Bibliometrix provides a variety of bibliometric functions which include co-authorship analysis, citation analysis, and visualisation of bibliomentric networks [26]. Visualisation and scientific literature analysis in a longitudinal framework, implying consideration of changes in the research landscape, can be done using SciMAT, an open-source software tool. SciMAT has the strength of providing researchers with modules of all steps of science mapping workflow, involving data collection, pre-processing analysis and visualisation [27].

VOSviewer allows researchers to view bibliometric data in various formats like co-authorship networks, co-citation networks and bibliographic coupling networks [28]. VOSviewer is handy for analysing and visualising large bibliographic data sets and identifying trends and patterns in literature [29]. This software tool allows the construction and visualisation of bibliometric networks, with journals, researchers or individual publications as actors, based on co-citation, bibliometric coupling, or co-authorship relations [28]. VOSviewer software is also used to identify specific research areas by discipline from keyword co-occurrences of the citing articles. Visibility through referencing and author keywords is limited despite that bibliometric software tools are making a noteworthy impact and contribution to research. Therefore, there is a need to raise awareness and initiate discussions on the citing practices of software tools in scholarly publications [30]. Notably, each bibliometric analysis software has advantages and disadvantages; hence, users should select the appropriate software for a particular analysis.

3. Bibliometric analysis linked opportunities

Academic endeavours to create knowledge and understand the world are dynamic targets which continuously change and, hence difficult to attain. This continuously provides opportunities for doing research. Therefore as long as humans are on earth, research will continue indefinitely. Irrespective of the field, research requires a research plan and the establishment of connections to prior knowledge [31]. As a process, research leads to new insights, discoveries and innovations; hence, national development requires research of all kinds [32]. In order to keep abreast with advances in any field, respective researchers need to be aware of current research publications. This will ensure that their research is up-to-date with the latest developments and technologies [33], which may impact their work and enable them to adjust their research plans appropriately [34]. Bibliometric analysis is important because it makes opportunities available to researchers, funders, institutions and countries. Some of these opportunities are discussed below.

3.1 Effective use of resources

Duplications waste financial and material resources for both researchers and funders. Therefore, avoiding duplications in research by identifying promising research possibilities is important because effort and resources are appropriately used. This ensures that resources are effectively used and quality research is conducted [10]. Research gaps and promising study fields can be identified using bibliometric analysis by considering the number and distribution of research publications and themes. This way, research areas that have gaps are identified. Mapping appropriate information for a study through bibliometric analysis in the initial phase can ensure that relevant literature is considered for the construction of new research [2]. Such an approach avoids duplication of research projects, which ensures optimum use of resources and focus of effort on promising areas of fields of study.

3.2 Partners or collaborators identification

Partners or collaborators can be identified through bibliometric analysis [35]. Through analysing co-authorship networks and collaboration patterns, bibliometric analysis can reveal researchers working on similar topics or having complementary skills, which provides opportunities for interdisciplinary collaborations and partnerships. Chiroma et al. [36] note that bibliometric analysis has the potential to allow researchers to determine areas that need further development, as well as identify potential collaborators at author, institutional and country levels. This encourages research networking among individual researchers, institutions and countries.

3.3 Funding

Funders are increasingly requiring evidence that the research they support has the potential to impact society's innovations [37, 38]. If properly analysed, bibliometric indicators give a research project consistency [8]. There is a possibility of presenting objectives and methods of research work precisely and concisely by a researcher who develops a research project based on bibliometric analysis. Gaps to be filled by the intended research will be illustrated [2]. This gives potential funders confidence that the proposed research project will succeed; hence, they are willing to fund.

3.3.1 Funding and impact of research nexus

As an evaluation methodology, bibliometrics analysis applies quantitative analysis to measure patterns of scientific publication and citation, typically focussing on journal papers. Case study analysis, peer review, surveys and consultations may be used to assess the impact of research in various fields [21]. Evaluation and tracing of research trends and scientific quality output are performed by application of bibliometric analysis. As a strategic approach, funding agencies seek to evaluate the impact of the research they fund in order to ensure that the intended objectives are achieved. Bibliometric analysis helps funders to evaluate the research impact of higher education institutions and make informed decisions on funding [39, 40].

Inequality in funding research is widespread. One of the causes of this inequality is the bias of evaluation and funding mechanisms since some funders are more inclined to known research areas or researchers. Therefore, upcoming researchers can use bibliometric analysis to identify possible partners [41]. However, it is important to note that promising areas of research or researchers may lose funding for not being well known. To address this inequality in funding research, governments should create policies which promote increase in funding. In addition, assessment of project applications should be done carefully. Therefore, there is a need for fair evaluation criteria that focus on supporting innovative and risky research projects, avoiding preference for known researchers [42].

3.3.2 Funding acknowledgements

Funding is critical for research to be done [40]. There is no standard way of acknowledging funders by researchers, resulting in inconsistencies between journals and research fields. However, a reliable way of linking publications to funding schemes and funders can be achieved through funding acknowledgement (FA) data available on databases in Thomson Reuters' Web of Science (WoS) [40]. One of the key limitations associated with use of FA data from the Thomson and Reuters database is that it began recently in in mid-2008 to index FA data, for only articles included in Science Citation Index. FA for the Social Science Citation Index (SSCI) became available in 2015. Another important limitation to the use of FA to link funding agencies and published articles is the exclusion by some researchers of FA [43]. In some cases, researchers may include FA even if the publication is not closely related to the funding received. Nevertheless, false positives are reduced through the use of FA data from WoS since it allows a more precise and direct linkage of funding agencies and published articles [40].

The use of citations in bibliometrics is a standard practice whose limitations are acknowledged. In order to inform decisions on who to fund based on research performance, there is a need for a credible way to do this. Therefore, when comparing the scientific impact of different publications or groups of publications, normalised citation counts are usually preferred to raw counts. The normalised citations are calculated by dividing the number of citations of that article by the average number of citations published in the same year in the same field.

3.4 Bibliometric analysis application in evaluation

Bibliometric analysis can be used to generate useful quantitative indicators of collaboration and measures of interdisciplinary research. Bibliometrics analysis is an approach for measuring research output anchored on the methodological reliability of bibliometric measures. If a paper has many authors, there is no clear way of distinguishing relative contributions made by each individual. In practice, citations on papers are attributed to all named authors during evaluations. In order to achieve high-quality bibliometric analysis, there is a need for a clear understanding of the strengths and limitations of each of these measures, as well as sensitivity to the contexts in which they are used [21].

Tied to review by experts, bibliometric analysis increases the objectivity of and confidence in evaluation. However, caution should be taken when using indicators derived from publication and citation data, since some fields publish faster than others and citation rates vary. This points to the need for citation counts to be carefully normalised to account for such variations by field. Usually, normalisation is done by reference to the relevant global average for the field and for the year of publication. Since citation counts grow over time, it is essential to account for growth by year [44].

3.4.1 Premise of citation assumptions used in evaluation

For evaluation purposes, an extensive range of measures of research performance have been developed in citation analysis. The development of measures for bibliometric analysis is underpinned by important assumptions, which are:

1. document citation suggests the use of the document by concerned authors;

2. merits like quality, significance or impact of the document are reflected by its citation;

3. best possible work is cited;

4. citing document is related to the cited document;

5. although field adjustments can be made to take account of the number of citations that a paper receives relative to others in the same field, all citations are considered equal [21].

3.5 H-index research output measurement

The h-index is an effective parameter in determining academic strength [11]. An indicator receiving a lot of attention for measuring the quality of researchers and organisations is the h-index, since it shows papers that are highly cited [45]. H-index can be used to determine the impact of papers. Data on publication can be obtained through bibliometric analysis from Web of Science, and most prolific countries or individual researchers can be established using paper productivity as a criterion [46]. A study by [46] established a strong positive correlation (r = 0.864) between the h-index and the number of papers published by the countries. H-index was developed for evaluating researchers, and it has been extended to include academic output and the widespread effects of publications by researchers or countries [47]. The h-index is also an effective parameter in determining academic strength [11].

A country's overall scientific achievements in a specific field can be consistently estimated by the h-index, since it includes the total number of publications and citations. In other words, the h-index is designed to assess both the quality and quantity of scientific papers in a cumulative approach. Premised on this, Sezgin et al. [46] report a positive correlation between the quality and quantity in the field of special education of publications of countries. Deviation of positive correlation, especially the journal quartiles (Q), the level of international collaboration (IC%) and the percentage of open access papers (OA%) have a significant effect. The USA is the leading country in terms of both the number of published papers and the h-index. However, it is crucial to note that countries which make the most impact in terms of the widespread impact of the publications (h-index) are not those with the highest number of publications [46].

3.6 Ranking of institutions

Progressively bibliometric analysis is being integrated into methods of evaluation to assist R&D policymakers in making decisions. In countries like United States, United Kingdom and Australia, there is evidence of gradual shift in the past 10 years towards a model of university assessment and ranking using bibliometic measures. The Department of Health in England (Britain) has shown interest in using bibliometric analysis to assist in making decisions in R&D; hence, it has engaged RAND Europe's expert in this [21].

3.7 Discovery of research opportunities/identifying gaps

3.7.1 Authors countries, institutions, articles and keywords analysis gap and research trends identification

A researcher can know the most referenced authors through analysis of the most cited authors. This analysis may indicate to the researcher opportunities for co-orientation partnerships and participation in international research groups. One way that can be used to identify gaps is analysing the most commonly used keywords in articles on a given topic. The high frequency of keywords in the portfolio of documents analysed in bibliometric analysis is the criterion for measuring the relevance of a particular topic. This way, it can be determined whether a topic has been sufficiently explored or gaps exist. Researchers should pay attention to keywords that were used previously in articles but no longer used with such frequency. This may be an indicator of the exhaustion of a theme in literature. VOSviewer software is appropriate for this analysis since it automatically counts the number of keywords that are occurring in selected articles [2]. The implication is that the researcher will not waste effort focussing on such areas for research. Similarly, funders will not fund research in such areas.

Reading research articles is a way of identifying gaps. Gaps which are explicit in the text of an article, usually in the conclusion section, can be easily identified. Also, difficulties faced in conducting a study can provide explicit gaps that may originate new research. If research with similar objectives is geographically limited, then the gap is in the application of the study in other regions, countries or continents. Reading is another way of identifying implicit gaps in text. In order to identify implicit gaps, the reader/researcher carefully analyses shortfalls which are implicit in the text. The reader's experience with the topic is important for easy identification of such gaps [2].

3.7.2 Grouping, timeline, and analysis of interactions: gap and research trends identification

Timeline analysis, grouping topics analysis, and searching for similarities between various groups can be done with bibliometric analysis to identify gaps and trends in research. Mastery in the state of the art of the field being studied is required when topics are grouped into sub-areas. Analyses of most cited authors and articles, countries and research centres are important because, through them, rich information is extracted that helps the perception of similarities, formation of groups and identification of research trends to be made. Content analysis is the appropriate technique used to make groups, as the researcher identifies the most recurring topics. Visualisation of analysis can be facilitated with a chart that shows the frequency of occurrence of particular elements in literature, hence revealing the most recurrent topics, which are then used to form groups.

3.7.3 Citation analysis for gap identification

Bibliometic analysis enables researchers to identify impactful publications in specific fields. Analysis of citation patterns can reveal the most highly cited publications, giving valuable insights into the development of a research field over time. Observed trends can inform the development of new research projects, guide researchers on potential collaborators, and inform policy decisions in various organisations. Bibliometric analysis can reveal the most highly cited publications, hence identifying the most influential authors in a study field. Also, bibliometric analysis enables researchers to understand the current state of a research field and identify the most pressing issues that need to be addressed.

Identifying the most highly cited publications in a study field assists in the identification of gaps for further study, as well as providing insights into potential collaborations or funding opportunities. By quantitatively analysing publication and citation data [17], bibliometric analysis can be utilised to discover research opportunities in various research fields [48, 49]. Through analysis of publication and citation data, researchers gain insights into the most trending research topics in a particular discipline [50]. This helps researchers to highlight research gaps and possibilities to inform future research trajectories. Therefore, bibliometric analysis is a tool that can initiate impactful original research in addressing crucial societal issues, as well as widen frontiers of knowledge in various areas.

4. Bibliometric analysis limitations

4.1 Citation data bias

Attending to the limitations of bibliometric analysis can increase its usefulness. One such limitation is bias in citation data. Bias can be in favour of high-impact articles or authors from prestigious institutions at the expense of upcoming ones. To mitigate these biases, one can use altmetrics or complex citation analysis algorithms that account for quality and relevance of the citations [51].

4.2 Exclusion of qualitative data

Bibliometric analysis provides quantitative data at the expense of qualitative components of research. Qualitative factors like the research's quality or its impact on society are not catered for in the provision of data by bibliometric analysis. To address qualitative factors, it is necessary to include qualitative criteria like peer review, societal influence and ethical considerations. Through peer review, rigour of scientific discoveries and validity is ensured.

4.3 Interdisciplinary nature of research

Research is interdisciplinary in nature, yet bibliometric analysis is discipline-specific and this can impede interdisciplinary research. Against this background, efforts should be made to promote interdisciplinary bibliometric analysis by introducing cross-disciplinary indicators that capture the diversity of research collaborations.

4.4 Limitations to use of bibliometrics

- Different methodologies for collecting and reporting bibliometric measures use citation-tracking databases. This may produce significant limitations to some disciplines when research publications from various fields of study are indexed.

- Not every type of publication can be indexed by a citation-tracking database, and comprehensive coverage of research publications is not possible. This limited coverage is reflected in the research analytic tools (such as InCites and SciVal) that draw on data from citation-tracking databases. Proprietary citation-tracking databases (such as Web of Science and Scopus) index different collections defined by the publications their commercial enterprises hold. Google Scholar, while not defined by proprietary collections, is limited by search conventions that can include non-scholarly works.

- Academic discipline outputs include patents, papers in conference proceedings, produced systems developed and widely used, data sets or hardware and software artefacts, policy papers, white papers and reports produced for government and other public organisations, books or works produced and exhibitions. However, not all of these outputs are indexed equally well by citation-tracking databases.

- There is poor coverage by citation-tracking databases of research that is not published in English. Therefore, the field-specific context for research outputs like the extent and type of some research collaborations cannot be provided.

- Across disciplines and fields, the practice of attributing citations and collecting citation data differs. Citations in some fields accrue within a few years after the publication of work, while in some fields, it takes many years. Differences in citation practices carry over into every bibliometric measure that uses citations as part of calculating the metric, including the h-index.

- Gender bias is evident in citation practices, thereby underestimating contributions made by women researchers. This should be considered when conducting bibliometric analysis.

- Meaningful comparisons cannot be made for bibliometric measures taken at different times. Citations, as a key research bibliometric measure, accrue with time after publication. Also, the time required to understand the impact of a paper using citations differs by discipline. Citation databases change their methodology and journal coverage over time.

- Changes which arise due to use of bibliometric measures include how researchers choose to publish, increase in opportunities for enhanced coverage in citation-tracking databases, and what they choose to research. It may provide opportunities and incentives to manipulate metrics. When using bibliometric tools, cross-disciplinary differences may be misinterpreted as cross-disciplinary differences in research activity or impact itself [52].

Also it is important to note that while absolute numbers/rankings are easy to understand, population-weighted figures allow smaller countries not to be drowned out of analysis by bigger countries [53]. Bibliometric analysis application is not universal or the same across disciplines; hence, context needs to be considered.

5. Discussion

Bibliometric analysis allows knowledge gaps to be identified and ideas for areas of inquiry to be developed. Due to continuous change in the research landscape, experts in any discipline must keep abreast with the most recent research output in their field [30, 33]. Identification of new areas of study ensures discoveries are still relevant. Policymakers and funding agencies allocate resources to promising areas, and they put effort wisely to sustain research. Also, to benefit society through research and innovation, bibliometric analysis identifies areas where more should be done. An important application of bibliometric analysis is the identification of the most influential journals and authors in an area of research. This information is useful in designing future studies, formulating policy, and selecting research partners [54]. Comprehension of current research status, identification of research gaps, and new research fields are possible through bibliometric analysis [55].

Most cited works and authors can be identified by bibliometric analysis, which may show how a particular field evolved or is evolving. Analysis of co-authorship networks and collaboration patterns in bibliometric databases can show scholars working on similar issues or complementary talent, hence promoting multidisciplinary collaborations and partnerships [34]. Quality of data and accessibility in bibliometric analysis could be improved by adopting standardised metrics and instituting data-sharing standards. Such improvements can make bibliometric analysis a very robust tool for assessing the quality of scholarly work [10].

6. Conclusion

Bibliometric analysis offers opportunities to do research, avoiding duplications by identifying promising research possibilities. This ensures that financial and material resources are not wasted for both researchers and funders. Through analysing co-authorship networks and collaboration patterns, bibliometric analysis can reveal researchers working on similar topics or having complementary skills, which provides opportunities for interdisciplinary collaborations and partnerships. Researchers use bibliometric software to analyse bibliometric data so that they can identify research trends, collaboration networks and citation patterns. Some prevalent bibliometric software include VOSviewer, ScientoPy, Bibliometrix and SciMAT. It is important for researchers to bear in mind that while the strengths of bibliometric software are applauded, each software has weaknesses, such that it is important to decide when it is appropriate to use each software.

Although bibliometric analysis has application opportunities, it also has its caveats which should be taken into account for effective application. For instance, it cannot capture research quality, so the accuracy and breadth of bibliometric analysis depend heavily on data sources. It is important to note that bibliometric analysis is not a substitution for content analysis or other methods of gaining insight into a research field. However, notwithstanding these limitations, bibliometric analysis remains an effective tool for discovering new areas of enquiry and making informed decisions by researchers on where to focus efforts.

Author details

Alois Matorevhu
Mutare Teachers' College, Mutare, Zimbabwe

*Address all correspondence to: amatorevhu@gmail.com

References

[1] Pritchard A. Statistical bibliography or bibliometrics. Journal of Documentation. 1969;**25**:348-349

[2] Oliveira JO, Silva FF, Juliani F, Motta FCL, Nunhes VT. Bibliometric method for mapping the state-of-the-art and identifying research gaps and trends in literature: An essential instrument to support the development of scientific projects. Scientometrics. 2019:1-20. DOI: 10.5772/intechopen.85856

[3] Putra RP, Rachmawati I, Cholifah YW. Digital information media of the Salman ITB halal center in improving marketing performance of halal lecture program. Mediator: Jurnal Komunikasi. 2021;**14**(1):42-53. DOI: 10.29313/mediator.v14i1.6992

[4] Akoka J, Comyn-Wattiau I, Laoufi N. Research on big data - a systematic mapping study. Computer Standards & Interfaces. 2017;**54**:105-115

[5] Dragos CM, Dragos SL. Bibliometric approach of factors affecting scientific productivity in environmental sciences and ecology. Science of the Total Environment. 2013;**449**:184-188. DOI: 10.1016/j.scitotenv.2013.01.057

[6] Bornmann L, Leydesdorff L. Scientometrics in a changing research landscape. Science & Society. 2014;**2014**(15):1228-1231. DOI: https://10.15252/embr.201439608

[7] Gumpenberger C, Wieland M, Gorraiz J. Bibliometric practices and activities at the University of Vienna. Library Management. 2012;**33**:74-183. DOI: 10.1108/01435121211217199

[8] Campbell D, Picard-Aitken M, Côté G, Caruso J, Valentim R, Edmonds S, et al. Bibliometricsasaperformancemeasurement tool for research evaluation: The case of research funded by the national cancer institute of Canada. American Journal of Evaluation. 2010;**31**:66-83. DOI: 10.1177/1098214009354774

[9] Vogel R. What happened to the public organization? A bibliometric analysis of public administration and organization studies. American Review of Public Administration. 2014;**44**:383-408. DOI: 10.1177/0275074012470867

[10] Abdullah HK, Roslan FM, Ishak SN, Ilias M, Dani R. Unearthing hidden research opportunities through bibliometric analysis: A review. Asian Journal of Research in Education and Social Sciences. 2023;**5**(1):248-259. DOI: 10.55057/ajress.2023.5.1.23

[11] Hancı V, Altuntaş Uzun AG, Aksoy M, Bozkurt S, Büşra Otl B, Özçelik M, et al. H-index and bibliometric analysis of scientific production parameters of the assistant academic anesthesiology and reanimation specialist in educational institutions in Turkey. Journal of Academic Research in Medicine. 2021;**11**(3):234-240. DOI: 10.4274/jarem.galenos.2021.42714

[12] Murni WA, Suryanti, Suprapto N. Use of bibliometric software to explore the relationship between scientific literacy and socio-scientific issues. In: E3S Web of Conferences 450, 03009, ICoSBi 2023. London: EDP Sciences; 2023. DOI: 10.1051/e3sconf/202345003009

[13] Donthu N, Kumar S, Mukherjee D, Pandey N, Lim WM. How to conduct a bibliometric analysis: An overview and guidelines. Journal of Business Research. 2021;**133**:285-296. DOI: 10.1016/j.jbusres.2021.04.070

[14] García-Villar C, García-Santos JM. Bibliometric indicators to evaluate scientific activity. Radiología (English Edition). 2021;**63**(3):228-235. DOI: 10.1007/s00778-019-00539-y

[15] Thayyib PV, Mamilla R, Khan M, Fatima H, Asim M, Anwar I, et al. State-of-the-art of artificial intelligence and big data analytics reviews in five different domains: A bibliometric summary. Sustainability. 2023;**15**(5):1-38. DOI: 10.3390/su15054026

[16] Gutiérrez-Salcedo M, Martínez MÁ, Moral-Muñoz JA, Herrera-Viedma E, Cobo MJ. Some bibliometric procedures for analyzing and evaluating research fields. Applied Intelligence. 2018;**48**(5):1275-1287. DOI: 10.1007/s10489-017-1105-y

[17] Ellegaard O, Wallin JA. The bibliometric analysis of scholarly production: How great is the impact? Scientometrics. 2015;**105**:1809-1831. DOI: 10.1007/s11192-015-1645-z

[18] Skute I, Zalewska-Kurek K, Hatak I, De-Weerd-Nederhof P. Mapping the field: A bibliometric analysis of the literature on university–industry collaborations. Journal of Technology Transfer. 2019;**44**(3):916-947. DOI: 10.1007/s10961-017-9637-1

[19] Fabregat-Aibar L, Barberà-Mariné MG, Terceño A, Pié L. A bibliometric and visualization analysis of socially responsible funds. Sustainability. 2019;**11**(9):1-17. DOI: 10.3390/su11092526

[20] Moral-Muñoz JA, Herrera-Viedma E, Santisteban-Espejo A, Cobo MJ. Software tools for conducting bibliometric analysis in science: An up-to-date review. El profesional de la información. 2020;**29**(1):e290103. DOI: 10.3145/epi.2020.ene.03

[21] Pech G, Delgado C. Assessing the publication impact using citation data from both Scopus and WoS databases: An approach validated in 15 research fields. Scientometrics. 2020;**125**(2):909-924. DOI: 10.1007/s11192-020-03660-w

[22] Ismail S, Nason E, Marjanovic S, Grant J. Bibliometrics as a Tool for Supporting Prospective R&D Decision-making in the Health Sciences: Strengths, Weaknesses and Options for Future Development. 2009. Available from: https://www.rand.org/content/dam/rand/pubs/technical_reports/2009/RAND_TR685.pdf

[23] Juliani F, Oliveira OJ. State of research on public service management: Identifying scientific gaps from a bibliometric study. International Journal of Information Management. 2016;**36**:1033-1041. DOI: 10.1016/j. ijinfomgt.2016.07.003

[24] Gil-Leiva I, Alonso-Arroyo A. Keywords given by authors of scientific articles in database descriptors. Journal of the American Society for Information Science and Technology. 2007;**58**:1175-1187. DOI: 10.1007/s00778-019-00539-y

[25] Ruiz-Rosero J, Ramirez-Gonzalez G, Williams JM, Liu H, Khanna R, Pisharody G. Internet of things: A scientometric review. Symmetry. 2017;**9**(12):1-32. DOI: 10.3390/sym9120301

[26] Aria M, Cuccurullo C. Bibliometrix: An R-tool for comprehensive science mapping analysis. Journal of Informetrics. 2017;**11**(4):959-975. DOI: 10.1016/j.joi.2017.08.007

[27] Cobo MJ, López-Herrera AG, Herrera-Viedma E, Herrera F. SciMAT: A new science mapping analysis software tool. Journal of the American Society for Information Science and Technology. 2012;**63**(8):1609-1630. DOI: 10.1002/asi.22688

[28] Van Eck N, Waltman L. Software survey: VOSviewer, a computer program for bibliometric mapping. Scientometrics. 2010;**84**(2):523-538. DOI: 10.1007/s11192-009-0146-3

[29] Orduña-Malea E, Costas R. Link-based approach to study scientific software usage: The case of VOSviewer. Scientometrics. 2021;**126**(9):8153-8186. DOI: 10.1007/s11192-021-04082-y

[30] Tomaszewski R. Visibility, impact, and applications of bibliometric software tools through citation analysis. Scientometrics. 2023;**28**:4007-4028. DOI: 10.1007/s11192-023-04725-2

[31] Snyder H. Literature review as a research methodology: An overview and guidelines. Journal of Business Research. 2019;**104**:333-339. DOI: 10.1016/j.jbusres.2019.07.039

[32] Patel M, Patel N. Exploring research methodology: Review article. International Journal of Research and Review. 2019;**6**(3):48-55. Available from: https://www.ijrrjournal.com/IJRR_Vol.6_Issue.3_March2019/IJRR0011.pdf

[33] Frazzetto D, Nielsen TD, Pedersen TB, Šikšnys L. Prescriptive analytics: A survey of emerging trends and technologies. The VLDB Journal. 2019;**28**:575-595. DOI: 10.1007/s00778-019-00539-y

[34] Kroon N, do Céu Alves M, Martins I. The impacts of emerging technologies on accountants' role and skills: Connecting to open innovation-a systematic literature review. Journal of Open Innovation: Technology, Market, and Complexity. 2021;**7**(3):1-27. DOI: 10.3390/joitmc7030163

[35] Abdullah KH, Sofyan D. Machine learning in safety and health research: A scientometric analysis. International Journal of Information Science and Management. 2023;**21**(1):17-37. DOI: 10.22034/ijism.2022.1977763.0

[36] Chiroma H, Ezugwu AE, Jauro F, Al-Garadi MA, Abdullahi IN, Shuib L. Early survey with bibliometric analysis on machine learning approaches in controlling COVID-19 outbreaks. PeerJ Computer Science. 2020;**6**:1-37. DOI: 10.7717/peerj-cs.313

[37] Gläser J, Laudel G. A bibliometric reconstruction of research trails for qualitative investigations of scientific innovations. Historical Social Research. 2015;**40**:299-330. DOI: 10.12759/hsr.40.2015.3.299-330

[38] Bornmann L. How are excellent (highly cited) papers defined in bibliometrics?A quantitative analysis of the literature. Research Evaluation. 2014;**23**:166-173. DOI: 10.1093/reseval/rvu002

[39] Hugar GJ, Bachlapur MMB, Gavisiddappa A. Research contribution of bibliometric studies as reflected in web of science from 2013 to 2017. Library Philosophy and Practice (e-journal). 2019:2319. Available from: https://digitalcommons.unl.edu/libphilprac/2319

[40] Rushforth AD, Yegros A, Mongeon P, van Leeuwen T. How does 'undone science' get funded? A bibliometric analysis linking rare diseases publications to national and European funding sources. In: EU-SPRI Early Career Researcher Conferences; November 21, 2016; Vienna. 2016. Available from: https://arxiv.org/ftp/arxiv/papers/1802/1802.05945.pdf

[41] Wanga BS, Wua BD. Evolution of research on funding inequality in science: A bibliometric analysis. Procedia Computer Science. 2023;**221**:1200-1207

[42] Bromham L, Dinnage R, Hua X. Interdisciplinary research has

consistently lower funding success. Nature. 2016;**534**(7609):684-687. DOI: 10.1038/nature18315

[43] Costas R, Leeuwen TN. Approaching the "reward triangle": General analysis of the presence of funding acknowledgments and "peer interactive communication" in scientific publications. Journal of the American Society for Information Science and Technology. 2012;**63**:1647-1661. DOI: 10.1002/asi.22692

[44] Innovative Medicines Iniriative Joint Undertaking (IMI JU). Bibliometric Analysis of Ongoing Projects: Fourth Report: April 2014. 2014. Available from: https://www.imi.europa.eu/sites/default/files/uploads/documents/reference-documents/BibliometricReport4_Final.pdf

[45] Bartneck C, Kokkelmans S. Detecting h-index manipulation through self-citation analysis. Scientometrics. 2011;**87**:85-98. DOI: 10.1007/s11192-010-0306-5

[46] Sezgin A, Orba K, Orbay M. On the widespread impact of the most prolific countries in special education research: A bibliometric analysis. Shanlax International Journal of Education. 2022;**10**(2):59-66. DOI: 10.34293/education.v10i2.4334

[47] Schubert A, Schubert G. All along the h-index-related literature: A guided tour. In: Glänzel W, Moed FH, Schmoch U, Thelwall M, editors. Springer Handbook of Science and Technology Indicators. Berlin: Springer International Publishing; 2019. pp. 301-334

[48] Topal Z, Bahsi I, Tufan AE. Evaluation of the psychiatric research output from Turkey via Web of Science database: A bibliometric analysis. Psychiatry and Clinical Psychopharmacology. 2020;**30**(4):1-33. DOI: 10.5455/PCP.20201117083927

[49] Veloutsou C, Mafe CR. Brands as relationship builders in the virtual world: A bibliometric analysis. Electronic Commerce Research and Applications. 2020;**39**:100901. DOI: 10.1016/j.elerap.2019.10090

[50] Sofyan D, Abdullah KH, Hafiar H. The philosophy of sport and physical education: Four decade publication trends via scientometric evaluation. Physical Education Theory and Methodology. 2022;**22**(3):437-449. DOI: 10.17309/tmfv.2022.3.20

[51] Shakeel Y, Alchokr R, Krüger J, Leich T, Saake G. Altmetrics and citation counts: An empirical analysis of the computer science domain. In: Proceedings of the 22nd ACM/IEEE Joint Conference on Digital Libraries. New York: ACM Place; 2022. pp. 1-11. DOI: 10.1145/3529372.3530939

[52] University of Waterloo Working Group on Bibliometrics. White Paper on Bibliometrics, Measuring Research Outputs through Bibliometrics. Waterloo, Ontario: University of Waterloo; 2016. Available from: https://uwspace.uwaterloo.ca/bitstream/handle/10012/10323/Bibliometrics%20White%20Paper%202016%20Final_March2016.pdf

[53] Know Space in Association with Digital Science. Bibliometric Analysis of Research Linked to UK Space Agency Funding. 2021. Available from: https://assets.publishing.service.gov.uk/media/61090144e90e0703ba3ca026/UKSA_Bibliometrics_Report_-_FINAL_300321.pdf

[54] Song Y, Chen X, Hao T, Liu Z, Lan Z. Exploring two decades of research on classroom dialogue by using bibliometric

analysis. Computers & Education. 2019;**137**:12-31. DOI: 10.1016/j.compedu.2019.04.002

[55] Abdullah KH. Publication trends in biology education: A bibliometric review of 63 years. Journal of Turkish Science Education. 2022;**19**(2):465-480. DOI: 10.36681/tused.2022.131

Chapter 2

Technical-Scientific Scenario Based on the Triple Helix: Innovative Approach beyond Bibliometrics

Otávio José de Oliveira, Aglaé Baptista Torres da Rocha, Ana Carolina Ferreira Costa and Maximilian Espuny

Abstract

In scientific research, obtaining reliable information, ideally from several sources of evidence, is crucial for a comprehensive understanding of the subject under study. This chapter introduces guidelines for creating the Technical-Scientific Scenario (T-SS), a valuable tool complementing traditional bibliometric studies. The T-SS incorporates the Triple Helix (TH) model, analyzing industry, government, and academia contributions and their interactions. T-SS mapping consists of collecting, interpreting, analyzing, synthesizing, and presenting information about the topic of study, which can be explored from the perspectives of the TH spheres. Its elaboration relies on the integrative review scientific method, which enables the exploration of diverse sources of evidence, such as articles, patents, organizational reports, government laws, research funding agencies, scientific projects from universities, etc. Consequently, it is possible to propose policies, strategies, and actions tailored to the TH spheres based on the T-SS, thereby contributing to the development or enhancement of the field of study.

Keywords: Technical-Scientific Scenario, integrative review, Triple Helix, bibliometrics, innovative scientific method

1. Introduction

In contemporary scientific research, the need for robust methods is urgent, especially in the constant social and technological evolution. The rapid advancement of scientific information further highlights the necessity for innovative methods that allow researchers to conduct their research from new perspectives. Quantitative scientific methods, such as bibliometric analysis, and qualitative ones, such as literature reviews, have been used to explore and advance the state of the art in various research fields [1, 2].

Bibliometric analysis is distinguished by its precision, enabling accurate research and data analysis within specific knowledge domains. This approach helps identify emerging research trends, pinpoint scientific gaps, leading journals, collaborations between universities, and the contributions of researchers, among other significant elements [1, 3]. The advancement of scientific databases, such as Scopus and Web of Science, has significantly contributed to the widespread adoption of this method. Moreover, tools such as VoSViewer, Gephi, and Bibliometrix have further enhanced and strengthened bibliometric analyses, ensuring their reliability and robustness [1, 3].

Complementing bibliometric analysis with qualitative methods is a promising strategy [1]. For example, the integrative review (IR), one of these methods, enables in-depth exploration and synthesis of a given field of research, making it possible to develop new theories and contribute to proposing policies and practices based on scientific evidence [2, 4]. This method allows for identifying and analyzing documents from different sources and types using a more rigid standard to conduct scientific research [4, 5]. When adopting IR as a research method, many authors summarize previous publications without the necessary in-depth analysis, lacking significant contributions to the field of study. Moreover, such works often need to meticulously demonstrate the steps used in data collection, compromising the transparency and replicability of the research process [4]. This absence of a methodological protocol, recurrent in IR studies, can be seen as an opportunity for approaches that better structure investigative works. However, it is unrealistic to base the methodology on data analysis to deal with the interaction among the main spheres of knowledge production. In this case, the Triple Helix model, introduced by Ref. [6], is a solid theoretical framework for synthesizing universities, industry, and government interactions. The model suggests an active partnership among these three spheres, which creates networks for the free movement of knowledge and technology, leading to innovation opportunities [6]. It creates an environment where scientific and technical innovations can thrive to address the problems that come with it effectively—as it evolves into what is now known as the knowledge economy [7].

Therefore, this chapter introduces the Technical-Scientific Scenario (T-SS) mapping method, which provides a panoramic view of the current state of knowledge in a specific area. TS-S is based on the IR method and stands out as a relevant tool, complementing traditional bibliometric analysis focusing on quantitative metrics and productivity analysis. The T-SS incorporates qualitative elements from various sources of evidence, providing a more holistic understanding of the current state of knowledge and generating significant and relevant contributions.

The T-SS integrates the Triple Helix (TH) model, a robust tool for identifying and analyzing industrial, government, and academic contributions and their dynamic interactions. The structuring of the T-SS allows for the meticulous exploration of various evidence sources, such as articles, prominent authors, research funding agencies, patents, organizational reports, government laws, funding announcements, and best practices from industry, government, and academia. Incorporating diverse information sources is crucial for achieving a more comprehensive understanding of phenomena and promoting consistency in research. This approach mitigates the bias observed in studies that exclusively emphasize positive aspects within a specific subject, especially those focused solely on scientific literature [5, 8]. To achieve this, it is necessary to establish rigorous and replicable criteria so that the search strategy and the selection, collection, and organization of data and information are structured and standardized [4]. This careful definition of criteria will ensure the reliability of the T-SS mapping. Moreover, conducting this search on reliable and well-structured platforms and individually identifying relevant documents is crucial. These steps are fundamental to ensure the credibility and relevance of the results. The rigorous application of established criteria underpins the research and strategically guides TH actors based on the most up-to-date and relevant findings in the field in question. Section 2 presents these criteria and the steps of the T-SS in detail.

T-SS mapping unfolds into two distinct and complementary processes, technical and scientific. Initially, mapping the technical scenario involves identifying and exploring patent records, company reports, and governmental documents. Such sources provide crucial information about technological and management solutions and address incentives and public policies that contribute, in an applicable and practical manner, to the development of the theme under analysis. Meanwhile, mapping the scientific scenario is based on the solutions and best practices highlighted in the most relevant articles, the contributions of the most influential authors, the scientific material produced by prominent academic institutions, and the innovations derived from projects assisted by funding agencies in the area. Integrating these two scenarios enhances the comprehension of the multidimensional panorama associated with the research theme. The meticulously collected material is a basis for benchmarking based on scientific theory and the authors' experience. This process culminates, for instance, in the formulation of guidelines or recommendations, which can be systematized in many ways depending on the research objective.

In previous publications that used T-SS mapping as a research method [9–13], guidelines were developed for each sphere of TH, including strategies and concrete actions designed to maximize their impact on the topic studied. This method facilitates effective interventions by industry, government, and academia by promoting a deep understanding of technical and scientific contexts. Moreover, the interaction and collaboration among these spheres enhance the formulation of policies, strategies, and initiatives, significantly advancing knowledge in relevant research areas.

The T-SS mapping method substantially contributes to scientific research, industry, and society. These significant contributions include identifying trends and gaps in knowledge on a specific topic, guidance for strategic decision-making, promotion of interdisciplinary collaboration, support for developing public policies, encouragement of scientific dissemination, and unveiling scientific discoveries and advancements. In summary, the T-SS mapping method plays a crucial role in guiding various research areas, in policy formulation, and in advancing society through the promotion of significant scientific discoveries and the encouragement of efficient resource use.

Thus, this chapter guides T-SS mapping, assisting researchers in the challenging activities of gathering, analyzing, and critiquing works of several types, resulting in solutions or strategies related to the study area. It is anticipated that using the T-SS mapping method will result in a greater volume and higher quality of research and initiatives, tangibly improving the body of knowledge in various fields of study.

2. T-SS mapping method

This section will discuss the T-SS mapping process, illustrating it with examples from published works for better comprehension. The process has three steps, as shown in **Figure 1**, which are explained in the following subsections. It is important to note that when incorporating the T-SS method into their studies, researchers must grasp the significance of their work and its contributions to the area in question. Identifying and addressing potential gaps is essential to achieving the intended results.

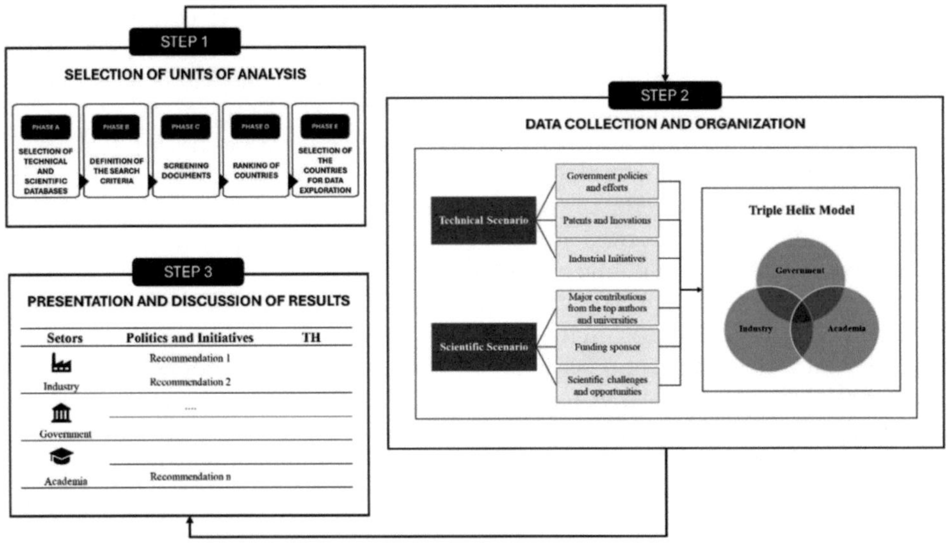

Figure 1.
Steps for developing the T-SS mapping. Source: Adapted from [10].

It is worth noting that the T-SS can take two primary forms: as an independent scientific work, with its mapping results constituting the research itself, or as the basis for broader studies, with the researcher using the information in the T-SS to support their study.

2.1 Selection of units of analysis

In this subsection, we detail Step 1, which involves selecting units of analysis before initiating data collection for the T-SS mapping. This selection is necessary because of the abundance of existing data, making a comprehensive analysis of all technical and scientific production in various areas impractical. In scientific research, the unit of analysis refers to the crucial elements under investigation. Researchers may designate countries, groups, industries, or individuals as the unit of analysis.

In this chapter, countries were used as units of analysis to procure varied information on the subject to describe the process of mapping the T-SS. The identification and ranking of prominent technical and scientific nations in the studied area were accomplished by cross-referencing data from relevant data platforms. By cross-referencing this information, researchers derive a new ranking from which the units of analysis are chosen. The number of units in a study varies according to its characteristics, available time, and number of researchers involved in the work. Following the selection of the units of analysis, the researchers gather country-specific data, as described in Step 2.

The process of selecting the units of analysis involves five distinct phases, as illustrated in **Figure 2**: selection of technical and scientific databases (Phase A), definition of the search criteria (Phase B), screening documents (Phase C), ranking of countries (Phase D), and selection of the countries for data exploration (Phase E). To aid understanding of the T-SS, we will use graphic elements from our published studies on Education 4.0 [10] and Solid Waste Management [9].

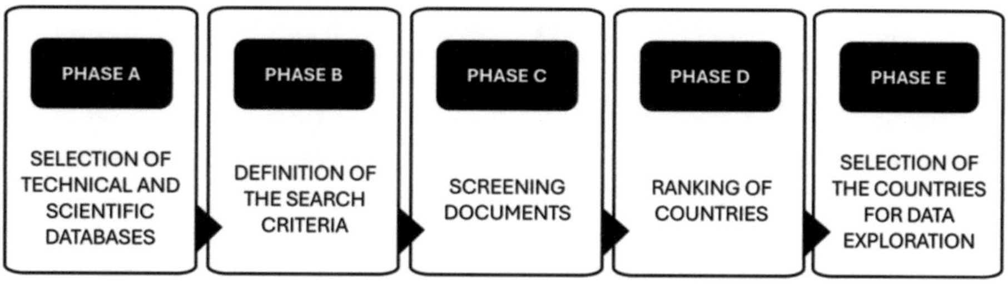

Figure 2.
Phases for selecting the units of analysis. Source: The authors.

In the Education 4.0 study, four countries were selected as the units of analysis, and a team of three researchers completed the research over 10 months. In the Solid Waste Management study, three countries were chosen as the units of analysis, and a three-member research team dedicated 18 months to the study.

In Phase A, researchers must determine the databases that will be used to select the units of analysis. It is advisable to use both technical and scientific databases during this stage to outline the countries to be chosen in Phase E. The technical database should be a reliable and comprehensive platform that enables the collection of patent information from various countries. In this respect, the Orbit Intelligence [14] and Lens [15] platforms stand out for their efficiency and reliability, making it possible to identify patents filed globally. For scientific data, the research team should use reputable platforms such as Scopus [16], Web of Science [17], and PubMed [18] to identify scientific articles and reviews. The first two databases cover content from various fields, whereas PubMed is focused on the medical domain. We use the Lens and Scopus platforms as examples to describe the T-SS method. The chosen platforms should ideally offer metrics such as the H-Index and impact factor. It is essential to mention that additional sources will be integrated later to gather more specific elements, as outlined in Step 3 (Data Collection and Organization).

In Phase B, researchers must establish precise search criteria by devising a strategy using specific terms related to the field of study [19]. In emerging topics where conventional databases may lack information, broadening search fields by including various term variations and using multiple datasets can enhance data collection. For example, in the article on E4 [10], the authors employed two search sets to identify documents directly or indirectly related to the topic, as depicted in **Figure 3**.

In this article, Set 1 comprises the term "Education 4.0" and its variations. Additionally, Set 2 combines terms related to Education and Industry 4.0 to provide a more comprehensive dataset. A second set of terms is recommended when a single set does not yield sufficient data. Boolean operators OR and AND establish relationships within the same set and between Set 1 and Set 2. For Set 1, researchers employ the OR operator to retrieve data containing terms like "Education 4.0," "Learning 4.0," "Teaching 4.0," or "Educational 4.0" in the title. The AND operator is employed when researchers narrow down a search to retrieve data containing multiple terms simultaneously. For instance, in Set 2, the AND operator connects two search subsets. This ensures that the results include terms from the first subset and those from the second subset, such as "Education" (from the first subset) and "Industry 4.0" (from the second subset). It is important to note that various operators, including AND NOT, PRE/, and W/, can be combined in different ways to align with the unique objectives of each researcher and the specific characteristics of their work. Scopus, for example, offers these additional operators.

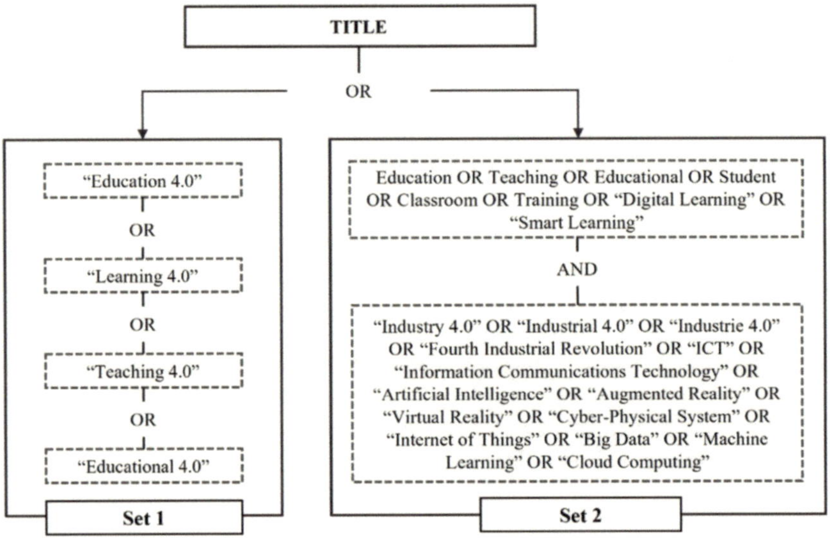

Figure 3.
Example of term sets for the search. Source: [10].

It is crucial to note that defining search criteria is an iterative process that requires multiple iterations on technical and scientific data platforms. After each search, researchers should evaluate whether the results align with the research topic. If needed, adjustments to the query, such as adding, changing, or removing terms and filters, should be made until the results accurately represent the state of the art on the topic. On the patent platform (technical data), it is recommended to conduct searches in the title for results closely related to the subject, as depicted in **Figure 4**. If the results are limited, searching for abstracts and claims of patents is suggested. We recommend limiting the search to the last decade to identify patents with recent contributions. The research team should also exclude discontinued, inactive, and expired patents.

On the scientific data platform, it is advisable to prioritize the search by focusing on the article's title, as this tends to result in more closely aligned documents. If the number of articles representing the state of the art is limited, researchers can enhance the search by adding keywords and abstracts. Defining filters such as time intervals,

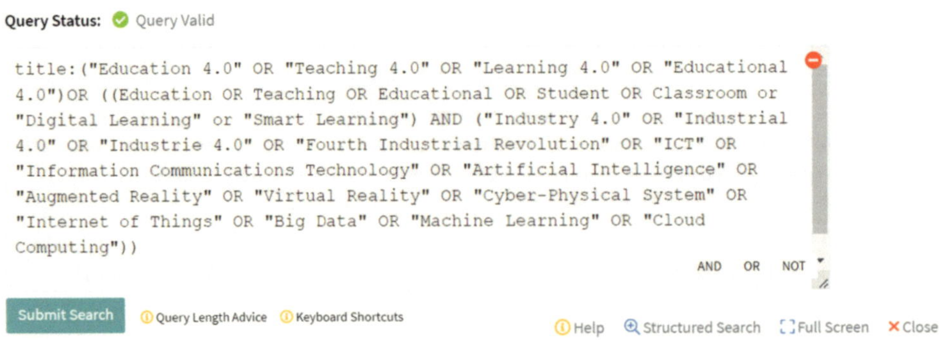

Figure 4.
Example of a query for searching patents on the Lens platform. Source: [10].

language, and document types is crucial. English, widely recognized as the predominant language in scientific communication, is recommended. For the time interval, prioritizing the last 5 years, including the current year, is suggested. However, this can be extended to 10 years or more in fields with low annual scientific production. Scientific articles or reviews are the preferred document types and are considered more relevant and reliable [19]. **Figure 5** depicts a sequence of queries in the Scopus database based on the terms used in the Education 4.0 article.

Screening the documents found on Phase C's technical and scientific data platforms is crucial. For the technical data platform, it is recommended that search results be exported to data management software, such as Excel, in "comma-separated values" (CSV) format. This allows researchers to evaluate patent information by eliminating duplicates, irrelevant documents, and those without the full text available, among other criteria.

On the scientific data platform, researchers are advised to review the title, abstract, and, if necessary, the entire article to assess its relevance to the research topic. Subsequently, researchers can use software such as Excel [20] or SciMat [21] to eliminate duplicate elements and irrelevant documents, simplifying material visualization and handling. Some platforms, such as Scopus, offer features to create lists, facilitating the sorting process directly within the platform. **Table 1** illustrates the process of creating a list using Scopus.

As a result of Phase C, the researchers will obtain two reliable datasets: patent data from the technical platform and scientific documents from the scientific platform. With this, the research team is ready to move on to the next phase, which aims to develop two-country rankings.

In Phase D, a first ranking must be drawn from the patent dataset. To do this, data management software, such as Excel, can be used to count and classify the patents by country, arranging them in descending order. If researchers choose to use Excel, it is recommended to use the "pivot table" tool to streamline this process. A second ranking should be drawn from the dataset of scientific documents (articles and reviews). It is recommended that this ranking be developed based on each country's H-Index. The H-Index measures the number of articles and reviews and their influence in the scientific field, considering their citations [19]. This enables the identification of the most productive countries in the subject based on the citations received. If the research team uses the "List" feature on the Scopus platform in the previous phase, they can obtain H-Index information for each country directly using the "Citation Overview" tool. This tool counts and displays the number of citations per scientific

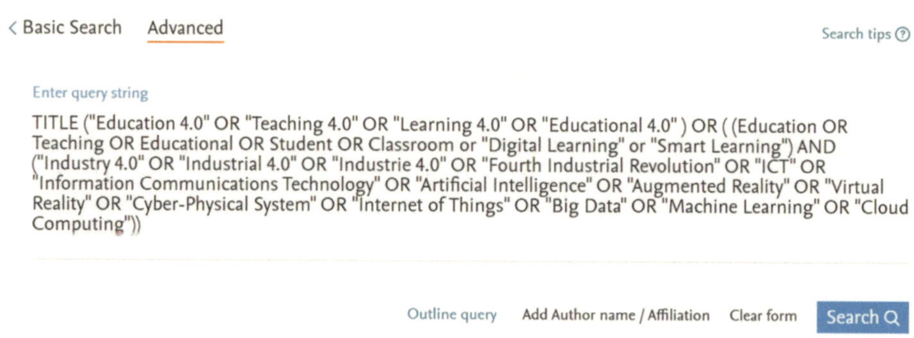

Figure 5.
Example of a query to search for articles and reviews on the Scopus platform. Source: [10].

Action	Explanation	Illustration
1	The research team should select the documents they want to create the list by clicking on the box next to the article number	
2	Then click on "... More" and select "Save to list"	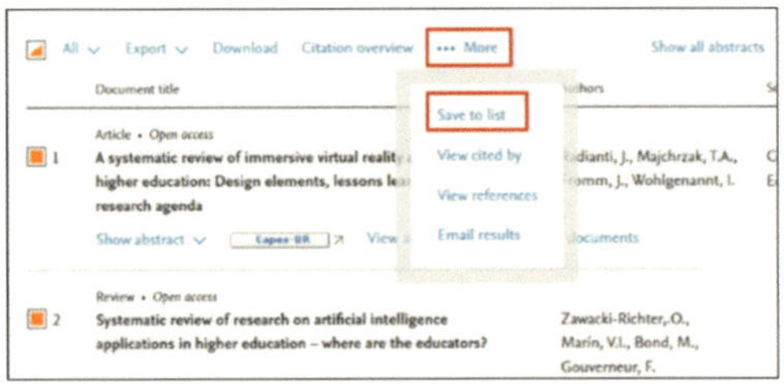
3	A window will open, and the research team should choose a name for the list and click on "Create new list"	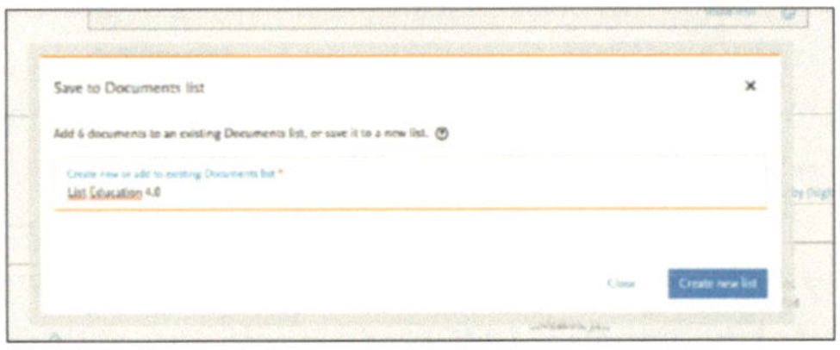
4	This will create a list that can be used by clicking on the icon with the researcher's initials and then "Saved List"	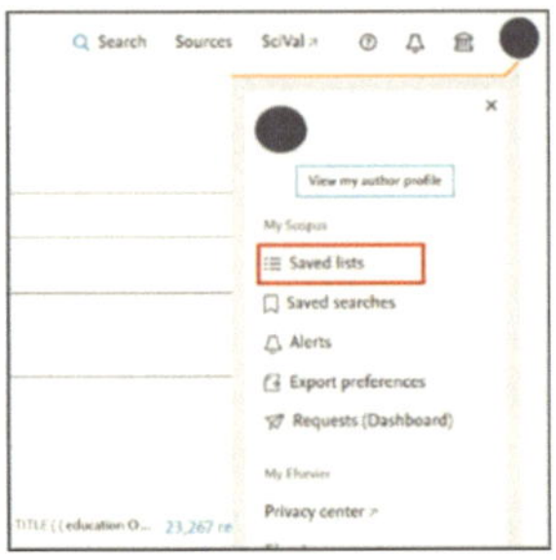
5	A page with all the saved lists will appear, and the researcher must click on the name of the previously created list	

Table 1.
Procedure for creating a list in Scopus. Source: Scopus.

document over the years. The research team should open the created list and select one country at a time to identify the H-Index of countries using the Scopus tool. This allows the creation of a ranking of countries in descending order on the H-Index. **Table 2** illustrates and details this process.

As a result of Phase D, researchers should obtain two different country rankings, the first with the number of patents per country and the second with the H-Index per country (**Figure 6**). The "Patent Position" ranks the top 10 countries with the most patents, while the "H-Index Position" ranks the top 10 countries based on the H-Index in the studied subject. The patent count is crucial for identifying innovative countries,

Action	Explanation	Illustration
1	Open the created list and select only one country to check its H-Index	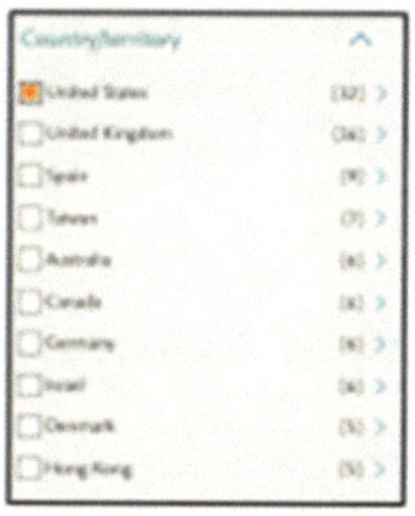
2	Click on "..." and select "View Citation Overview"	
3	A Citation overview window will open and show the country's H-Index, considering its publications on the topic saved in the list	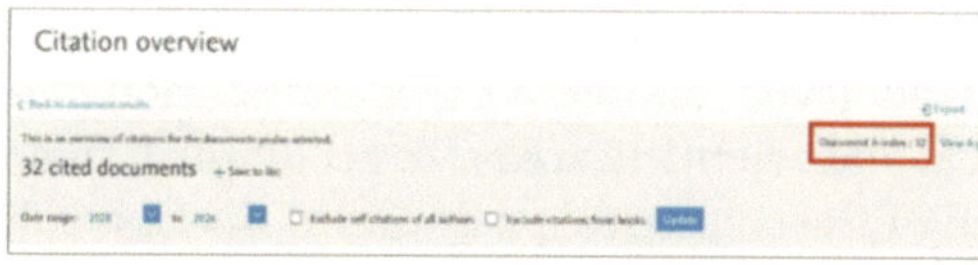

Table 2.
Procedure for obtaining the H-Index of countries on the Scopus platform. Source: Scopus.

Patent Position

N°	Countries	Patents
1	United States	273
2	China	271
3	India	178
4	South Korea	120
5	Canada	100
6	Japan	99
7	Australia	74
8	Brazil	50
9	Mexico	40
10	Singapore	27

H-Index Position

N°	Countries	H-Index
1	China	26
2	India	23
3	Italy	23
4	United Kingdom	22
5	United States	18
5	Spain	18
7	Brazil	17
8	Australia	16
9	Japan	15
10	Malaysia	13

Figure 6.
Country rankings. Source: Adapted from [9].

and focusing on those with the highest H-Index includes world leaders in research and innovation. This approach provides a representative and comprehensive basis for analysis.

Researchers can use this information to initiate Phase E, which involves selecting countries by cross-referencing the data. By integrating patent count with H-Index

Patent Position

N°	Countries	Patents
1	United States	273
2	China	271
3	India	178
4	South Korea	120
5	Canada	100
6	Japan	99
7	Australia	74
8	Brazil	50
9	Mexico	40
10	Singapore	27

H-Index Position

N°	Countries	H-Index
1	China	26
2	India	23
3	Italy	23
4	United Kingdom	22
5	United States	18
5	Spain	18
7	Brazil	17
8	Australia	16
9	Japan	15
10	Malaysia	13

Final Position Index

Final Position	Average	Main Countries	Patents	H-Index
1	1.50	China	271	26
2	2.50	India	178	23
3	3.00	United States	273	18
4	7.50	Japan	99	15
5	7.50	Australia	74	16
6	7.50	Brazil	50	17

$$Average = \frac{H\text{-}Index\ Position + Patent\ Position}{2}$$

Figure 7.
Final ranking of countries. Source: Adapted from [9].

data, a comprehensive understanding of a country's research and innovation capabilities is achieved, allowing the identification of global competencies in specific technological and scientific areas. To accomplish this, researchers calculate the arithmetic mean of the countries' positions in the first column of both rankings. This generates a new ranking of countries, where each country's position is determined based on the calculated average. **Figure 7** illustrates an example of this calculation used in the Solid Waste Management study [9].

As shown in **Figure 7**, the United States, China, India, Japan, Australia, and Brazil appear in both rankings and are therefore considered in the "Final Position Index." Their positions were determined by calculating the "Final Position Index," the average of the "Patent Position" and "H-Index Position." The resulting average is presented in the "Average" column and organized in ascending order. The lower the number, the more relevant the country is in the technical-scientific field, indicating good positions in both rankings. China, India, and the United States emerge as standout performers with the highest number of patents and a substantial H-Index compared to the other countries.

Consequently, these three countries were selected as the units of analysis for data collection in Step 2. In the case of this work used as an example, three distinct countries were considered. However, the number of countries analyzed can vary according to the number of researchers and the time allocated to the research. This approach facilitates the identification of countries that link theory with the practical aspects of the studied topic, reflecting national priorities in research and development. The "Final Position Index" helps identify current leaders in research and innovation, offering insights into areas with robust technological development and opportunities for international research collaborations.

2.2 Data collection and organization

After selecting countries, the research team initiates Step 2, involving the collection and organization of data. Researchers should strive to find relevant information from various sources in the selected countries that can enrich and boost the development of the topic under study. This includes exploring databases previously used in Step 1, consulting official government websites at the federal, regional, and municipal levels, and analyzing business reports. These technical and scientific data should be analyzed, synthesized, and organized according to the TH spheres (**Figure 8**). This universal collaboration model encompasses academia, which can also be called "university," government, and industries [22]. Consequently, the inputs from these three spheres, in which the participants define their specific roles and come together to achieve a shared goal, drive the technological and scientific development of the research field.

Figure 8 depicts the technical scenario encompassing policies and initiatives from governments and industries. The research team collects data from various sources, including official government websites, reports, and patents. Researchers should look for government policies, laws, and incentives that directly or indirectly boost progress in the field. For industries, the analysis of patents can reveal technological innovations relevant to the field of study. In addition, companies' Global Reporting Initiatives (GRI) may contain initiatives to develop the topic. It is recommended that researchers define a criterion for choosing the companies to be explored, such as those with the highest number of published patents. Alternatively, rankings drawn up by reliable business industries that provide financial information and analysis of corporate performance reports, such as S&P Global, can be used [23]. Alongside conventional companies, startups represent another source of valuable insights. They stand out by developing products and services that can offer innovative alternatives and emerging technological solutions. It should be noted that many data sources can be explored, and the choice depends on the specific characteristics of the topic or the amount of data available.

The scientific scenario comprises contributions from academia and its partners. Researchers must access scientific databases, universities' websites, and research funding bodies for data collection. Based on the H-Index, the research team can choose a specific number of authors, universities, and funding agencies for each investigated country *via* the scientific data platform used in Step 1. The volume of documents selected should be manageable according to the team size, time available, and other resources dedicated to the research. Researchers can select the most cited articles and scientific reviews to identify and analyze their most relevant aspects and explore their findings.

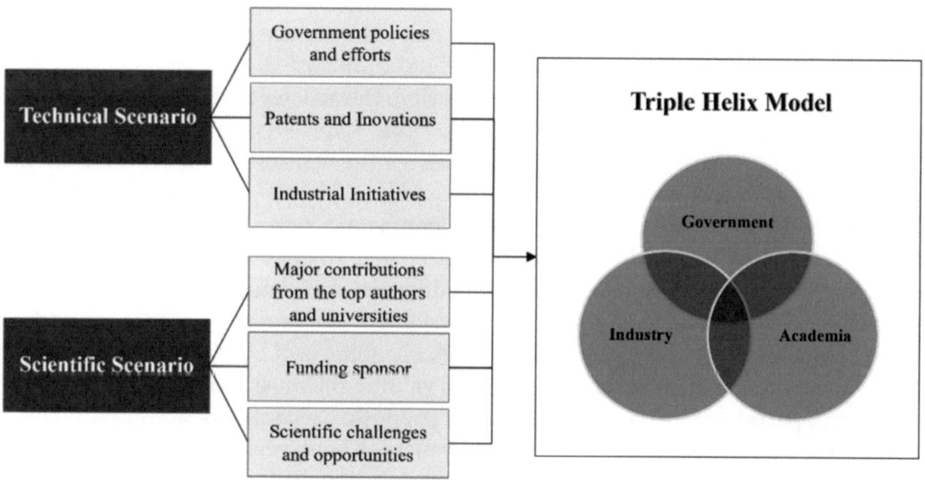

Figure 8.
Organization of data into the TH spheres. Source: Adapted from [10].

In this context, it is essential to determine and evaluate scientific opportunities and challenges related to the topic based on these scientific documents. This makes it possible to identify emerging or related topics that still require research and theoretical and practical barriers that may restrict the advancement of knowledge in the area studied. These opportunities and challenges should be grouped to make identifying significant patterns and trends in the field of study easier. This process highlights the current situation in the research area and serves as a guide for directing future research efforts.

Thus, the most relevant technical and scientific information collected in each country must be carefully selected and organized according to the TH model, with the most significant contributions being classified within each sphere (industry, government, and academia). This classification will serve as the basis for benchmarking, drawing up a framework with recommendations, and discussing the results, a process detailed in the following subsection (Step 3).

2.3 Presentation and discussion of results

In Step 3, researchers must focus on systematizing results in a logical, intelligible, and applicable manner. Additionally, it involves a comprehensive discussion of the implications of these results in the context of the existing scientific literature. It is crucial to emphasize that the scientific work developed using the IR method associated with the T-SS mapping goes beyond being a mere synthesis of previous works. It should provide relevant and valuable outcomes, contributing to the production of discoveries and the resolution of practical problems [4]. For this purpose, researchers need to integrate the knowledge derived from the T-SS mapping and scientific theory with their expertise, aiming to perform benchmarking leading to the formulation of recommendations, propositions, and the development of new theories and practical solutions tailored to the TH spheres.

Results should be systematized according to the topic's characteristics. This can take different forms of representation, such as conceptual models, frameworks, and research agendas. Authors should systematically present and discuss their findings in a way that effectively addresses the research question and fills the research gap, thus driving the advancement and development of the topic. Incorporating graphical elements, such as figures, tables, and diagrams, can enhance the clarity and objectivity of complex concepts, facilitating a better understanding of the results.

The results were systematized as a framework in the articles employed as examples for applying the T-SS mapping method [9–13]. **Table 3** presents a framework developed based on the TH that contains recommendations for the development of Education 4.0 (E4) [10]. These recommendations were proposed based on the analysis of information extracted from scientific articles, patents, company reports, and government laws, among others, combined with the authors' experience. To this end, the authors adapted and expanded the information collected from different data sources, considering their experiences on the topic and aligning it with insights from the scientific literature. This approach is particularly suited to the TH model, characterized by dynamic collaboration between industry, government, and academia, valuing the most innovative and best practices in a particular field of knowledge. By proposing recommendations based on the Technical-Scientific Scenario, the aim is to enable TH players to create development strategies, promoting innovation and tackling society's challenges [7]. It is worth noting that this framework is just one example, and each researcher should systematize and present their results according to the characteristics of their work and their skills.

Spheres	Domains	Politics and initiatives	Triple Helix interactions
Industry	Training	Create online training platforms for internal and outsourced employees	Industry and academia
		Use E4 tools in training for activities that provide risks to worker safety or that are difficult to implement and replicate	Industry and academia
		Partner with universities and schools to modernize curricula and conduct internships to develop the skills required by I4 in future professionals	Industry, government, and academia
	Technology	Partner with universities and schools for the development and commercialization of E4 technologies	Industry and academia
		Develop and commercialize educational platforms to enable personalized and adaptive education	Industry, government, and academia
Government	Politics and legislation	Develop a national policy with guidelines, objectives, and action plans for the modernization of education based on E4, which includes activities of training people, educational management, and development of infrastructure	Industry, government, and academia
		Develop legislation to ensure access to quality education with the development of students' digital skills	Government and academia
	Education	Boost the use of E4 approaches and technologies at all levels of education	Government and academia
		Create centers that support public and private universities to develop online learning platforms based on E4	Government and academia
	Economy	Create technological infrastructure for E4 development in public education	Government and academia
		Support financially the development of projects and research centers on E4 technologies	Industry, government, and academia
		Create financing programs and partnerships with companies to capacitate future professionals in I4 technologies	Industry, government, and academia
Academia	Education	Develop approaches for inserting E4 in teacher training	Government and academia
		Use E4 technologies to include students with disabilities in schools, universities, and the job market	Industry, government, and academia
		Use E4 in educational approaches to teach STEM areas	Government and academia
		Include and offer blended learning in their courses and programs	Academia
	Research	Investigate the impacts and challenges of integrating I4 technologies into education	Academia
		Propose solutions for integration of I4 technologies to teaching	Industry, government, and academia
		Map the skills and competencies needed for professionals to work in I4 and introduce them in the curricula	Industry, government, and academia

Table 3.
Example of proposed framework using the T-SS method. Source: [10].

As presented in **Table 3**, the proposed framework was systematically organized and directed toward the TH spheres highlighted in the first column. The second column specifies a domain of interest for each sector, a subdivision that becomes necessary to link the recommendations to a specific theme. The third column displays recommendations for policies and initiatives to be implemented by the TH spheres. In the example provided, these actions aim to overcome challenges, explore opportunities, and drive the development of Education 4.0. Finally, the fourth column pertains to the potential interactions between the TH spheres. Following the presentation of the framework, the authors examine and discuss each recommendation, considering the literature and highlighting its theoretical and practical implications.

Although each of the three spheres of TH has different roles, it is through collaboration that the most significant impact is generated. The university contributes to research and develops new ideas, the industry transforms these ideas into products and services, and the government creates policies and regulations encouraging this collaboration. When these three forces come together around a common goal, the innovation potential is amplified, resulting in more significant economic and social benefits than if each sphere acted in isolation. The interactive dynamic created by this cooperation is crucial for tackling complex challenges and promoting sustainable development [24].

As such, the TH model fosters the creation of collaborative research centers and encourages strategic alliances that break down traditional barriers, allowing for co-creating knowledge and solutions to overcome transdisciplinary challenges. By adopting this model, the spheres of TH expand beyond their original functions, promoting an integrated ecosystem that accelerates technological advancement grounded in sustainability principles [6, 24].

There has been considerable discussion about incorporating a fourth, fifth, or even more helices into innovation models to enhance understanding of the dynamics that drive innovation, particularly in sustainable development. By including dimensions such as the political, economic, educational, natural, and public spheres, the three traditional TH spheres, once central, would now share the same level within the expanded system. This shift could dilute the central role of these spheres, reinterpreting them as equal components alongside the new dimensions, potentially distorting the original model's value [22]. Although a system with additional spheres is still not entirely satisfactory, there is a clear need for an expanded model that reconciles innovation and sustainability, offering a more comprehensive framework for addressing contemporary global challenges [22].

3. Conclusion

This chapter outlines the steps of the T-SS mapping method, which is a valuable complement to traditional bibliometric studies. The T-SS integrates qualitative elements from diverse sources, including articles, renowned authors, research funding notices, patents, organizational reports, government laws, and research projects. These elements, framed within the TH model, facilitate the integration of initiatives across industry, government, and academia. Consequently, they provide essential inputs for proposing and discussing the work results.

Thus, the T-SS emerges as a crucial tool for researchers, enhancing the relevance and scope of their studies. Its capability to integrate qualitative elements enables the proposal of impactful solutions for the TH spheres, significantly advancing the topic under investigation. Throughout the T-SS mapping process, emphasis is placed on the vital aspects of properly defining search criteria, selecting units of analysis, and conducting replicable procedures. This emphasis aims to enhance the reliability and rigor of scientific work. While the definition is crucial, it remains flexible, allowing researchers to choose alternative criteria for unit selection, such as identifying critical industrial, governmental, and academic leaders. This flexibility is essential for adapting the method to the nuances of each field of study and enhancing the applicability of propositions grounded in the T-SS. Furthermore, based on the authors' experience and benchmarking of best practices, the proposed actions are adapted to the TH model, considering the inherent characteristics of its three helices and the capacity for mutual collaboration.

The T-SS contributes in a theoretical-scientific way to the development and deepening of the research field by conducting a comprehensive and integrative analysis of diverse data sources. Beyond identifying scientific opportunities, challenges, and technological trends, the T-SS fosters increased collaboration among industry, government, and academia on specific research topics.

From a managerial-applied perspective, the T-SS provides a strategic roadmap for shaping public policies, steering industrial initiatives, and directing academic research agendas. Through its emphasis on interactions among TH spheres, the T-SS facilitates the identification of priority areas for investment and collaboration, thereby promoting technological and scientific development. This pragmatic approach can guide the strategic allocation of resources and research efforts to maximize innovations' socioeconomic and scientific impact.

Future studies should explore integrating new data sources with analytical approaches to further advance and refine the T-SS. This exploration enhances accuracy and broadens the scope of the proposed method. Specifically, research using data from digital platforms, such as social networks and specialized forums, can provide novel insights into trends and prevalent themes across industry, government, and academia. The evolution of sophisticated analytical tools that integrate artificial intelligence and machine learning techniques can discern intricate patterns and intersectoral relationships within TH. These studies enhance T-SS's theoretical and practical comprehension and reinforce the groundwork for more efficient collaboration among the involved spheres. Furthermore, future research should prioritize exploring the implications of T-SS in diverse cultural and economic contexts and evaluating its adaptability and effectiveness in promoting sustainable development and innovation at both local and global scales. We also suggest that future research seek to deepen discussions and propose solutions for the inclusion of additional helices to the traditional Triple Helix model, considering both their theoretical contributions and empirical applications.

Acknowledgements

This study was financed in part by the Coordenação de Aperfeiçoamento de Pessoal de Nível Superior—Brasil (CAPES)—Finance Code 001; Conselho Nacional de Desenvolvimento Científico e Tecnológico [Grant number: 314918/2023-0]; and Fundação de Amparo à Pesquisa do Estado de São Paulo [Grant Number 2023/16971-7].

Conflict of interest

The authors declare no conflict of interest.

Author details

Otávio José de Oliveira, Aglaé Baptista Torres da Rocha*, Ana Carolina Ferreira Costa and Maximilian Espuny
Production Department, FEG-UNESP Sao Paulo State University, Guaratinguetá, Brazil

*Address all correspondence to: aglae.baptista@unesp.br

References

[1] Donthu N, Kumar S, Mukherjee D, Pandey N, Lim WM. How to conduct a bibliometric analysis: An overview and guidelines. Journal of Business Research. 2021;**133**:285-296. DOI: 10.1016/j.jbusres.2021.04.070

[2] Cronin MA, George E. The why and how of the integrative review. Organizational Research Methods. 2023;**26**:168-192. DOI: 10.1177/1094428120935507

[3] Ellegaard O, Wallin JA. The bibliometric analysis of scholarly production: How great is the impact? Scientometrics. 2015;**105**:1809-1831. DOI: 10.1007/s11192-015-1645-z

[4] Snyder H. Literature review as a research methodology: An overview and guidelines. Journal of Business Research. 2019;**104**:333-339. DOI: 10.1016/j.jbusres.2019.07.039

[5] Hopia H, Latvala E, Liimatainen L. Reviewing the methodology of an integrative review. Scandinavian Journal of Caring Sciences. 2016;**30**:662-669. DOI: 10.1111/scs.12327

[6] Etzkowitz H, Leydesdorff L. The Triple Helix—University-industry government relations: A laboratory for knowledge based economic development. EASST Review. 1995;**14**:14-19

[7] Cai Y, Etzkowitz H. Theorizing the Triple Helix model: Past, present, and future. Triple Helix Journal. 2020;**7**:1-38. DOI: 10.1163/21971927-bja10003

[8] Paez A. Gray literature: An important resource in systematic reviews. Journal of Evidence-Based Medicine. 2017;**10**:233-240. DOI: 10.1111/jebm.12266

[9] Anuardo RG, Espuny M, Costa ACF, Oliveira OJ. Toward a cleaner and more sustainable world: A framework to develop and improve waste management through organizations, governments and academia. Heliyon. 2022;**8**:e09225. DOI: 10.1016/j.heliyon.2022.e09225

[10] Costa ACF, Santos VHM, Oliveira OJ. Towards the revolution and democratization of education: A framework to overcome challenges and explore opportunities through Industry 4.0. Informatics in Education. 2022;**21**:1-32. DOI: 10.15388/infedu.2022.01

[11] Nunhes TV, Garcia EV, Espuny M, Santos VHM, Isaksson R, Oliveira OJ. Where to go with corporate sustainability? Opening paths for sustainable businesses through the collaboration between universities, governments, and organizations. Sustainability. 2021;**13**:1-33. DOI: 10.3390/su13031429

[12] Reis JSM, Espuny M, Nunhes TV, Sampaio NAS, Isaksson R, Campos FC, et al. Striding towards sustainability: A framework to overcome challenges and explore opportunities through industry 4.0. Sustainability. 2021;**13**:5232. DOI: 10.3390/su13095232

[13] Santos VHM, Campos TLR, Espuny M, Oliveira OJ. Towards a green industry through cleaner production development. Environmental Science and Pollution Research. 2022;**29**:349-370. DOI: 10.1007/s11356-021-16615-2

[14] Questel. Orbit Intelligence—Patent Search & Analytics Software. Questel; 2024 https://www.questel.com/patent/ip-intelligence-software/orbit-intelligence/

[15] Lens. The Lens—Free & Open Patent and Scholarly Search. 2024. Available from: https://www.lens.org/

[16] Elsevier. Scopus | Abstract and Citation Database | Elsevier. Scopus Comprehensive, Multidisciplinary, Trusted Abstract and Citation Database. 2024. Available from: https://www.elsevier.com/products/scopus?dgcid=RN_AGCM_Sourced_300005030

[17] Clarivate. Web of Science Platform. Clarivate; 2024. Available from: https://clarivate.com/products/scientific-and-academic-research/research-discovery-and-workflow-solutions/webofscience-platform/

[18] National Library of Medicine. PubMed. 2024. Available from: https://pubmed.ncbi.nlm.nih.gov/

[19] Oliveira OJ, Silva FF, Juliani F, Barbosa LCFM, Nunhes TV. Bibliometric method for mapping the state-of-the-art and identifying research gaps and trends in literature: An essential instrument to support the development of scientific projects. In: Kunosic S, Zerem E, editors. Scientometrics Recent Advances. London: IntechOpen; 2019. p. 21. DOI: 10.5772/intechopen.85856

[20] Microsoft. Free Online Spreadsheet Software: Excel. Microsoft 365; 2024. Available from: https://www.microsoft.com/en-us/microsoft-365/excel

[21] Cobo MJ, López-Herrera AG, Herrera-Viedma E, Herrera F. SciMAT: A new science mapping analysis software tool. Journal of the American Society for Information Science and Technology. 2012;**63**:1609-1630. DOI: 10.1002/asi.22688

[22] Etzkowitz H, Zhou C. Triple Helix twins: Innovation and sustainability. Science and Public Policy. 2006;**33**:77-83. DOI: 10.3152/147154306781779154

[23] S&P Dow Jones Indices. Performance Reports | S&P Dow Jones Indices. Perform Reports. 2024. Available from: https://www.spglobal.com/spdji/en/research-insights/performance-reports/

[24] Leydesdorff L, Etzkowitz H. Emergence of a Triple Helix of university—Industry—Government relations. Science and Public Policy. 1996;**23**:279-286. DOI: 10.1093/spp/23.5.279

Chapter 3

Automating Research Problem Framing and Exploration through Knowledge Extraction from Bibliometric Data

Christian-Daniel Curiac, Mihai Micea, Traian-Radu Plosca, Daniel-Ioan Curiac, Simona Doboli and Alex Doboli

Abstract

The steep rate at which the number of research outputs has been growing (e.g., books, journal articles, conference proceedings, patents, and other work in digital format) produces not only many intriguing opportunities but also significant challenges. Efficiently managing the research outputs in various very large digital databases has become much more difficult and error-prone than before. It is hard to precisely track all published documents in a way that is usable by humans to frame and explore new research problems. Methodologies and software tools are necessary to automate the time and resource-consuming activities in research. This chapter overviews the existing work and envisioned opportunities to automate the analysis of the research outputs available in digital databases to maximize the research quality and impact. A novel system architecture is also suggested to support research problem framing and exploration. The architecture includes smart recommender modules that also address other research activities, like researcher and institution assessment, bibliography recommendation, and research team formation.

Keywords: bibliometric data, research trend analysis, research problem framing, research team formation, publication latency

1. Introduction

The needs of modern economies and societies have continuously increased the importance of research work in science, engineering, humanities, and social sciences [1–3]. Research has uncovered new fundamental knowledge and formulated novel theories about the physical world; has learned new insight into living organisms and produced new treatments in the medical fields; has devised new engineering solutions that are faster, cheaper, more robust, and less energy-hungry; and has produced new studies and products that express human nature in both individual and social settings. The broad set of topics tackled by research endeavors has involved an increasing number of researchers and required an increasing amount of resources allocated by societies [4]. Often scientific opportunities and accomplishments capture the attention of the broad public across all demographics, bringing research to the attention of the media and other news-oriented platforms [5–7]. This situation not only creates unique opportunities and gives research a large visibility but also produces increasing expectations and responsibilities for the outcomes of research work.

The unprecedented pace at which the volume of research outputs has increased not only the produced opportunities but also the difficulty of the challenges must be addressed. Some of the research outputs in digital format include books, book chapters, journal articles, conference proceedings, patents, student theses, technical reports and documents, blogs, web pages, podcasts, design descriptions, computer code, and many more [8–10]. Ubiquitous, fast, and often free access to research documents in digital format supports a quick dissemination of the result. Democratizing the access to scientific outcomes has enabled interested professionals to stay updated with respect to the state-of-the-art knowledge in a domain and to participate to further improving and extending the knowledge. Moreover, new high-return research problems have emerged across multiple domains, hence requiring researchers from different domains to jointly work on common topics in bioinformatics, biomedical sciences, intelligent manufacturing, AI-driven medicine, and many more [5, 11–13].

Simultaneously, the challenges of effectively managing the huge volume of research outputs have also become much harder, less accurate, and more error-prone. For example, continuously and precisely keeping track of the published results is likely impossible due to the sheer size of the results and the difficulty of summarizing it in a way that is usable by humans for analysis, reasoning, and creative problem solving [8]. Even if somebody could somehow read all publications produced on a topic, it would be arguably impossible to cognitively produce a mental representation of the work. It is likely that important aspects and features of the work will be missed or misunderstood. Moreover, such a cognitive effort would be unsustainable for a longer period of time. Another issue is that different researchers have other perspectives and understandings of the importance of the research problems as well as diverse preferences and priorities on the available topics [14, 15]. Aggregating these different subjective perspectives into an accurate and comprehensive "map" of a research community is difficult [13]. Finally, as research work also has significant societal importance, like to give an advantage in the market competition, increased security, higher geo-strategic influence, and so on, the positions and roles of researchers and research groups are quite different: some are more altruistic, aiming to address *objective needs*, for example, scientific problems on understanding fundamental problems in physics, while some pursue *subjective needs*, which are tightly linked to the goals and objectives of the funding agencies, like research with a heavy commercial character [12]. Exploiting the opportunities while navigating around the difficulties is difficult and unsustainable without proper methodologies and software instruments that support the automated execution of the time and resource-consuming activities in research.

The chapter offers an overview about the envisioned opportunities of using software tools to automate the analysis of the published research outcomes, such as digital books, book chapters, journal articles, conference proceedings, and so on, to maximize the quality and impact of new research activities. A novel system architecture is presented to support two main research activities, problem framing and exploration. The chapter describes the main bibliographic databases used in research work, including their characteristics, like conciseness, relevance, selectivity, and objectivity, as well as the defining features of databases, like IEEE Xplore, PubMed, Web of Science, and others. A discussion of the impact of outdated bibliometric data is given, too. The chapter enumerates research activities that can benefit from automated bibliometric data analysis, that is, publication content categorization, research trend analysis, research gap discovery, researcher and institution assessment, research problem framing, bibliography recommendation, and research team formation. The research knowledge development process is also summarized, as a starting point for creating novel smart recommender systems to aid the activities of knowledge development.

The main contributions of the chapter are as follows:

- We have discussed an important aspect that must be considered during the creation of new automated tools for using bibliometric databases in research, which is that bibliographic information reflects a past state of research and not the current state. This time lag is important for highly dynamic domains. To mitigate this aspect, prediction techniques should be employed (see Subsection 2.1).

- We have presented the main bibliometric metadata fields that are available to support the research-related activities (see **Table 1**).

Paper Metadata Field	**publication content categorization**	**research trend analysis**	**research gap discovery**	**researcher/ institution assessment**	**research theme framing**	**bibliography recommendation**
title	✓	✓	✓	✓	✓	✓
abstract	✓	✓	✓	✓	✓	✓
keywords	✓	✓	✓	✓	✓	✓
document ID	—	—	—	✓	✓	✓
document type (e.g., review, article)	—	—	—	—	—	✓
access (e.g., open, close, unavailable)	—	—	—	—	—	✓
author name	—	—	—	✓	✓	✓
author affiliation	—	—	—	✓	—	✓
author ID	—	—	—	✓	✓	✓
references	—	—	—	—	—	✓
citation count	—	✓	—	✓	✓	✓
citing patent count	—	✓	—	✓	✓	✓
downloads count	—	✓	—	✓	✓	✓
year	✓	✓	✓	✓	✓	✓

Table 1.
Metadata Fields Used in research-related activities.

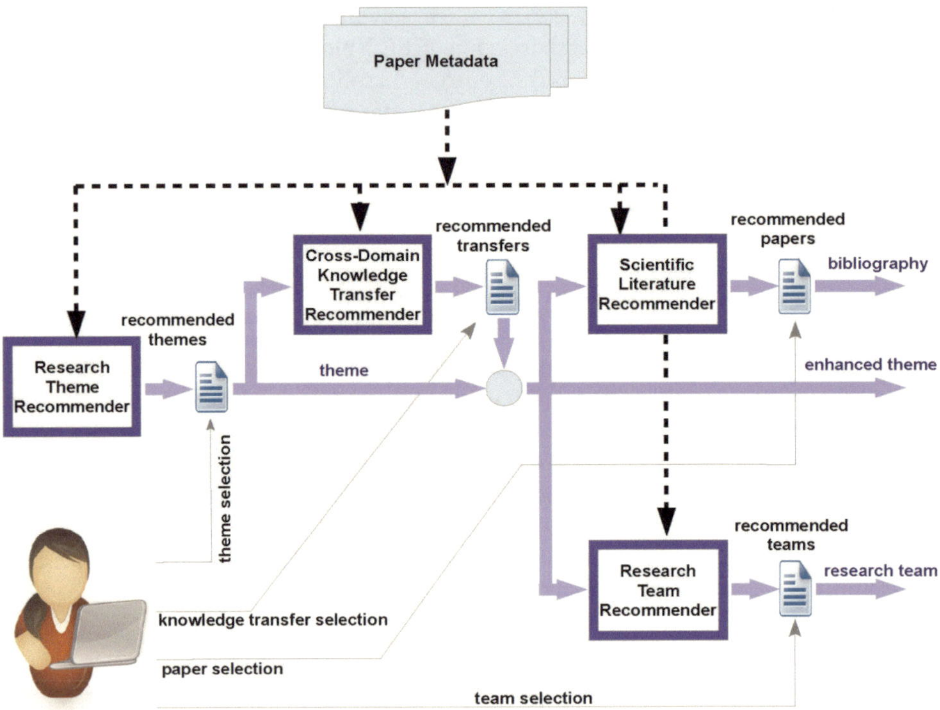

Figure 1.
System architecture for automated research problem framing and exploration.

- We have described a novel framework for encapsulating insights from bibliometric metadata into research activities (e.g., the multi-recommender system in **Figure 1**).

The chapter has the following structure. Section 2 describes the characteristics of the bibliographic metadata used in summarizing research documents in databases. Section 3 focuses on enumerating the research activities that can benefit from bibliometric information. Section 4 explains the research knowledge development process. A proposed system architecture for automated research problem framing and exploration is offered in Section 5. Conclusions end the chapter.

2. Bibliographic metadata as a research marker

The fast growth in the number of scientific achievements, projects, and researchers, as well as the continuous emergence of new scientific fields, has resulted in an unprecedented expansion in the number of research publications, including journals, conference proceedings, technical reports, patents, dissertations, and books. Comprehensively surveying a very large number of publications becomes increasingly time-consuming, error-prone, and arguably unsustainable without resorting to the already processed, analyzed, and summarized content indexed in bibliographic databases. As they are a collection of uniform descriptors of scientific documents (like metadata records) that usually include specific data elements to identify the publication, for example, title, authors, publisher, year, and additional supporting information, such as keywords, abstract, citation counts, and references, bibliographic databases provide a rich and valuable source of research-related information. The information has the following characteristics:

- Conciseness and accuracy: Bibliographic records are compact and robust representations of the publications and the research that supports them.

- Relevance: The information included in bibliographic records provides the means to not only identify the publications but also summarize its scientific content based on publication title, keywords, and abstract.

- Selectivity: Grounded in the impossibility of following the entire body of scientific publications and in the need to eliminate irrelevant, duplicate, fake, and low-quality publications, major bibliographic databases have devised means to control their content, for example, by selecting and adopting a whitelist of reputable publications.

- Objectivity: The bibliographic records are usually not subjected to outside influence and contamination.

The mentioned characteristics are the key support for guiding, shaping, and sustaining scientific research, even though some drawbacks, such as the subscription-based access to highly regarded bibliometric databases (e.g., Scopus and Web of Science), a limited access to full-text, the usage of other languages than English, and outdated bibliographic data, are also possible.

2.1 Addressing outdated bibliometric data

Besides the discussed benefits, a possible limitation of bibliometric data characteristic, outdated data, can limit its effective utilization in research-related activities, mainly in the case of fast-paced domains. This limitation has its roots in the time lag δ between the research completion and the moment the related publications are indexed in bibliometric databases, as expressed by:

$$\delta = \delta_{MWT} + \delta_{PL} + \delta_{PIL}, \tag{1}$$

where parameters δ_{MWT}, δ_{PL}, and δ_{PIL} represent the manuscript-writing time, the research publication latency, and the publication indexing latency, respectively.

The manuscript-writing time δ_{MWT} is the time interval between completing the research and submitting the related paper. It includes specific activities, including writing the original draft, reviewing, editing, and finding the right publication to submit the manuscript. Its value depends on the authors' expertise and experience and the type of publication, having lower values for short communications, and which is gradually increased for regular-length papers, book chapters, and books, that is, from a few days or weeks to months or even years.

The publication latency δ_{PL}, also known as publication time or editorial handling time, is a specific characteristic of the publication (e.g., journal) to which the research results are submitted for review and publication. It is defined as the average time interval between the moment a manuscript is submitted and the moment the manuscript is published [8]. Since this information is not stored in bibliometric databases, it needs to be either acquired from the publication's website, if this information is available, or approximated by averaging the time needed to publish the most recent corpus of research papers. In the latter case, the submission date and publication date must be manually extracted from each of the published versions of the papers. In a recent study for biomedical journals, the publication time is between 91 and 639 days [16].

The publication indexing latency δ_{PIL} represents the time lag between the manuscript publication and the time it appears in a bibliometric database. It depends not only on the bibliometric database indexing services but also on the time it takes the publication to send the manuscript-related record in the appropriate format to be indexed in the database. This time interval may vary from a few days to a few months.

As a consequence of the delays, bibliometric data do not reflect the present state of scientific research but a past moment. The effect of the delayed representation needs to be mitigated through appropriate techniques to increase the accuracy in estimating and understanding the status of the current scientific research and its related trends. Such techniques can utilize suitable forecasting methods to evaluate the current state from bibliometric data. Hence, we need to derive the number of prediction steps N, which depends on the delay δ and on the time step size Δt. The following formula can be used:

$$N = \lfloor \frac{\delta}{\Delta t} \rceil, \tag{2}$$

where function $\lfloor . \rceil$ is the rounding function (i.e., nearest integer function), and the two quantities of the right side of the Eq. (2) have the same time measurement unit (e.g., year).

To exemplify how the influence of parameter δ can be reduced by using forecasting techniques, we compared the research trends with and without δ-correction against the real trend (ground truth). We considered the time evolution of occurrences for the key term 'automatic test pattern generation' in the bibliographic metadata for papers published in IEEE Transactions on Computer-Aided Design of Integrated Circuits and Systems (TCAD). The paper metadata were acquired from the IEEE Xplore database. To identify the given key term in fields 'Title,' 'Keyword,' and 'Abstract,' a TagMe procedure with a link-probability, $lp = 0.1$, was utilized, following the same methodology as the one described in Ref. [8].

Figure 2 plots the time series of the normalized document frequency *ndf* [17] for the mentioned key term during the years 2013–2023. We started with devising the number of prediction steps N according to Eqs. (1) and (2):

$$N = \lfloor \frac{\delta_{MWT} + \delta_{PL} + \delta_{PIL}}{\Delta t} \rceil = \lfloor \frac{0.2 + 0.55 + 0.1}{1} \rceil = 1\,[year], \tag{3}$$

where the manuscript-writing time δ_{MWT} and the publication indexing latency δ_{PIL} were considered to be about 2 month and 1 month, respectively, and the research publication latency about 0.55, as computed in Ref. [8].

To find the trend for year 2022 without correction (shown as a black line), we considered only the observations from the years 2013–2022 (depicted using light-blue bars). For the trend with correction (the red-dotted line), we added the pink bar having the value obtained using an autoARIMA prediction method with the best parameters, $(p, d, q) = (1,0,0)$. Finally, the real trend (the blue-dashed line) was computed using the observed value from year 2023 (the dark-blue bar). The figure

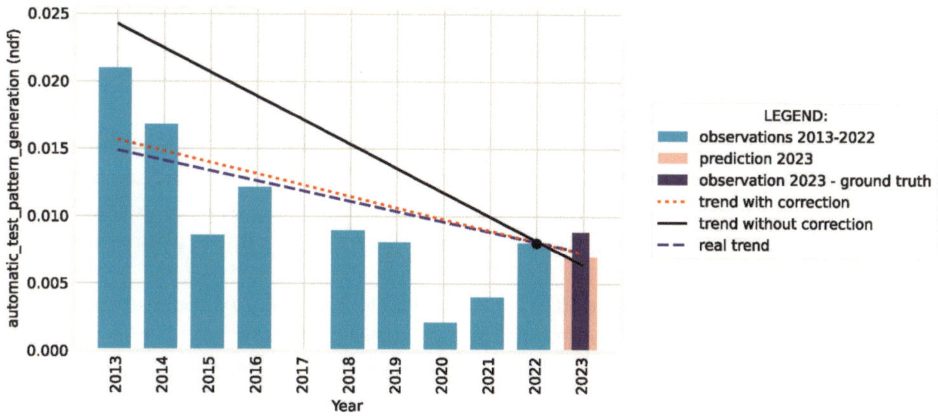

Figure 2.
Trend comparison for the key term 'Automatic test pattern generation.'

shows that the trend with δ-correction ($slope = -0.0007647$) is closer to the real trend ($slope = -0.0006856$) than the uncorrected trend ($slope = -0.0016226$).

A more stringent issue refers to the impact that the delays expressed in Eq. (1) have on the evolution of a research community. Let us assume a return model for the published work that follows a diminishing return model, in which the returns, for example, the received attention from the community, including citations, increase until it reaches a maximum followed by a decrease over time [5]. The time delay δ_{MWT} mainly affects the authors of a work and close collaborators that have access to the work before being published. In case of high-impact results delayed by a long value δ_{MWT}, authors and their collaborators might originate a pool of work to utilize the high-impact results, hence increasing their total expected impact. However, other researchers will not be impacted. A similar comment is valid for the next delay δ_{PL}, too. Hence, any derivative work performed during the delay $\delta_{MWT} + \delta_{PL}$ is bound to be partially outdated, as it was not using the insight of the high-impact result. While this delay has impact on the usefulness of some derivative work, it can be argued that the impact is not critical. However, the impact of the indexing delay δ_{PIL} can be much more disadvantageous for researchers who track the research outputs through bibliometric databases. As many other researchers will have become aware of the critical results after the time $\delta_{MWT} + \delta_{PL}$, they will be able to get some of the still available return during the interval δ_{PIL}. Hence, the remaining return after the bibliometric indexing time will be likely low. This stresses the need for a very short indexing delay δ_{PIL} as a necessary requirement for any indexing database.

2.2 Bibliometric databases as main sources of research insight

Bibliometric databases are systematic and extensive digital collections of bibliometric records (i.e., metadata) referring to the published work. They cover journals, conference proceedings, patents, books and book chapters, standards, reports, and many more. Their role in assessing various research-related facets has become critical mainly due to the difficulty to tackle the continuously increasing number of scientific materials published every year and the way academic communities quantify the quality and impact of the scientific work and, thus, evaluate researchers or research teams [6]. This subsection investigates the types of bibliometric metadata fields used to provide research insight. We selected three popular, domain-related databases (i.e., DBLP, IEEE Xplore, and PubMed) and three more general, multi-domain databases (e.g., Clarivate's Web of Science, Scopus, and Google Scholar). The databases are summarized next.

DBLP was established at the University of Trier in 1993 as an open bibliographic database devoted to the computer science literature. The general structure of a publication metadata record is inspired by the BibTeX syntax and is simple because it includes only essential elements, like title, author names, and publication-related specifications.

IEEE Xplore was launched in 2000 and has since become a reliable source of information for researchers who are looking for timely information on current trends and advances in the specific field of electrical and electronics engineering, computer science, telecommunications, and other related technical areas. It hosts content published under the aegis of the Institute of Electrical and Electronics Engineers (IEEE) and other affiliated associations. The bibliographic metadata record for each indexed publication provides a rich set of data fields, including publication keywords and abstract, different fields for citation counts and patent citation counts, download counts, authors' affiliations, and so on.

PubMed is an open archive dedicated to biomedical and life sciences journals. It is supported by the U.S. National Institutes of Health (NIH). It has been available since year 1996 and uses a complex journal paper metadata structure, which besides fields, like article title, keywords, abstract, authors, affiliations, publication specifications, and citation count, also includes a publication type element (e.g., Journal Article, Letter, Review, Retracted Publication) and an element describing the state of a publication (i.e., ppublish - printed on paper, epublish - digital publication, or ahead of print).

Web of Science was established in 1997 as a multidisciplinary subscription-based bibliographic database that encloses a wide spectrum of scientific fields and disciplines in the humanities. Its content is filtered using an evaluation and inclusion procedure that considers a comprehensive set of criteria including peer review, influence, opportuneness, and geographic coverage of publications. Besides giving a complex bibliographic record for publications, Web of Science also gives a set of related instruments, for example, Journal Citation Reports to present information about the impact factors of scientific journals.

Scopus is a large and multidisciplinary indexing, abstract, and citation bibliographic database, established in 2004 by Elsevier. It covers a large variety of scientific topics from social and human sciences to science, technology, and medicine. Such broad topics were previously curated by independent consultants and subject-matter experts. Scopus utilizes a comprehensive publication metadata structure that is made available to the public through subscription.

Google Scholar is a multidisciplinary and free of charge database that stores scholarly publication metadata since year 2004. It uses a search methodology based on website crawling and indexing and not human expert-curated cataloging. Therefore, querying Google Scholar may often provide inconclusive or sometimes misleading results, hence being up to the researchers to determine if the obtained metadata records are relevant and suitable for their goals. For Google Scholar, the publication metadata structure is reduced, as it does not incorporate some standard indexing fields, like Digital Object Identifier (doi), authors' unique IDs of their affiliations, ISSN or ISBN, and so on.

There is a large set of bibliometric metadata fields that are likely to be used to support research-related activities. Their coverage in the bibliometric databases is

Paper Metadata Field	DBLP	IEEE Xplore	PubMed	Clarivate's WoS	Scopus	Google Scholar
title	✓	✓	✓	✓	✓	✓
abstract	—	✓	✓	✓	✓	—
keywords	—	✓	✓	✓	✓	—
document ID	—	✓	✓	✓	✓	—
document type (e.g., review, article)	—	—	✓	✓	✓	—
access (e.g., open, close, unavailable)	✓	—	—	✓	✓	—
author name	✓	✓	✓	✓	✓	✓
author affiliation	—	✓	✓	✓	✓	—
author ID	—	✓	✓	✓	✓	—
references	—	✓	✓	✓	✓	—
citation count	—	✓	✓	✓	✓	✓
citing patent count	—	✓	—	—	—	—
downloads count	—	✓	✓	—	—	—
year	✓	✓	✓	✓	✓	✓

Table 2.
Journal Paper Metadata Fields to support research-related activities.

different, as summarized in **Table 2**. Due to the specifics of each database (e.g., covered domains and existing metadata fields), the type and depth of insights can vary, sometimes needing the accessing of more databases to acquire the needed insightful and precise information.

The specific usage of bibliographic metadata fields in research activities can be classified into the following categories:

- **Publication content categorization** is generally based on summarizing the content of a publication based on its fields 'Title,' 'Keywords,' and 'Abstract' and sets of key terms. Text representations, like the classic bag-of-words [18] and bag-of-entities [9], are used. As a result, the scientific output is categorized depending on the purpose of its use into either fine-grained themes (e.g., Multi-Factor Authentication or Generative Adversarial Networks) or coarse-grained research areas (e.g., Information Security or Machine Learning) [10]. Specific Natural Language Processing (NLP) techniques are used to support bibliographic data acquisition and preprocessing, key term extraction, key term frequency analysis, topic modeling, and text classification [19–21].

- **Research trend analysis** is a systematic procedure meant to reveal and understand scientific trends and detect hot topics in research. Two different approaches have been pursued; one considers the time evolution of the number of publications associated with the key term and set of key terms characterizing the research domain [11], and one utilizes the citation analysis of the domain-relevant publications and any resulting bibliographic coupling [13, 22]. Both types of methods rely on time series modeling and prediction techniques, such as Mann–Kendall test or Sen's slope estimator, or on burst detection algorithms [11].

- **Research gap discovery** requires the analysis of the bibliographic metadata to unveil non-existent or weak links inside sets of key terms during a specified time interval [5, 12]. If there is sufficient scientific knowledge to support each individual key term and the links between them remain insignificant, a possible research gap may have been identified [23]. The endeavor to discover research gaps is generally based on evaluating the time distribution of key term times and their co-occurrences in a given publication metadata corpus.

- **Researcher and institution assessment** is the continuous process to characterize the research activities of both individuals and organizations. This process is increasingly data-driven and reliant on metrics [24]. The evaluation generally relies on investigating scientific production in terms of quantity, quality, and impact based on carefully selected bibliometric-related criteria and indicators (e.g., h-index and Field-Weighted Citation Impact (FWCI)) [7].

- **Research theme framing** is a complex process that is tightly linked to the scientific gap discovery and the research trend evaluation but must also consider the experience and expertise of the researchers possibly involved in these themes. Because not every research gap is a feasible starting point for new research initiatives, it is critical to choose research gaps that provide sufficient scientific innovation prospects at that particular time moment. Various NLP and machine learning (ML) techniques and available bibliographic resources can be utilized [23].

- **Bibliography recommendation** assumes searching for the most appropriate references to start surveying the state-of-the-art in a given scientific domain. According to Ref. [25], it can be formalized as a ranking problem with two steps: (i) publication selection, where a set of candidate references are identified, and (ii) publication ranking, where candidate documents are sorted based on carefully predefined criteria. The process generates a reference list characterized by the appropriate domain coverage, representativeness, and timeliness. It contains a list of review papers to offer a broad perspective on the given domain and a set of research articles to give deeper insight into the research topic. To obtain a higher accuracy, this recommendation model has to rely not only on paper metadata but also on indirect features, like citation analysis over time and scientific quality assessment [26, 27].

- **Research team formation** is an important task when dealing with new scientific themes for which there is still no established community. If the research project is complex, multidisciplinary, or the number of candidates is large, then the bibliographic information can be a solid starting point [28]. The candidates are selected based on a quantitative and qualitative analysis that considers both the technical expertise and teamwork traits of the candidates. This information can be extracted from bibliometric data [29].

Table 1 describes the metadata fields that, we think, are suitable for research activities.

3. Importance of using bibliometric information to improve research activities

There has been an unprecedented increase over the last decades in the research activity and research outputs. This includes traditional areas, like physics, computer science, electrical engineering, medicine, and so on, as well as new, emerging areas, such as machine learning, neuroscience, biochemistry, bioinformatics, and other areas. The sheer volume of new information and knowledge produced every single day originates new challenges and opportunities. For example, the large number of published research outcomes can complicate the process of tracking the studied ideas, the objective and comprehensive comparison of the ideas to understand their merits and limitations, and the discovery of any research gaps in a field of study. These issues become more acute in cross-disciplinary research. Therefore, effective framing of new research questions in a timely and systematic way is increasingly difficult and arguably still pursued in an empirical way guided by personal experience and preferences. Subsequently, identifying research teams with an expected high success rate for a new research problem is difficult without more advanced automated support to quantify the existing literature, the current research needs, and the available pool of expertise. Hence, it is possible that the existing research resources, for example, the research funding, are utilized in a less than optimal way.

Transforming the way in which research communities operate to address research needs by using existing resources requires a new way of processing and utilizing the outputs of a research community, for example, its publications, driven by automated or semi-automated algorithms that assess the evolution of the research needs and ideas, track problems that are over-studied and topics that are ignored, describe the expertise and team-working skills of researchers, and possibly suggest collaborators and team structures. Existing work, including our own research [23, 30], has studied these needs, often based on NLP of electronic documents to perform activities, like topic modeling, document clustering, keyword extraction, trend modeling, identifying high-impact papers and researchers, characterizing the implicit and explicit structure of research domains, and so on. Existing work has achieved some notable results, like defining new metrics to describe the impact of papers and authors [30, 31], topic modeling [32], and document summarizing [33]. Still, many open problems remain, especially related to using semantic information in characterizing and optimizing research work.

4. Research knowledge development process

Research is often characterized as the process of investigating the available knowledge sources and materials to establish facts and suggest new research needs [4]. Novel research results often reuse, link, and combine fragments of the existing body of knowledge [5, 34] and, less often, restructure the existing knowledge to formulate new theories and models in purely creative processes (e.g., through sudden insight) [1].

Figure 3 summarizes the knowledge flow of this process.

The system in **Figure 3** for automating and optimizing the new knowledge development process first must collect all the results created by a research field, including electronic publication in peer-reviewed databases, repositories, blogs, company

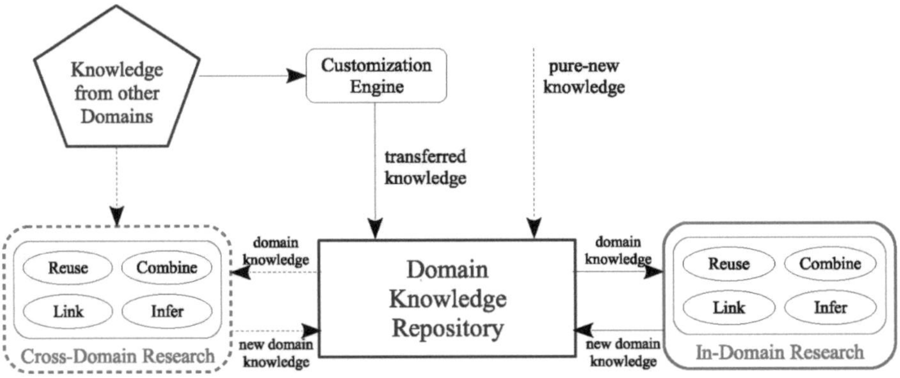

Figure 3.
Knowledge development process for a specific research field.

publications, and other documents. The repository arguably contains the entire body of knowledge acquired during the time and includes theories, methods, datasets, experiments, case studies, and the scientific literature. This repository should be in a format that is easy to inquire, possibly including variants based on large language models (LLMs). We argue that there are several ways in which this repository can be developed:

1. In-domain research

2. Knowledge transferred from other domains

3. Inter−/trans- and multi-domain research

4. Pure-new knowledge coming from sudden insights

In-domain research refers to incremental research, as the needed knowledge is already available within the domain under investigation. This is why such research work mainly focuses on reusing, linking, and combining in a new way the existing ideas in order to obtain novel research outcomes.

A second possibility to extend the body of knowledge in the domain under investigation is to transfer and adapt knowledge from other fields. This is popular in applied domains, where traditionally research outcomes in the theoretical domains were mapped to solve applications. Arguably, an effective way to originate new research ideas can be achieved, if possible, by transferring knowledge from related fields, that is, conceptually similar topics, methodologies, and algorithms. Also, important contributions may come from fields that are on an upward trend or which are expected to be peak domains in the near future, that is, emerging domains.

Also, collaborations between researchers from distinct fields address cross-disciplinary research needs, which includes multi-, inter-, or trans-disciplinary research, where parts of the results may enhance the knowledge repository of the domain under investigation [35].

The last way to grow the repository is through emergent innovative knowledge, that is, sudden insight [1]. Such insight can be disruptive and spawn new opportunities and ideas to be studied.

5. System architecture for automated research problem framing and exploration

This section discusses our methodology as well as other existing approaches to automate the process of framing new and feasible research problems, recommend relevant scientific literature, and suggest possible teams to study the problem. Existing approaches differ by the degree of human participation, that is, the level of human supervision, as the human expert is expected to guide the process according to her/his goals and expectations.

The input to the system is a dataset containing scientific paper metadata (i.e., titles, keywords, and abstracts) from significant publications, which may effectively illustrate the research work in the field of study and in related or emerging domains. To acquire the needed dataset, various metadata and records are typically extracted from influential bibliometric databases, like Clarivate Web of Science, Scopus, PubMed, and IEEE Xplore. Our system, since it targets research in information technology and electric and electronic engineering, uses IEEE Xplore as its bibliometric data source. The previous sections summarized the main datasets and explained their pros and cons in terms of the offered information. Our ideas on effective organization of such datasets to aid automated research problem framing and exploration are also presented here.

Our system incorporates four modules that can act either together, as shown in **Figure 1**, or as standalone modules:

1. Research theme recommender module
2. Cross-domain knowledge transfer recommender module
3. Scientific literature recommender module
4. Research team recommender module

5.1 Research theme recommender module

This module provides a list of main and feasible research themes by analyzing the state of research within the domain and by evaluating the opportunity and feasibility of the themes by carrying out trend and statistical analysis. The corpus of relevant paper metadata is employed to identify a comprehensive list of domain-specific key terms, discover the research gaps within the domain, and evaluate the opportunity and feasibility of investigating a topic corresponding to such research gaps.

Framing new research themes has historically been grounded in three fundamental scientometric methodologies and their combinations [23, 36]: (i) investigating the trends in scientific output to reveal the evolutionary dynamics that govern the scientific production in a specific field [37], a typical instance being the employment of Mann–Kendall test, Sen's slope assessment, and Kleinberg's burst method to investigate key terms' popularity and trends [11]; (ii) analyzing citation networks by tracking the scientific community's interest on a given topic based on the number of citations or co-citations to map the intellectual structure and evolution of a scientific field [2, 38]; and (iii) conducting content analysis either on the paper metadata fields, like 'Title,' 'Keywords,' and 'Abstract,' or on full-text documents by employing topic modeling coupled with co-word analysis to extract scientific topics and explore their time evolution [39, 40]. While the aforementioned methods may provide valuable insights into the dynamics of a research domain to aid scientific theme framing, they do not directly tackle the discovery of research gaps.

In order to formulate new and viable research themes from bibliographical metadata, we proposed a practical methodology that relies on formulating the discovery of feasible research gaps as a graph theoretical problem centered on key term co-occurrences [23]. Starting from the assumption that a scientific domain can be mapped to an integer-weighted undirected graph, where the nodes represent the domain's key terms and the co-occurrence matrix extracted from paper metadata is the graph's cost adjacency matrix, we model the identification of viable scientific gaps as a particular sub-graph extraction problem, where the weights associated to the edges need to be confined to a specified interval to assure a desired level of innovation- and success-related prospects. In our view, to automatically identify feasible research gaps to work on, we must follow the following sequence of steps:

Step 1: Acquire a paper metadata corpus corresponding to the journals and conference proceedings that characterize the considered scientific domain.

Step 2: Using entity linking techniques (e.g., TagMe) applied to the metadata fields 'Title,' 'Keywords,' and 'Abstract,' identify a finite set of key terms that characterize the scientific domain, and compute their co-occurrences to build the domain's weighted undirected graph;

Step 3: Employing a double-threshold procedure that presumes deriving a success threshold α and a novelty threshold β from statistical data, drop the edges from the domain's weighted undirected edges that do not lie in an interval $[\alpha, \beta]$;

Step 4: Extract all connected subgraphs (i.e., models of research gaps) having a predefined number of nodes, rank them according to the mean co-occurrence value μ (i.e., average of all subgraph weights), and present these recommendations to the user.

This research theme recommender is presented in detail in Ref. [23] along with an illustrative case study from the Electronic Design Automation (EDA) domain.

5.2 The cross-domain knowledge transfer recommender module

This module identifies potential sources of relevant knowledge transfers that help solving the recommended research problem. Document similarity assessment and topic modeling techniques can point toward twin and emerging domains to find methods or materials that relate to the current research theme.

The interest in developing automatic techniques to identify suitable inter-domain knowledge transfers is arguably still in a pioneering stage, even though such methods may provide feasible and straightforward solutions to a wide spectrum of research problems. For example, employing a citation network extracted from scientific publications belonging to aviation and sustainability fields, Nakamura et al. proposed a recognized-unrecognized matricial model to highlight the neglected problems and identify suitable knowledge for developing an innovative water/air transport system [41]. A similar approach was adopted by Ogawa and Kajikawa [42]. They fused knowledge identified for the fields of fuel cell technology and ammonia synthesis to propose novel research topics based on time-series analysis of citation networks and keyword similarity. An interesting experiment was reported by Ittipanuvat et al., which investigated hidden knowledge connections between two totally different scientific areas, namely robotics and gerontology, to develop new robotic applications for disabled and elderly people assistance [3]. As it may be observed, these studies focus on specific situations rather than trying to offer methods for generic cross-domain knowledge transfers.

In the context of design of electronic analog and mixed-signal (AMS) circuits, our previous work has devised a new model and the necessary circuit schematic mining algorithms to describe representing AMS design metaknowledge [43]. The representation has three parts: the associative component expresses the hierarchy of the concepts used in the circuit designs; the part to present the performance of the AMS circuits, like performance tradeoffs and bottlenecks; and the causal modeling part that presents the likely starting ideas and steps used to design a circuit. The same approach used to devise the metaknowledge representation for AMS circuits was then utilized to design a metaknowledge representation for other open-ended problems, including architectural engineering and general-domain problems [44]. Finally, a cognitive architecture, called InnovA, was suggested to use the metaknowledge representation to automatically generate new AMS circuit designs, either by incrementally modifying circuits in the representation or by combining features of distinct circuits from the knowledge representation [45].

In our view, a cross-domain knowledge transfer recommender should be based on the following key aspects: (a) scientific domains and research themes may effectively be modeled by sets of key terms; bibliographic metadata are authoritative and comprehensive sources of information about scientific output; and (b) NLP techniques can effectively extract and interpret information from textual data to identify hidden links or patterns between the bodies of knowledge of two different domains. Our suggested approach is centered around the concept of 'twin scientific domains' (i.e., scientific areas sharing similar or related research topics, notions, theories, materials, and methods), since the similarity of such domains is likely to provide reasonable knowledge transfers. Thus, to discover feasible knowledge transfers, we have to follow three phases:

1. *Bibliographic metadata acquisition and processing* to build a domain-characteristic text file for each of the scientific domains (i.e., both target and potential twin domains) under investigation. This stage employs an entity linking method to construct a document containing the list of all key terms encountered in the paper metadata fields 'Title,' 'Keywords,' and 'Abstract' for each of the mentioned scientific domains.

2. *Twin domain identification*, where a document similarity method is applied to rank the potential twin domains, based on their document-characteristic text file similarity with the one corresponding to the target domain.

3. *Investigating the body of knowledge in each of the best-ranked twin domains by evaluating the key term co-occurrences and suggesting the knowledge transfers*, which are characterized by considerably higher co-occurrences in the twin domain as compared to the one in the target domain.

5.3 Scientific literature recommender module

To help researchers establish a suitable starting point from where to conduct the literature review, the proposed system directs the search in two directions: an in-domain exploration to find high-impact work on a research theme and twin/emerging domain explorations to find relevant papers on the knowledge we intend to transfer.

Previous work has focused on devising metrics to describe the research impact of individuals, like the well-known h-index. However, there has been significantly less effort to characterize the role of a research group in a community. Our work has focused on this gap by conducting an extensive experimental study on the role a group plays to the flow of ideas in a research community [30]. The study considered the contribution of groups to the impact research ideas make on other groups and the way a group contributes to linking a community together. Experiments have also indicated that groups can be clustered into four categories based on the count of the references to their work. Groups of the two mid-tier categories have a main role in bridging between groups, thus in linking them in a well-connected community. This insight is important as more fragmented communities, like those with fewer mid-tier groups, are likely to be less effective.

This recommender system is meant to aid researchers in reducing the number of publications that are subjected to (manual) literature review and is based on exploring the bibliographical databases with carefully tailored search strategies that are implemented in search queries. To provide a reliable starting point for the research theme, a scoping review procedure [46] that offers a structured and comprehensive image of the research theme with respect to all its facets has to be carried out [14, 47]. Hence, the user has to pursue the following steps [48]: (i) choose the appropriate bibliographical database to search by investigating the databases' domain specificity and adequateness; (ii) pick key terms to search for by considering both the research theme needs and the bag of key terms likely to be extracted from the metadata fields 'Title,' 'Keywords,' and 'Abstract' (e.g., by using TagMe, WikiMiner, or RedW entity linking methods for which the key terms should represent Wikipedia mentions); (iii) decide the boundaries of the systematic review by targeting only a defined set of publications (i.e., employing 'publication title' metadata field) and/or publications from a given time interval (i.e., using the metadata field 'Year'); and (iv) select the type of papers to be explored, namely surveys and/or research papers, this information being made available by the metadata field 'Article type.' The search query configuration is neither a simple nor an easy task, as it relies on the user's experience and expertise.

Recently some interesting literature recommending environments, suited for the biomedical field, have been made available. LitSuggest employs a large set of classifiers (e.g., ridge classifier, elastic net classifier, etc.) to decide, based on a user-provided list of papers, if other publications existing in PubMed database are relevant, irrelevant, or ambiguous. For this, the metadata fields 'Title,' 'Abstract,' 'Keywords,' 'Journal,' and 'Publication type' are utilized in a bag-of-words representation [49]. Another Web-based software tool to suggest scientific literature is RobotAnalyst, which combines ML algorithms (i.e., classifiers and topic modeling) and the metadata field 'Abstract' text-mining to classify and rank references by their semantic similarity [15]. While effective in biomedical domains, such approaches have some inherent limitations (e.g., the inability to cope with different research theme granularities, the reduced adaptability to other scientific domains, ignoring the influence of high-visibility individuals and groups in the field, and reduced explainability and transparency due to the type of used ML models). Hence, a more in-depth analysis of the literature recommending process is needed.

5.4 Research team recommender module

A set of possible teams to carry out a specific research theme can be automatically proposed by solving a complex and multi-objective team formation optimization problem by analyzing the corpus of paper metadata to extract information about the expertise and teamwork skills associated to researchers in a database.

Among the first to employ bibliographic metadata in research team formation are Lappas et al. [28]. Based on four paper metadata fields acquired from DBLP database (i.e., fields 'Title,' 'Authors,' 'Publication year,' and 'Publication name'), they took into account each candidate's technical proficiency to complete the task requirements as well as their teamwork skills to build effective research teams. Since then, despite its limited topic coverage and simplified publication metadata structure, the DBLP bibliographic database has been extensively utilized as a source of information for computer science researchers to assess diverse team-shaping strategies [29, 50]. Although several studies suggested obtaining data from more extensive databases including PubMed [51] or Google Scholar [52], they remain grounded in the same limited selection of metadata fields, which may offer an imprecise and insufficient depiction of potential team members. Therefore, the full potential of the use of bibliographic information for effective team formation has not yet been realized, requiring ongoing efforts to build new or improve upon existing techniques. In our opinion, the focus should be directed toward developing new theoretical and computational models of collaborative research work and finding a suitable set of candidate-related metrics that can be computed from bibliographic information. For this, the number of considered bibliographic metadata fields has to be increased by employing the citation and download counts, authors' affiliations, or publication abstract when extracting personal and interpersonal candidates' competencies. Moreover, appropriate multi-objective team formation optimization procedures relying on candidate-related indicators derived from bibliographic metadata need to be devised and adapted to particular research theme contexts.

5.5 Using the proposed architecture in research

This section discusses a possible procedure of using the system architecture in **Figure 1** for automated research problem framing and exploration. Other alternatives of using the architecture can be devised, too.

The first step in the procedure is the selection of a potential research theme by the likely principal investigators (PIs) of a future research project. The Research Theme Recommender module is used for this task. Using keywords describing current, main research themes, the PIs identify a set of themes, like three to five research topics, that cover the keywords but are less studied by the existing scientific literature. The method in Ref. [23] or other similar methods can be used for this step. For the selected themes, opportunities for transferring knowledge across the related domains are then identified using the Cross-Domain Knowledge Transfer Recommender module. The feasibility of these opportunities is analyzed next, such as an algorithm already used in effectively describing Integrated Chip layouts is identified as an interesting approach to represent any visual data, too. The next two steps select the scientific literature for the project and make recommendations on possible research teams. The Scientific Literature Recommender module offers a starting point on the research papers that support an identified cross-disciplinary theme. New related papers are identified as the research work is carried out. Team selection utilizes the Research Team Recommender module. A dataset available to form cross-disciplinary teams of members from "Politehnica" University Timisoara is available at Ref. [53]. The procedure can be repeated to adjust the keywords used for research theme recommendation or to select other research themes among those recommended and explore other cross-domain knowledge transfer opportunities.

6. Conclusions

This chapter discussed the current opportunities and challenges in using automated methodologies and software tools to analyze published research outcomes present in bibliometric databases, like digital books, book chapters, journal articles, conference proceedings, and so on. The goal is to maximize the quality and impact of new research. The chapter enumerated the main features of the most frequently used bibliographic databases, like DBLP, IEEE Xplore, PubMed, Web of Science, Scopus, and Google Scholar. The main characteristics of the databases were also introduced, for example, conciseness, relevance, selectivity, and objectivity. The impact of outdated bibliometric data was mentioned, and a correction method was suggested. The chapter proposed a novel system architecture to automatically support the research knowledge development process. The system is a collection of recommender modules that target the different activities of the knowledge development process, for example, publication content categorization, research trend analysis, research gap discovery, researcher and institution assessment, research problem framing, bibliography recommendation, and research team formation. Future work is expected to address each of the enumerated activities, so that the potential of automated processing of bibliometric data is fully harnessed.

Author details

Christian-Daniel Curiac[1†], Mihai Micea[1†], Traian-Radu Plosca[1†], Daniel-Ioan Curiac[1*†], Simona Doboli[2†] and Alex Doboli[3†]

1 Politehnica University of Timisoara, Timisoara, Romania

2 Hofstra University, Hempstead, NY, USA

3 Stony Brook University, Stony Brook, NY, USA

*Address all correspondence to: daniel.curiac@aut.upt.ro

† These authors contributed equally.

References

[1] Kuhn TS. The Structure of Scientific Revolutions. Chicago, IL, USA: University of Chicago; 1996

[2] Upham S, Small H. Emerging research fronts in science and technology: Patterns of new knowledge development. Scientometrics. 2010; **83**(1):15-38

[3] Ittipanuvat V, Fujita K, Sakata I, Kajikawa Y. Finding linkage between technology and social issue: A literature based discovery approach. Journal of Engineering and Technology Management. 2014;**32**:160-184

[4] Leedy PD, Ormrod JE. Practical Research. Saddle River, NJ, USA: Pearson Education; 2005

[5] Liu X, Doboli A, Doboli S. Bottom–up modeling of design knowledge evolution: Application to circuit design community characterization. IEEE Transactions on Computational Social Systems. 2020; **8**(3):689-703

[6] de Oliveira OJ, da Silva FF, Juliani F, Barbosa LC, Nunhes TS. Bibliometric method for mapping the state-of-the-art and identifying research gaps and trends in literature: An essential instrument to support the development of scientific projects. In: Scientometrics Recent Advances. London, UK: IntechOpen; 2019

[7] Campbell D, Picard Aitken M, Côté G, Caruso J, Valentim R, Edmonds S, et al. Bibliometrics as a performance measurement tool for research evaluation: The case of research funded by the National Cancer Institute of Canada. American Journal of Evaluation. 2010;**31**(1):66-83

[8] Curiac CD, Banias O, Micea M. Evaluating research trends from journal paper metadata, considering the research publication latency. Mathematics. 2022; **10**(2):233

[9] Gonzalez, Pinto JM, Balke WT. Demystifying the semantics of relevant objects in scholarly collections: A probabilistic approach. In: Proceedings of the 15th ACM/IEEE-CS Joint Conference on Digital Libraries. Knoxville TN, USA: IEEE; 2015. pp. 157-164

[10] Zhang Y, Jin B, Chen X, Shen Y, Zhang Y, Meng Y, et al. Weakly supervised multi-label classification of full-text scientific papers. In: Proceedings of the 29th ACM SIGKDD Conference on Knowledge Discovery and Data Mining. Long Beach, CA, USA: ACM; 2023. pp. 3458-3469

[11] Marrone M. Application of entity linking to identify research fronts and trends. Scientometrics. 2020;**122**(1): 357-379

[12] Juliani F, de Oliveira OJ. State of research on public service management: Identifying scientific gaps from a bibliometric study. International Journal of Information Management. 2016; **36**(6):1033-1041

[13] Boyack KW, Klavans R. Creation of a highly detailed, dynamic, global model and map of science. Journal of the Association for Information Science and Technology. 2014;**65**(4):670-685

[14] Azarian M, Yu H, Shiferaw AT, Stevik TK. Do we perform systematic literature review right? A scientific mapping and methodological assessment. Logistics. 2023;7(4):89

[15] Przybyła P, Brockmeier AJ, Kontonatsios G, Le Pogam M-A,

McNaught J, von Elm E, et al. Prioritising references for systematic reviews with robot analyst: A user study. Research Synthesis Methods. 2018;**9**(3): 470-488

[16] Andersen MZ, Fonnes S, Rosenberg J. Time from submission to publication varied widely for biomedical journals: A systematic review. Current Medical Research and Opinion. 2021; **37**(6):985-993

[17] Happel HJ, Stojanovic L. Analyzing organizational information gaps. In: Proceedings of the 8th International Conference on Knowledge Management. Graz, Austria. 2008. pp. 28-36

[18] Joorabchi A, Mahdi AE. An unsupervised approach to automatic classification of scientific literature utilizing bibliographic metadata. Journal of Information Science. 2011;**37**(5): 499-514

[19] Akundi A, Euresti D, Luna S, Ankobiah W, Lopes A, Edinbarough I. State of industry 5.0–analysis and identification of current research trends. Applied System Innovation. 2022;**5**(1):27

[20] Curiac C-D, Micea MV. Identifying hot information security topics using LDA and multivariate Mann-Kendall test. IEEE Access. 2023;**11**:18374-18384

[21] Chen H, Wang X, Pan S, Xiong F. Identify topic relations in scientific literature using topic modeling. IEEE Transactions on Engineering Management. 2019;**68**(5):1232-1244

[22] Hopcroft J, Khan O, Kulis B, Selman B. Tracking evolving communities in large linked networks. Proceedings of the National Academy of Sciences. 2004;**101**(suppl_1):5249-5253

[23] Curiac C-D, Doboli A, Curiac DI. Co-occurrence-based double thresholding method for research topic identification. Mathematics. 2022;**10**(17):3115

[24] Hicks D, Wouters P, Waltman L, De Rijcke S, Rafols I. Bibliometrics: The Leiden manifesto for research metrics. Nature. 2015;**520**(7548):429-431

[25] Bhagavatula C, Feldman S, Power R, Ammar W. Content-based citation recommendation. arXiv:1802.08301. 2018. DOI: 10.48550/arXiv.1802.08301

[26] Nair AM, Benny O, George J. Content based scientific article recommendation system using deep learning technique. In: Inventive Systems and Control: Proceedings of ICISC. Singapore: Springer; 2021. pp. 965-977

[27] Chaudhuri A, Sinhababu N, Sarma M, Samanta D. Hidden features identification for designing an efficient research article recommendation system. International Journal on Digital Libraries. 2021;**22**(2):233-249

[28] Lappas T, Liu K, Terzi E. Finding a team of experts in social networks. In: Proceedings of the 15th ACM SIGKDD International Conference on Knowledge Discovery and Data Mining. Paris, France: ACM; 2009. pp. 467-476

[29] Hamidi Rad R, Fani H, Bagheri E, Kargar M, Srivastava D, Szlichta J. A variational neural architecture for skill-based team formation. ACM Transactions on Information Systems. 2023;**42**(1):1-28

[30] Liu X, Doboli A, MacCarthy T, Doboli S. Understanding the significance of mid-tier research teams in idea flow through a community. IEEE Transactions on Computational Social Systems. 2023;**10**(6):3422-3432

[31] Kim D, Lee B, Lee HJ, Lee SP, Moon Y, Jeong MK. Automated

detection of influential patents using singular values. IEEE Transactions on Automation Science and Engineering. 2012;**9**(4):723-733

[32] Blei DM. Topic modeling and digital humanities. Journal of Digital Humanities. 2012;**2**(1):8-11

[33] Allahyari M, Pouriyeh S, Assefi M, Safaei S, Trippe ED, Gutierrez JB, et al. Text summarization techniques: A brief survey. arXiv:1707.02268. 2017. DOI: 10.48550/arXiv.1707.02268

[34] Doboli A, Umbarkar A, Subramanian V, Doboli S. Two experimental studies on creative concept combinations in modular design of electronic embedded systems. Design Studies. 2014;**35**(1):80-109

[35] Vugteveen P, Lenders R, Van den Besselaar P. The dynamics of interdisciplinary research fields: The case of river research. Scientometrics. 2014; **100**:73-96

[36] Mazov NA, Gureev VN, Glinskikh VN. The methodological basis of defining research trends and fronts. Scientific and Technical Information Processing. 2020;**47**:221-231

[37] Liu X, Jiang T, Ma F. Collective dynamics in knowledge networks: Emerging trends analysis. Journal of Informetrics. 2013;**7**(2):425-438

[38] Shiau WL, Wang X, Zheng F. What are the trend and core knowledge of information security? A citation and co-citation analysis. Information & Management. 2023;**60**(3):103774

[39] Sivanandham S, Sathish Kumar A, Pradeep R, Sridhar R. Analysing research trends using topic modelling and trend prediction. In: Soft Computing and Signal Processing: Proceedings of 3rd ICSCSP 2020. Vol. 1. Singapore: Springer; 2020. pp. 157-166

[40] Mohammadi E, Karami A. Exploring research trends in big data across disciplines: A text mining analysis. Journal of Information Science. 2022; **48**(1):44-56

[41] Nakamura H, Ii S, Chida H, Friedl K, Suzuki S, Mori J, et al. Shedding light on a neglected area: A new approach to knowledge creation. Sustainability Science. 2014;**9**:193-204

[42] Ogawa T, Kajikawa Y. Generating novel research ideas using computational intelligence: A case study involving fuel cells and ammonia synthesis. Technological Forecasting and Social Change. 2017;**120**:41-47

[43] Jiao F, Montano S, Ferent C, Doboli A, Doboli S. Analog circuit design knowledge mining: Discovering topological similarities and uncovering design reasoning strategies. IEEE Transactions on CADICS. 2015;**34**(7): 1045-1058

[44] Doboli A, Umbarkar A, Doboli S, Betz J. Modeling semantic knowledge structures for creative problem solving: Studies on expressing concepts, categories, associations, goals and context. Knowledge-Based Systems. 2015;**78**:34-50

[45] Li H, Liu X, Jiao F, Doboli A, Doboli S. Innova: A cognitive architecture for computational innovation through robust divergence and its application for analog circuit design. IEEE Transactions on Computer-Aided Design of Integrated Circuits and Systems. 2017;**37**(10):1943-1956

[46] Arksey H, O'Malley L. Scoping studies: Towards a methodological

framework. International Journal of Social Research Methodology. 2005;**8**(1): 19-32

[47] Booth A, Sutton A, Clowes M, Martyn-St JM. Systematic Approaches to a Successful Literature Review. 3rd ed. London, UK: SAGE Publications; 2022

[48] Wanyama SB, McQuaid RW, Kittler M. Where you search determines what you find: The effects of bibliographic databases on systematic reviews. International Journal of Social Research Methodology. 2022;**25**(3):409-422

[49] Allot A, Lee K, Chen Q, Luo L, Lu Z. LitSuggest: A web-based system for literature recommendation and curation using machine learning. Nucleic Acids Research. 2021;**49**(W1):W352-W358

[50] Juang MC, Huang CC, Huang JL. Efficient algorithms for team formation with a leader in social networks. The Journal of Supercomputing. 2013;**66**: 721-737

[51] Neshati M, Beigy H, Hiemstra D. Expert group formation using facility location analysis. Information Processing and Management. 2014;**50**(2):361-383

[52] Srivastava B, Koppel T, Paladi ST, Valluru SL, Sharma R, Bond O. ULTRA: A data-driven approach for recommending team formation in response to proposal calls. In: 2022 IEEE International Conference on Data Mining Workshops (ICDMW). Orlando, FL, USA: IEEE; 2022. pp. 1002-1009

[53] Curiac CD, Micea M, Plosca TR, Curiac DI, Doboli A. Dataset for bibliometric data-driven research team formation: Case of Politehnica University of Timisoara scholars for the interval 2010-2022. Data in Brief. 2024; **53**:110275. DOI: 10.1016/j. dib.2024.110275

Chapter 4

Bibliometric Analysis of Dubious Research

Muhammad Asif Khan, Humaira Farid and Imtiaz Ali

Abstract

Retracted papers are scientific or scholarly works officially withdrawn by the publisher or journal after their initial publication. The primary goal of retractions is to rectify the literature and alert readers about articles containing substantially flawed or erroneous content or data, or due to ethical concerns, rendering reported findings and conclusions unreliable. Retraction notices are typically issued for various reasons, including scientific misconduct, genuine mistakes, or problems with peer review. This chapter provides a systematic analysis of the dubious research identified in the Web of Science Core Collection. Bibliometric analysis was conducted on dubious research to assess the magnitude and influence of the questionable work on the pool of knowledge. The contingency matrix between countries and Web of Science categories of retracted papers reveals correlations between certain domains and the countries. To counter this growing tendency, a multi-pronged approach is essential. Robust policies, vigilant watchdogs, and targeted interventions by institutions are necessary to uphold the integrity of scholarly literature. Academia cannot afford to remain silent in the face of this threat to its credibility.

Keywords: retractions, bibliometrics, scientific integrity, research misconduct, evaluation

1. Introduction

The number of retractions in journals is on the rise, posing a significant challenge to scientific integrity [1]. Retraction notices are typically issued due to various factors, including scientific misconduct, genuine mistakes, and problems with peer review, among others. The primary purpose of retractions is to rectify the literature and apprise readers about articles with substantially flawed or erroneous content, and ethical concerns, rendering their findings and conclusions unreliable [2]. The increasing trend in retractions in recent years has raised concerns about the quality of the peer-review process.

Typically, a retraction comprises the original article and the retraction announcement, often accompanied by explanations [3]. Traditional print journals lack a mechanism to remove retracted articles, unlike online-only journals, which can eliminate such articles from all repositories. Eliminating all copies, especially those shared on personal websites, proves impractical many times. Consequently, there is an ongoing risk that certain readers may not identify a retracted article.

The dissemination of erroneous research findings, as exemplified by the chloroquine study, has far-reaching negative impacts on the scientific community, society, and the authors themselves, posing a threat to their professional standing [4]. When a mistake or misconduct is identified, publishing a retraction of the fraudulent article becomes essential [5]. This serves to rectify the literature, inform the scientific community, and underscore the commitment of the scientific community to correct its errors. The "publish or perish" culture jeopardizes the integrity and honesty of researchers. To ensure ethical practices in academic publishing and preserve the integrity of researchers and accessible knowledge, the Committee on Publication Ethics (COPE) has established comprehensive guidelines and measures. Included in these guidelines is the Code of Conduct, which strives to integrate ethical practices into the editorial culture. One notable measure is the promotion of error reporting by researchers and publishers to maintain journal reliability. Through this approach, COPE aims to tackle various aspects of scientific misconduct, including duplicate publication, plagiarism, falsification and fabrication, ethical concerns, authorship disputes, and fraudulent peer reviews. Furthermore, the COPE guidelines establish the criteria for ethical publication practices and offer guidance to editors, authors, and publishers [6].

Through proficient utilization of bibliometrics, the causes of retractions can be identified, trust can be restored, and the integrity of scientific knowledge can be protected. This endeavor goes beyond mere academic analysis; it is a mission to safeguard the very fabric of scientific progress.

The following provides operational definitions [7, 8] for the key reasons behind retracted papers as available in the academic literature:

Plagiarism: The author published work that included unacknowledged text, data, images, or ideas borrowed from other authors, violating academic integrity by not providing appropriate citations.

Duplicate publication: The author repeatedly failed to provide proper citations to their previous work when publishing their own texts, images, or data, presenting them as new content. Submitting the same work to multiple journals, i.e., accepted by a journal while still undergoing peer review by the initial journal, is considered a violation. In a similar case, five papers of an author were retracted, as the journals detected resemblances in titles, content, and data by individuals from distinct university affiliations [9, 10]. This behavior makes up a breach of professional ethics and the COPE code of conduct. According to COPE guidelines, submitting a paper implies that the work is neither published before nor being considered for publication elsewhere.

Falsification and fabrication: Falsification pertains to the deliberate manipulation or selective omission of the data by the author(s) to support their hypothesis. The act of fabrication involves the creation or alteration of data by author(s), which is then documented and disseminated in the results and later published.

Error: The scope of this category extends to encompass genuine mistakes or technical errors that arose during the publication process, legitimate errors made by authors, unavailability of raw data, inability to reproduce results, and errors in data that authors subsequently accepted with apologies in notices. Authors in coordination with the journals start voluntary withdrawals in this category. The term "heroic act" pertains to retractions that are requested by the authors themselves [11].

Misconduct: This terminology was specifically employed to refer to papers that were retracted because of issues pertaining to authorship, ethics, funding, or falsified peer reviews. The Medical Research Council (MRC) [12] and the US Office of Research Integrity (ORI) [2, 7] identify duplicate publication, plagiarism, falsification and fabrication, ethical issues, authorship issues, and fake peer reviews as forms of intentional misconduct.

Retraction Watch, a blog that has documented approximately 51k retracted papers, has observed a significant increase in retractions since its establishment 13 years ago, which is believed to be vastly underestimated [1, 13]. Confidence in researchers, universities, journals, and the scientific community can be undermined by unethical research. Intending to uphold the quality of accessible knowledge, the peer-review process, alongside the responsible and transparent correction of articles, serves this purpose [14].

2. Methodology

The data were accessed from the Web of Science Core Collection on January 20, 2024, using the following Boolean string in advanced search:

DT = (Expression of Concern OR Retracted Publication OR Retraction OR Withdrawn Publication OR Publication with Expression of Concern) AND PY = (1986–2023). All instances of retraction, including publications with expressions of concern and withdrawn, were included in this analysis. The time period for the publications was specified as 1986–2023.

For further investigation, connections between retractions and diverse bibliometric factors, including institutions, countries, and author/journal/publisher attributes, were explored using various tools, including bibliometrix, VoSviewer, Gephi, and CorText.

3. Results and discussion

In this section, a comprehensive analysis of the results obtained from an in-depth examination of retracted papers from Web of Science Core Collection database during 1986–2023 is presented. The analysis encompasses a detailed exploration of the descriptive characteristics, subject areas, journals, publishers, and the geographical distribution associated with these retracted publications.

3.1 Descriptive analysis

Understanding the landscape of retracted papers is crucial for the scholarly community as it provides insights into the factors contributing to retractions and their implications for scientific integrity. By delving into the descriptive analysis of retracted papers, the goal is to identify patterns and commonalities that can illuminate the underlying causes leading to retractions. This knowledge is essential for developing strategies to uphold the rigor and reliability of scientific research.

The information regarding editorial notices issued to dubious publications reveals that "Retraction" is the most prevalent notice, comprising 16,188 (55.33%) of the total count, while "Retracted Publication" accounts for 11,073 (37.85%). "Expression Of Concern" constitutes 1300 (4.44%), and "Publication with Expression Of Concern" accounts for 709 (2.42%) of the total count. Editorial notices for "Withdrawn Publication" and "Item Withdrawal" represent the smallest proportions, with 238 (0.81%) and 63 (0.22%), respectively. Consistency in the notices issued by journals or publishers may enhance the bibliometric data, aiding in identifying the real root cause of these retracted papers [7].

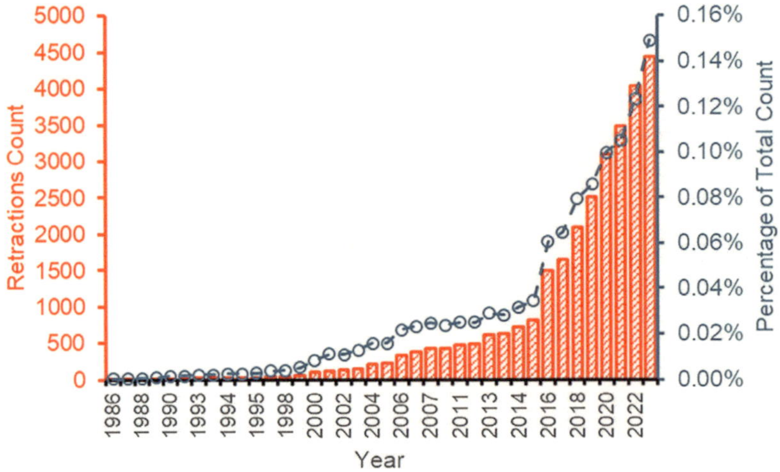

Figure 1.
Temporal evolution of retracted papers from 1986 to 2023 according to Web of Science.

Figure 1 illustrates the temporal evolution of retractions from 1986 to 2023. The retraction count was relatively low between 1986 and 2007. There was a consistent rise from 2008 to 2015, followed by a period of exponential growth. In 2023, the number of retractions reached 4429, making up 0.15% of the total publications for that year alone.

3.2 Subject areas

The examination of subject areas associated with retracted papers offers insights into the specific fields where retractions are more prevalent. Identifying these subject areas is essential for targeted interventions and improvements in research practices to mitigate the occurrence of retractions.

Despite being more prevalent in countries with a strong research background and reputable journals, retractions are not limited to specific fields of study and can be found in diverse areas such as medicine, engineering, and the social sciences [15]. Nonetheless, recent studies on retractions in the Web of Science database have revealed elevated rates in the domains of chemistry, biomedical sciences, and engineering [16, 17].

The word cloud displayed in **Figure 2a** visualizes the prevailing terms correlated with retracted papers in a range of academic disciplines. Each term's frequency is depicted by its respective size. Terms like "oncology," "biochemistry & molecular biology," and "multidisciplinary sciences" are prominently featured, suggesting they are common topics associated with retracted papers. To categorize them into wider fields, an overlay map was created.

Figure 2b displays a network map of a retracted paper across various Web of Science categories, grouped into five main disciplines. The field of Biology & Medicine is visually represented by the color red, while Chemistry & Physics are depicted in blue. Environmental Science & Technology is associated with the color yellow, Psychology & Social Sciences in green, and Engineering & Mathematics showcased in a purple-colored cluster. Nodes in each discipline represent

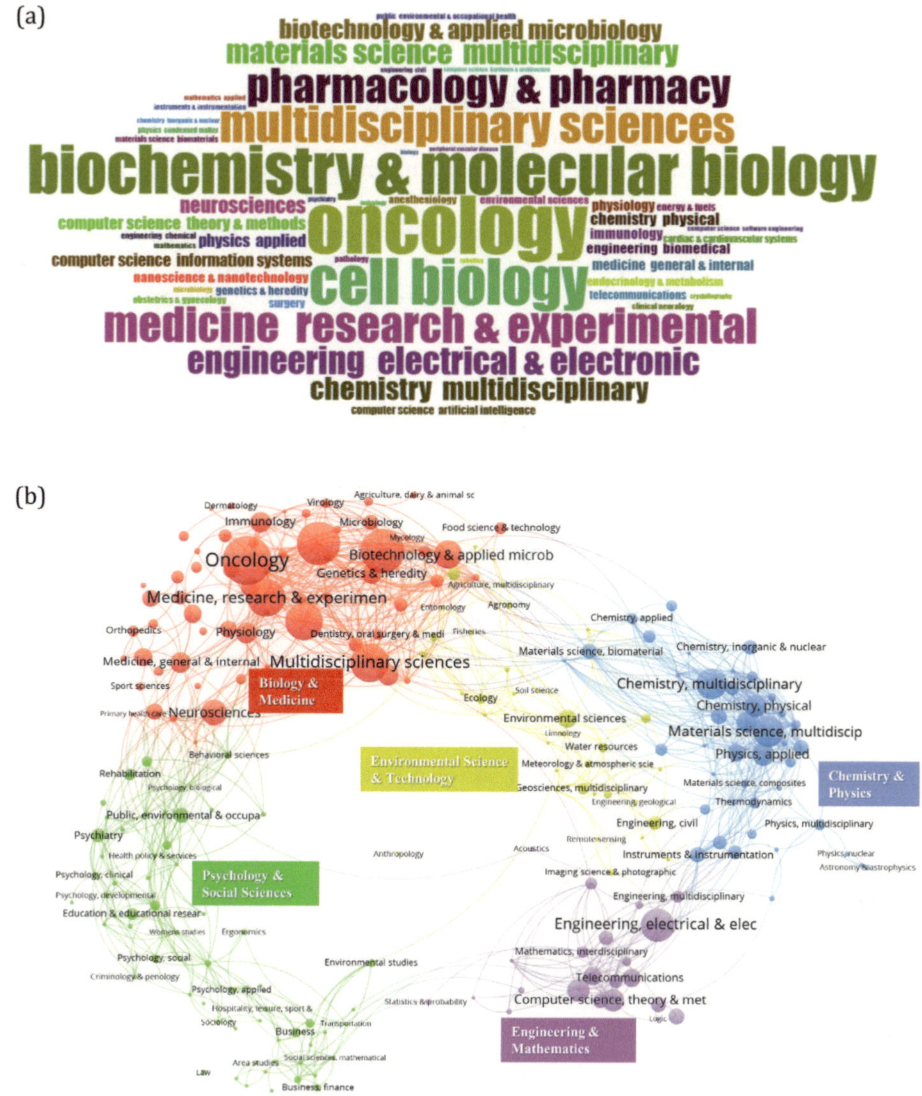

Figure 2.
(a) Word cloud of most frequent Web of Science subject categories, and (b) overlay map of retracted papers across Web of Science categories, grouped into five main disciplines: Biology & Medicine, Chemistry & Physics, Environmental Science & Technology, Psychology & Social Sciences, and Engineering & Mathematics.

sub-domains identified from journal listings, such as "Oncology" and "Genetics & heredity" within "Biology & Medicine." Lines connecting nodes indicate relationships or overlaps between categories, with the size of each node corresponding to the frequency of retractions in that category.

Results indicate that the majority of retractions come from Biology & Medicine, Chemistry & Physics, and Engineering & Mathematics, while retractions in Environmental Science & Technology and Psychology & Social Sciences are relatively low in volume.

3.3 Journals

An analysis of the journals and publishers involved in disseminating retracted papers provides valuable information about the platforms through which potentially problematic research has been communicated. This scrutiny is essential for understanding the role of academic publishing in maintaining the quality and credibility of scientific knowledge.

When considering the impact factor, establishing a direct correlation between higher-impact-factor journals and an increased number of retractions was not feasible. A study by Rubbo et al. [15] demonstrated a direct relationship between the impact factor of journals and the occurrence of retractions. However, contrary to this, some studies have asserted that journals with a lower impact factor are more prone to retracting articles [18, 19].

Table 1 describes the count of retractions in different scientific journals. PLoS One has a significantly higher number of retractions, with 1056 counts (3.54%), while other journals such as J Biol Chem, J Cell Biochem, and RSC Adv have fewer retraction counts, with 425 (1.42%), 347 (1.16%), and 343 (1.15%) respectively.

The correlation between this expansion and the retraction of articles by journals does not necessarily imply a surge in scientific misconduct. A meticulous study emphasized the need to understand whether there has been an actual increase in misconduct or if the rise in cases is solely a result of enhanced detection tools [20].

Figure 3 illustrates the trend of retractions in five scientific journals from 1996 to 2023. These journals retracted most of their published papers at different times. The last decade witnessed significant retractions in PLoS One, the Journal of Biological Chemistry, the Journal of Cellular Biochemistry, RSC Advances, and Tumor Biology. PLoS One and the Journal of Cellular Biochemistry show alarming spikes in retractions in 2021 and 2022, respectively.

3.4 Publishers

Publishers serve as guardians of scholarly integrity, wielding significant influence in preventing and addressing retractions. Through stringent manuscript vetting,

Journals	Retractions count	Percent of total retractions (%)
PLoS One	1056	3.54
J Biol Chem	425	1.42
J Cell Biochem	347	1.16
RSC Adv	343	1.15
Biomed Res Int	325	1.09
Tumor Biol	293	0.98
Eur Rev Med Pharmacol Sci	283	0.95
Onco Targets Ther	265	0.89
Sci Rep	263	0.88
Appl Bionics Biomech	247	0.83

Table 1.
Retraction counts from various scientific journals.

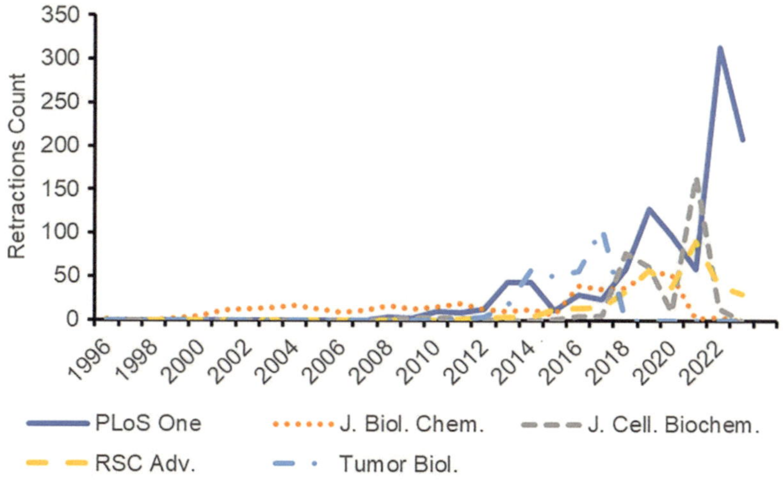

Figure 3.
Temporal evolution of retracted papers for five scientific journals from 1996 to 2023.

plagiarism detection tools, and clear ethics guidelines, they establish a foundation for trustworthy academic content. Editorial boards, appointed by publishers, play a pivotal role in upholding ethical standards within journals.

Publishers also contribute to fostering a culture of research integrity by providing educational resources for authors and actively monitoring post-publication discussions. The role of readers in developing a research culture cannot be undermined. For example, in the case of 33 papers, readers assumed the role of whistleblowers, identifying cases of misconduct and bringing them to the attention of the journal editor [21].

Table 2 presents the number of retractions and the corresponding percentage by various publishers. According to the data, Elsevier has the highest retraction count at 5529, which makes up 18.9% of the total retractions, followed by Springer Nature and Wiley with 4299 (14.7%) and 2440 (8.3%) retractions, respectively.

3.5 Countries

The geographical distribution of retracted papers offers a global perspective on the prevalence of retractions across different regions. Recognizing patterns in the distribution of retractions can inform efforts to address region-specific challenges and promote international collaborations for research integrity.

Publisher	Retractions count	Percent of total retractions (%)
Elsevier	5529	18.9
Springer Nature	4299	14.7
Wiley	2440	8.3
Hindawi Publishing Group	1598	5.5
Taylor & Francis	1577	5.4

Table 2.
Retractions by five publishers and the corresponding percentage of total retractions by each publisher.

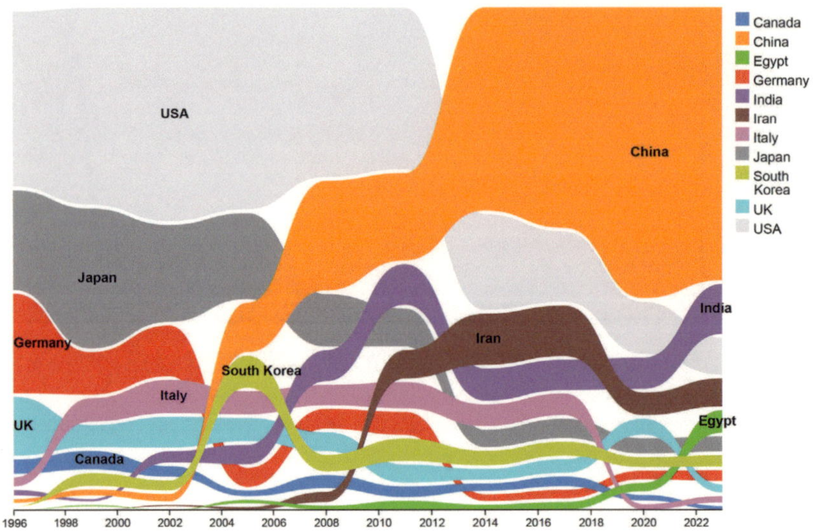

Figure 4.
Temporal evolution of retracted papers for different countries from 1996 to 2023.

Figure 4 shows the temporal evolution of retracted papers for different countries, normalized at each period between 1996 and 2023. Each country is represented by a unique color, and the magnitude of each color corresponds to the percentage of retractions from that country at any specific point in time. Notable temporal fluctuations/bumps are observed in countries such as the USA, Germany, Japan, the UK, Canada, Italy, India, China, Iran, Egypt, and South Korea. For instance, in the 1990s and 2000s, the USA had a relatively high volume of retractions compared to other countries. However, in the early 2010s, the volume of retractions in China began to increase, surpassing that of the USA by the mid-2010s. The percentage of retractions from most of the developed countries saw a decline after 2015, whereas China, Iran, and India witnessed an increase during that period.

Further investigation is required to explore this trend, which may be influenced by a range of factors including research metrics and roles within the ranking system.

Table 3 presents a compilation of leading countries with retractions, encompassing the overall document count, publications from a single country (SCP), publications involving multiple countries (MCP), the proportion of retractions attributed to each country in relation to the global total, and the MCP ratio determined by dividing MCP by the total documents from that country. China leads in terms of total retractions and SCP, although its MCP ratio is relatively lower compared to other countries. Interestingly, the USA is second, and the list includes scientifically strong countries such as Germany, Italy, the UK, Japan, and Korea.

Based on the research conducted by Ribeiro and Vasconcelos [22], an analysis of retracted articles documented in Retraction Watch from 2013 to 2015 revealed that 85% of these articles were associated with 15 distinct countries. It can be inferred that this problem exhibits uneven distribution across different countries.

Figure 5 demonstrates co-authorship patterns among authors from various countries. The figure displays the co-authorship network of authors' affiliated countries, with a threshold of 50 documents receiving at least 100 citations. Using VOSviewer and Gephi applications, the analysis was conducted for the period 1986–2023. The

Country	Documents	Proportion	SCP	MCP	MCP ratio
China	7783	0.267	7016	767	0.099
USA	2396	0.082	1819	577	0.241
India	1249	0.043	1104	145	0.116
Iran	912	0.031	723	189	0.207
Japan	888	0.031	791	97	0.109
UK	508	0.017	384	124	0.244
Korea	451	0.015	365	86	0.191
Germany	381	0.013	285	96	0.252
Italy	360	0.012	255	105	0.292

Table 3.
Countries wise share of retractions.

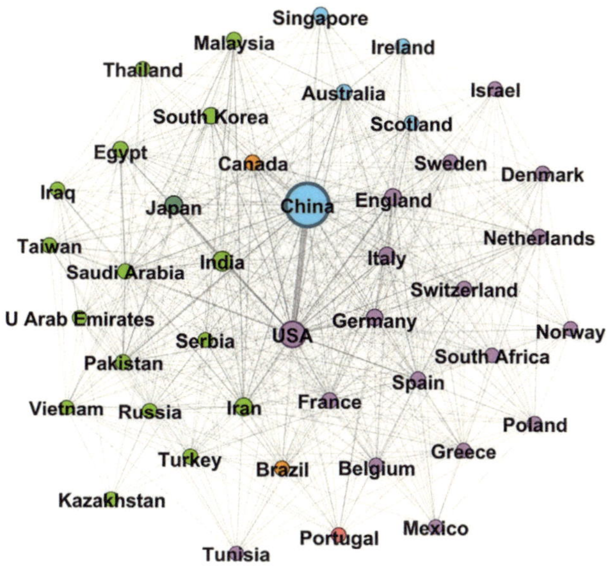

Figure 5.
Co-authorship of authors from various countries.

clusters (modularity class) of authors' affiliated countries can be determined by the color of the nodes, visually conveying the size and prominence of the countries within the network. The strength of the links or arrows signifies co-authorships. Notably, China, positioned at the center of the network, was found to collaborate strongly with the USA for dubious research. The data confirms earlier research findings, indicating that predominant retractions originate from countries with a notable research legacy, including the United States and China.

Figure 6 depicts the co-authorship network of authors' affiliating institutions from 1986 to 2023, with a threshold of 75 documents and at least 100 citations. The color of the nodes represents the clusters (modularity class) corresponding to the authors' affiliations. The varying size of the nodes visually conveys the degree or prominence of the institutions within the network, while the thickness of the lines

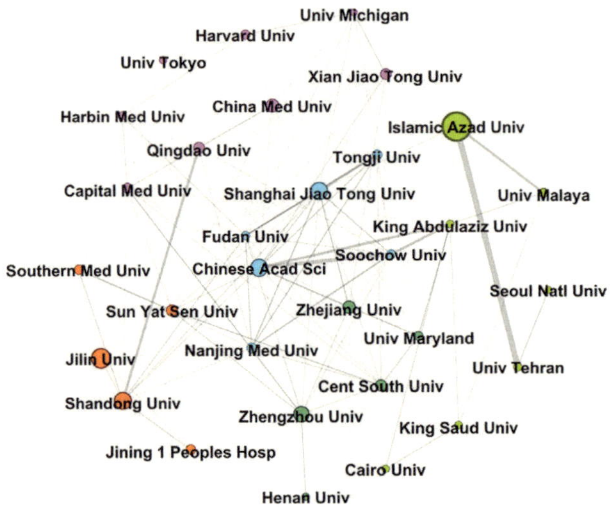

Figure 6.
Co-authorship of authors-affiliated institutions.

or arrows indicates the strength of co-authorships. Islamic Azad University and the University of Tehran, along with Qingdao University and Shandong University, demonstrated the highest level of collaboration in dubious research.

Liu and Lei [23] conducted a thorough bibliometric analysis examining the factors contributing to the rise in retractions in the Middle East over the past two decades. The study identified plagiarism, duplicate publishing, fabricated peer review, approval from institutions/researchers, and fraud as the leading factors behind retractions. Instances of plagiarism and duplicate publications often originate from

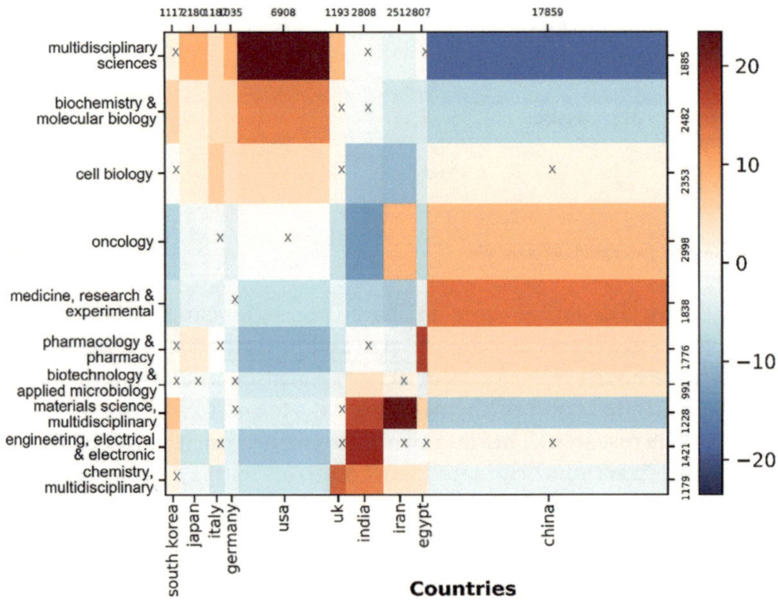

Figure 7.
Contingency matrix between countries and Web of Science categories of retracted papers.

countries that have recently entered the research field and are associated with journals of low impact factor.

The study conducted by Brainard [20] demonstrates a correlation between implementing comprehensive research misconduct policies in countries or institutions and a decrease in the number of retractions.

Figure 7 shows the contingency matrix of countries and Web of Science categories for retracted papers. The y-axis lists various science categories, including "multidisciplinary sciences," "biochemistry & molecular biology," "cell biology," "oncology," "medicine, research & experimental," "pharmacology & pharmacy," "biotechnology & applied microbiology," "materials science, multidisciplinary," and "chemistry, multidisciplinary," etc. Significant retractions from the USA are highly correlated with "multidisciplinary sciences," whereas Iranian retractions are strongly correlated with "materials science, multidisciplinary." Retractions from India fall within the domain of "engineering, electrical & electronic," while Egyptian retractions show high deviation in "pharmacology & pharmacy."

4. Conclusions

In concluding this analysis of retracted publications accessed from the Web of science Core Collection database for the period of 1986–2023, it becomes evident that understanding the intricate dynamics of retractions is paramount for sustaining the credibility of scholarly literature. The preceding sections have unveiled patterns in the descriptive analysis, subject areas, journals, publishers, and the global distribution of retractions, shedding light on the multifaceted challenges faced by the academic community. Such as

Rising trend of retractions: Between 2000 and 2019, a 15-fold increase has been witnessed. The overall number of dubious publications has increased exponentially, especially after 2015.

Focus areas and reasons: Retractions are not limited to specific fields. Biology & Medicine, Chemistry & Physics, and Engineering & Mathematics have higher retraction rates.

Journal and publisher landscape: PLoS One leads in retractions as a journal, whereas major publishers like Elsevier, Springer Nature, and Wiley are the main publishers with retractions.

Geographical distribution: The temporal distribution fluctuates across countries with a notable research legacy, such as the USA, Germany, Japan, the UK, Canada, Italy, and China. China leads in total retractions and single-country publications, but its multiple-country publication ratio is lower than other countries. Strong collaboration for dubious research exists between certain institutions, such as Islamic Azad University and the University of Tehran. International collaboration in dubious research also exists.

5. Recommendations

There is a pressing need for targeted interventions to address this growing issue. The primary onus, however, lies with publishers to enact measures aimed at averting retractions and upholding the trustworthiness and credibility of scholarly work. Publishers should:

i. Implement rigorous manuscript vetting processes to ensure that submitted articles meet high standards of quality and accuracy.

ii. Establish clear ethics guidelines for authors, reviewers, and editors.

iii. Use plagiarism detection tools to detect any instances of plagiarism in submitted articles.

iv. Provide training and education for authors, reviewers, and editors on best practices in academic publishing in order to ensure they understand their responsibilities and avoid common mistakes.

v. Implement post-publication review processes to identify any errors or issues in published articles before they become widespread.

vi. Strive for transparency in the publishing process by providing clear and detailed information about the review process, the authors, and the funding sources for the research.

vii. Encourage error reporting by researchers and publishers to maintain journal reliability.

Apart from these, it is imperative for institutions to establish rigorous policies and procedures to handle instances of research misconduct. They should also appoint vigilant watchdogs to monitor the research process and ensure that all ethical guidelines are being followed.

Acknowledgements

We gratefully acknowledge the financial support provided by Northumbria University for this research project.

Conflict of interest

The authors declare no conflict of interest.

Author details

Muhammad Asif Khan[1]*, Humaira Farid[1] and Imtiaz Ali[2]

1 Faculty of Business and Law, Department of Marketing, Operations and Systems, Newcastle Business School, Northumbria University, United Kingdom

2 Department of Chemical and Materials Engineering, King Abdulaziz University, Rabigh, Saudi Arabia

*Address all correspondence to: m.asif.khan@northumbria.ac.uk

References

[1] Candal-Pedreira C, Pérez-Ríos M, Ruano-Ravina A. Retraction of scientific papers: Types of retraction, consequences, and impacts. In: Faintuch J, Faintuch S, editors. Integrity of Scientific Research: Fraud, Misconduct and Fake News in the Academic, Medical and Social Environment. Cham: Springer International Publishing; 2022. pp. 397-407. DOI: 10.1007/978-3-030-99680-2_40

[2] Eldakar MAM, Shehata AMK. A bibliometric study of article retractions in technology fields in developing economies countries. Scientometrics. 2023;**128**(11):6047-6083

[3] Hesselmann F, Graf V, Schmidt M, Reinhart M. The visibility of scientific misconduct: A review of the literature on retracted journal articles. Current Sociology. 2017;**65**(6):814-845

[4] Mongeon P, Larivière V. Costly collaborations: The impact of scientific fraud on co-authors' careers. Journal of the Association for Information Science and Technology. 2016;**67**(3):535-542

[5] Sox HC, Rennie D. Research misconduct, retraction, and cleansing the medical literature: Lessons from the Poehlman Case. Annals of Internal Medicine. 2006;**144**(8):609-613

[6] Committee on Public Ethics. Committee on Publication Ethics (COPE). Guidelines on good publication practice. Journal of Postgraduate Medicine. 2000;**46**(3):217-221

[7] Definition of Research Misconduct. ORI – The Office of Research Integrity [Internet]. 2024. Available from: https://ori.hhs.gov/definition-research-misconduct

[8] Sharma P, Sharma B, Reza A, et al. A systematic review of retractions in biomedical research publications: Reasons for retractions and their citations in Indian affiliations. Humanity Social Science Communication. 2023;**10**:597

[9] Polymers Editorial Office, Abdalla S, et al. A bio polymeric adhesive produced by photo cross-linkable technique. Polymers. 2016;**8**:292. DOI: 10.3390/polym8080292

[10] Abdalla S et al. Controlled light cross-linking technique to prepare healable materials. Polymers. 2017;**9**:241. DOI: 10.3390/polym9060241. Polymers. 2017;**9**(8):382

[11] Alberts B, Cicerone RJ, Fienberg SE, Kamb A, McNutt M, Nerem RM, et al. Self-correction in science at work. Science. 2015;**348**(6242):1420-1422

[12] Evans I. The medical research council's approach to allegations of scientific misconduct. Science and Engineering Ethics. 2000;**6**(1):91-94

[13] Oransky I. Retractions are increasing, but not enough. Nature. 2022;**608**(7921):9-9

[14] Fang FC, Steen RG, Casadevall A. Misconduct accounts for the majority of retracted scientific publications. National Academy of Sciences of the United States of America. 2012;**109**(42):17028-17033

[15] Rubbo P, Helmann CL, Bilynkievycz dos Santos C, Pilatti LA. Retractions in the engineering field: A study on the web of science database. Ethics and Behavior. 2019;**29**(2):141-155

[16] Vuong QH, La VP, Ho MT, Vuong TT, Ho MT. Characteristics of retracted articles based on retraction data from

online sources through February 2019. Science Education. 2020;7(1):34-44

[17] Tang L, Hu G, Sui Y, Yang Y, Cao C. Retraction: The "Other Face" of research collaboration? Science and Engineering Ethics. 2020;**26**(3):1681-1708

[18] Furman JL, Jensen K, Murray F. Governing knowledge in the scientific community: Exploring the role of retractions in biomedicine. Research Policy. 2012;**41**(2):276-290

[19] Lei L, Zhang Y. Lack of improvement in scientific integrity: An analysis of WoS retractions by Chinese researchers (1997-2016). Science and Engineering Ethics. 2018;**24**(5):1409-1420

[20] Brainard J. Rethinking retractions. Science. 2018;**362**(6413):390-393

[21] Vuong QH. The limitations of retraction notices and the heroic acts of authors who correct the scholarly record: An analysis of retractions of papers published from 1975 to 2019. Learned Publishing. 2020;**33**(2):119-130

[22] Ribeiro MD, Vasconcelos SMR. Correction to: Retractions covered by Retraction Watch in the 2013-2015 period: Prevalence for the most productive countries. Scientometrics. 2018;**114**(2):735-735

[23] Liu W, Lei L. Retractions in the Middle East from 1999 to 2018: A bibliometric analysis. Scientometrics. 2021;**126**(6):4687-4700

Section 2

Bibliometrics Applications

Chapter 5

Teacher Training in Science Education: Insights into Research Trends through a Bibliometric Approach

Konstantinos Karampelas

Abstract

The primary objective of this study is to offer comprehensive insights into the current research trends concerning teacher training in the field of science education. By employing a bibliometric approach, this investigation explores a domain that has received limited scrutiny in previous studies. The data collection process involves querying the Scopus platform, resulting in the acquisition of 3695 articles spanning the publication years from 1967 to 2024. A detailed analysis of these articles reveals valuable information regarding the increasing output over time, geographic distribution of research, affiliations of contributors, diverse fields of study, and predominant themes explored by researchers. The data derived from this bibliometric analysis sheds light on the evolving landscape of teacher training in science education. It provides insights into the growing interest in this area, global distribution of research activities, key contributors from various affiliations, and diverse range of topics explored within the realm of science education. By examining the patterns and trends identified in the collected articles, this research contributes to a more nuanced understanding of the current state of teacher training in science education and highlights potential areas for further exploration and development in this critical field.

Keywords: teacher training, science teaching, higher education, bibliometrics, universities, higher education

1. Introduction

This research endeavors to furnish comprehensive insights into the examination of combined topics, namely teacher training and science education. In other words, it is an attempt to shed light on the research trends on these two topics. Teacher training is an important institution since it relates to the education, competencies, and qualities that future teachers will hold. Therefore, it is highly relevant to the effectiveness of their work and ability to deliver knowledge [1–3]. Science teaching is also very important. There has been significant research focusing on it, by examining several aspects of it, such as the content of science that has to be taught within education, the appropriate methods and conditions along with the role of teachers, schools, and society [4–6].

The study begins by presenting an overview of the major theories and literature relevant to these two interconnected subjects. Subsequently, an amalgamation of bibliometric studies independently focusing on teacher training and science education is provided. This synthesis aims to offer a consolidated understanding of the existing body of literature surrounding these topics. Building upon the insights gained from individual bibliometric studies, the research proceeds to outline a methodology that accentuates commonalities identified in the findings of these studies. This methodological approach seeks to bridge the existing knowledge gaps and explore the intersections between teacher training and science education. The distinctive identity, research questions, and methodology of the study emerge from this comprehensive synthesis.

The subsequent section delves into the outcomes and results derived from the research. By combining and contextualizing findings from various bibliometric studies, this study strives to contribute a holistic perspective on the synergies and intersections between teacher training and science education. Through this nuanced exploration, the research aims to provide valuable insights that can inform future investigations, policy development, and educational practices in the realm of science education and teacher training, allowing researchers to adopt an accomplished bibliometric approach [7].

2. Investigating teacher training and science teaching

2.1 Teacher training

Teacher training is widely recognized as a crucial factor in determining the quality of an education system. The promotion of teacher qualifications and competencies is a fundamental condition for achieving effective learning results across all levels of education. Teacher training is closely associated with teaching quality and productivity, and it is regarded as a complex issue that can influence and be influenced by a variety of factors and challenges. One such factor is the institutions responsible for providing teacher training, which are typically universities and higher education foundations. These institutions play a role in shaping the content and evaluation of teacher training programs. Additionally, these programs significantly impact the professional development or experience of educators [2].

The studies on teacher training highlight the influence of education and professional qualifications, including undergraduate and postgraduate degrees as well as teacher training courses. Researchers have emphasized the correlation between the fundamental undergraduate studies of teachers and their effectiveness. These studies suggest that teachers who hold undergraduate degrees from specific universities may outperform their counterparts [8, 9]. Moreover, studies have underscored the importance of formal qualifications in facilitating effective teacher training. These studies have stressed that teachers with master's degrees in education or social sciences are generally more efficient than those without such qualifications [1, 10]. However, this finding has sparked considerable debate [2, 9]. Finally, certain studies emphasize the significance of teacher training and preparation courses or programs. Although these studies seem relatively limited in scope, they consistently advocate for the inclusion of subjects that focus on the content knowledge that future teachers will have to deliver, such as language, mathematics, history, science, Information and Communication Technologies (ICT), along with subjects that focus on pedagogy, teaching methods, and instruction [2, 9].

There is a growing body of research that highlights the role of actual, context-based experience in teacher training. These studies point out that effective teacher training can rely on experiential learning. Such studies usually support the finding that teacher training should be based on a collaborative effort between schools and universities to provide trainee teachers with a comprehensive understanding of teaching and instruction from both theoretical and practical perspectives. This finding is drawn from relevant pilot studies that aim to bridge the gaps between theory and practice. By engaging teachers in actual teaching situations, these studies enable them to witness firsthand how research findings on effective teaching can be used to approach students, prepare materials, utilize resources, deliver instructions, and achieve desired outcomes. However, it is important to note that while experience is crucial, it should not undermine the importance of education and qualifications. A balanced combination of academic study and practical experience is key to developing effective educators [2, 3].

When considering the topics that should be included in teacher training, it is important for authors to acknowledge the insights of researchers such as Teo et al. [11], who emphasize the need for contemporary teachers to possess the required skills to respond to society's demands, especially in relation to the growing technological progress. Additionally, teachers should be equipped to provide learners with relevant knowledge, skills, attitudes, and competencies. In this context, it is critical for teacher training programs to prioritize the importance of Technological, Pedagogical Content Knowledge (TPACK), as described by Koehler et al. [12]. TPACK serves as a comprehensive framework of knowledge, skills, and abilities across three fields. First, the teachers must be well-versed in technology. Second, they must possess a deep understanding of the content they are delivering. Third, they should be proficient in pedagogy. TPACK should not be treated solely as a body of knowledge. Instead, it should be seen as means for teachers to become familiar with problem-solving, inquiry, active learning, and other effective teaching strategies with the aim of achieving improvement and development in student lives. By incorporating TPACK into the teacher training syllabus, educators can learn how to deliver new knowledge and qualities through the prism of critical thinking, project-based learning, problem-based learning, metacognition, creativity and innovation, collaboration, communication, and digital and information skills. Integrating these elements can not only achieve the teachers' primary goal of imparting knowledge but also assist in other desired goals of citizenship, such as ethical awareness, respect, personal and social competence, cultural consciousness, self-reflection, and adaptability to reform [11, 13].

Le Cornu [14] put forward the idea that effective teacher training must satisfy three basic conditions. First, the program should be well structured and include subjects related to the curriculum, pedagogy, education, and professional experience. Such an efficient structure is achieved with a carefully designed syllabus that provides ample opportunity for continuous learning, diverse professional development, and experience, as well as holistic assessment and validation of both the trainee teachers and the program. This approach aligns with the idea of developing TPACK [11, 12], while also incorporating both theory and experience [2, 3].

The second condition necessitates effective management. In this case, management encompasses aspects such as the placement of future teachers in schools and other institutions that facilitate the acquisition of necessary experiences. Neglecting this condition brings on negative impact on trainee teachers, potentially leading to negative experiences with the teaching profession and routine. Such a failure in teacher training programs would be highly consequential. To prevent this, effective management requires a specialized leadership team, collaboration between institutions, timing, and clear policies and guidelines [2, 14].

The third condition emphasizes the importance of robust support. This support includes the provision of appropriate human resources and infrastructure to accommodate the courses and all associated functions, primarily from the university or institution running the program, as well as all other collaborative institutions. For instance, if there is a shortage of teaching staff or classrooms, and if the schools where trainee teachers are placed do not provide sufficient attention, then the program is unlikely to succeed. Effective support should include formal accreditation of the program, appointment of directors, academic, and administrative staff, equal opportunities for development compared to other departments and courses, as well as funding and scholarships for students [14, 15].

In short, effective teacher training is expected to encompass the acquisition of appropriate knowledge [2, 9]. This is usually provided in courses run by universities or higher education institutions [1, 10]. At the same time, gaining experience from actual contexts of education organizations is considered necessary for trainee teachers, as a more holistic approach in their preparation for the educators' work [11, 13]. Moreover, teachers must acquire Technological Pedagogical Content knowledge, which encompasses the integration of pedagogy, subject knowledge, and technology in their teaching practices [12]. Bearing that in mind, higher education institutions offering teacher training courses should have well-designed curriculum, structure, and collaborations to ensure optimal outcomes [2, 14].

2.2 Science education

Research in science education, over the last decades, has focused on the development of concepts such as scientific literacy. According to Laugksch [4], defining scientific literacy is a complicated task. In essence, it reflects the ultimate goal of science education. This, however, is very complicated as the goals of science education can change depending on the social context and demands. The content of scientific literacy and the mission of teaching science can encompass several topics: the interrelationship between science and other fields such as humanities, technology, and social sciences; the ethics of science; the basic concepts of science; and the nature of science. More specifically, scientific literacy entails a set of seven dimensions. The first is understanding basic scientific knowledge, along with its nature and characteristics. The second is the ability to apply concepts, principles, laws, and theories appropriately while interacting, observing, and analyzing the natural world or the universe. The third is the ability to employ scientific knowledge, processes, and inquiry in problem-solving or decision-making, with the aim of further understanding the natural world. The fourth is the ability to use or implement science while considering values and ethics that define scientific work and nature. The fifth is the ability to appreciate the interrelationship between science and technology, as well as the significance of both in society and in general progress. The sixth dimension is the development of a rich, fundamental background of science, which can aid the formation of friendly attitudes toward this field, which can motivate and assist further learning. Finally, the seventh is the development of manipulative skills regarding science and technology, such as experimenting, asking questions, and critical thinking [4, 16].

The Organisation for Economic Co-operation and Development (OECD) [17] has endeavored to explain these findings in a practical manner, aiming to provide teachers with a comprehensive understanding of the essence of science teaching. In doing so, it has shed light on certain points that scientific literacy and experts engaged in science teaching should prioritize. First, the OECD emphasizes the relevance of the content in which science knowledge is applied. This content can span several contexts, whether it be personal, local, or global. In order to use this knowledge in any context, it is imperative to develop certain competencies. The first competency entails the ability to explain scientific phenomena by discerning, constructing, applying, and evaluating explanations for a range of natural and technological issues. The second competency revolves around the skill of constructing and evaluating designs for scientific inquiry, as well as critically interpreting scientific data and evidence. The third competency encompasses the aptitude to research, evaluate, and apply scientific information in the context of decision-making and action.

The development of these competencies relies on individuals' set of knowledge of science. This knowledge can be of many types. It can be content knowledge, which encompasses concepts, laws, and phenomena, procedural knowledge, which entails the process of scientific work and inquiry, or epistemic knowledge, which pertains to the nature of science and its mission. Epistemic knowledge interacts with wider approaches around science, such as the general beliefs about its rationale and contributions, attitudes, as well as dispositions and awareness in relation to wider issues like technology development and environmental challenges.

Policy and research around science teaching led the National Research Council of the United States, in cooperation with other institutions such as the National Science Teacher Association and American Association for Advancement in Science, to develop a basic framework, which includes fundamental goals, known as the Next Generation Science Standards (NGSS) [5, 6]. The rationale behind establishing this framework is to propose a set of science and engineering practices, as well as crosscutting concepts that link science, engineering, and other fields within the units being taught; additionally, this framework aims to provide fundamental ideas in the areas of natural science, life science, earth, space, engineering, technology, and applications of science [6].

The basic practices from the NGSS include the following: asking questions and defining problems; developing and using models; planning and carrying out investigations; analyzing and interpreting data; using mathematics and computational thinking; constructing explanations and designing solutions; engaging in argument from evidence; and obtaining, evaluating, and communicating information. These practices are expected to introduce a shift in teaching methods compared to mainstream curricula. They are designed to reflect fundamental outcomes that learners need to gain in order to connect science with their real-world experiences. For that purpose, these practices are structured to prioritize performance. The standards clearly outline the specific performance expectations for learners in relation to each practice or goal. These expectations are complemented by target and assessment methods. Moreover, these standards are coherent with other essential subjects, such as language, literacy, arts, and mathematic. This integration ensures that learners receive comprehensive instruction, fostering a holistic, deep understanding, appreciation, and practical use of science [5, 6].

Another contemporary innovation in science education is the introduction of Science, Technology, Engineering, Arts, and Mathematics (STEAM) in schools. This innovative approach integrates these five subjects, building upon the STEM model by incorporating arts and recognizing the importance of creativity in problem-solving. The key innovation lies in fostering skills applicable to real-life situations, encouraging a deeper understanding of contemporary issues related to scientific and technological progress [18–21].

The effective implementation of STEAM in education depends on well-trained teachers. These educators must undergo appropriate training to conduct relevant activities, considering the specific context in which they work. Teaching STEAM involves three primary axes. First, hands-on activities, projects, and inquiry-based scenarios challenge learners with real-world problems, requiring interdisciplinary knowledge. Second, technology-based teaching emphasizes digital skills and understanding modern technology, promoting competencies like critical thinking and information evaluation. Lastly, the arts and creativity axis encourages learners to think beyond traditional knowledge, fostering the ability to deal with unknown situations and connect fields through artistic patterns.

Teachers need specific qualities to teach STEAM successfully. They must appreciate and apply problem-based learning, be proficient in ICT, and cultivate creative thinking to transfer these skills to their students. Overall, STEAM education aims to prepare learners for a dynamic future by integrating diverse disciplines and nurturing essential skills for problem-solving and innovation [20, 22, 23].

In brief, the field of science teaching theory and research is oriented toward approaches and practices that can enhance the comprehension of science and improve learning outcomes. This objective relies on knowledge, skills, and attitudes toward science. Among the various teaching methods, inquiry-based learning is widely considered the most appropriate [4, 16, 17]. To effectively achieve these goals, teachers must possess appropriately designed teaching goals, policies, and curricula. Recognizing this need, the NGSS have been developed to provide teachers with practical guidance for implementing effective science teaching methods in a holistic and profound manner. The standards offer clear guidelines on clarified practices and desired levels of knowledge, competencies, skills, and attitudes that learners are expected to achieve in science during all levels of education [5, 6]. Simultaneously, STEAM as an interdisciplinary innovative approach is being introduced in schools [22, 23].

2.3 Bibliometric studies on teacher training

Teacher training has been a subject of great interest among bibliometricians for decades, as they strive to map the basic research trends in this field. Since 2020, there have been several studies on this topic. For instance, Zhang et al. [24] conducted a bibliometric analysis examining the trends around the identity development of teachers between 2001 and 2021. Utilizing the Web of Science database, they collected 848 articles. Their findings revealed that there is a growing interest surrounding this topic. The articles primarily explored themes such as professional development, teacher identity, higher education, curriculum, gender, teaching, and science education. Notably, the countries that made the most contributions were the United States of America, the United Kingdom, the Netherlands, China, Australia, Canada, Portugal, Finland, Israel, and Spain, with the majority of publications emerging from universities.

In a similar vein, Hursen [25] published a bibliometric study on teacher education and the role of critical thinking within it. A query in the Web of Science identified 2717 articles, published between 1989 and 2022. Remarkably, the rate of publications in this area has witnessed an acceleration during this time span. The majority of these articles came from the USA, Spain, Australia, Turkey, England, Brazil, China,

Canada, South Africa, and Russia. The themes of these articles, as reflected by the most frequent keywords, were critical thinking, education technology, engineering, technology integration, teaching strategies, distance education, teacher knowledge, innovation, creativity, science teaching, teacher development, inquiry, project-based learning, practices, and learning strategies.

Hallinger et al. [26] executed a study on the trends in teacher education, with a specific focus on leadership and professional learning. Utilizing the Scopus platform, they gathered 793 articles, published between the 1970s and 2010s. Notably, the publication rate experienced a surge after 1990. The majority of these articles came from the USA, the UK, Australia, Hong Kong, Canada, South Africa, the Netherlands, China, New Zealand, Israel, Thailand, and Spain. Further, the articles predominantly appeared in journals focusing on education and social studies, particularly those centered around education leadership and management. The primary themes explored in these studies revolved around teachers' professional development, school leadership, and administration.

Cretu et al. [27] conducted a bibliometric study around teacher training in the context of inclusive education. They collected 440 documents by leveraging the Web of Science. The results of their study revealed a rising trend in the number of publications. The countries with the largest number of contributions were the US, Australia, Spain, Canada, England, China, Germany, South Africa, Turkey, and Ireland. Universities emerged as the primary contributors to this body of knowledge. The majority of these articles were published in journals oriented toward education and teacher education. The predominant topics encompassed teacher education, self-efficacy, practices, teacher knowledge, higher education, technology, teacher attitudes, beliefs, special needs, and collaboration.

Gavinolla et al. [7] examined trends in teacher education in relation to sustainability. The authors gathered 1782 articles on the Scopus platform, published between 1991 and 2020. These articles were primarily sourced from journals that focused on sustainability, education, environmental studies, environmental education, and teacher education. The researchers, predominantly affiliated with universities, worked in fields such as social sciences, environmental sciences, health sciences, education, mathematics, computing, arts, and humanities. The countries with the greatest contributions were the USA, the UK, Brazil Taiwan, Portugal, and China. The analysis revealed several recurring keywords and themes within the articles, including sustainability, teacher education, curriculum, professional development, e-learning, teacher knowledge, training, teaching methods, and health.

These bibliometric studies highlight a growing interest in the field of teacher training [24, 26]. Many of these articles are published in journals that are relevant to social sciences or education, either in general or in specific areas such as education management or teacher education [26, 27]. The countries with the highest number of publications in this area are the USA, the UK, Australia, Canada, China, Turkey, Germany, and Spain. Moreover, universities are the primary affiliations providing these articles [27, 28]. The topics covered in these articles, as indicated by the keywords, are relevant to teacher education: e-learning, technology, higher education, curriculum, technology, teaching practices, pedagogical content knowledge, and teacher attitudes [25, 27, 28].

2.4 Bibliometric studies on science education

Bibliometricians have been endeavoring to identify precise research trends around science teaching and science education. Dogan [1] conducted a bibliometric analysis using a query on the Web of Science, which yielded 1096 articles published between 2000 and 2020. The majority of these articles were written by researchers working in universities, originating from English-speaking countries such as the USA, Canada, the UK, and New Zealand and non-English-speaking countries such as China, Brazil, Germany, Spain, France, Turkey, and Scandinavian countries. The themes, as defined by clustering keywords, were science teaching, professional development, socio-scientific issues such as the Nature of Science, inquiry-based teaching, and curriculum.

Wang et al. [29] attempted to map the evolution of science education research from 2001 to 2020. By searching specific journals, the authors gathered 6278 articles published between 2021 and 2020. The institutions at the forefront of research trends were mostly universities, with many articles resulting from collaborations between institutions. The countries with the most publications were the USA, Australia, England, Turkey, Canada, Taiwan, Germany, Israel, Sweden, and China. The major themes that emerged were STEAM, STEAM education, inquiry-based learning, motivation, achievement, scientific literacy, teacher education, professional development, pedagogical content knowledge, teacher education, socio-scientific issues, and the nature of science.

Effendi et al. [30] carried out research around trends in scientific literacy, collecting 644 studies published between 1984 and 2020 with the help of the Scopus database. Over this period, there was a notable increase in the number of publications on this subject. The themes that dominated the studies were science teaching, motivation, information literacy, curriculum, media, media education, computers, technology, health studies, learning strategies, NGSS, and pedagogical content knowledge. The main finding of the authors was that researchers have been linking scientific literacy and education. The USA was the country with the highest number of publications, followed by Canada, Australia, Turkey, and Indonesia.

Moving onto another study, Maryanti et al. [31] conducted a computational bibliometric analysis around science teaching. The authors collected 1000 articles containing the term science education in their keywords, which were published between 2017 and 2021. One significant finding of their analysis was the impact of central socio-economical and health topics, particularly those related to the COVID-19 pandemic, on research trends in this field. The identified themes were grouped into five different clusters. The first cluster centered around socio-scientific topics, such as education, teaching practices, history, and humanities in relation to science and technology. The second cluster focused on relating science with learning and subjects and contained topics such as inquiry-based learning, STEAM, mathematics, perception, performance, and problem-solving techniques. The third cluster entailed research topics in science teaching such as literature review, scholarship, and intervention. The fourth cluster examined the intersection of science teaching with technology and higher education topics, encompassing subjects such as computer science, engineering, communication, and integration. The fifth cluster revolved around the topics of teacher education and science issues, such as experience, attitude assessment, environment, technology teaching, COVID-19, and perspective.

Pham et al. [32] examined the research trends around the professional development of science teachers. By employing the Scopus database, the authors collected 431 articles published between 2001 and 2021. This time period saw a significant growth in the number of publications each year. Most articles were published in journals focusing on education and social sciences. The countries with the greatest number of contributions were the USA, the UK, South Africa, Australia, Israel, Germany, South Korea, and Turkey. The authors of these articles were primarily affiliated with universities. The most frequent themes were professional development, teacher education, science education, pedagogical content knowledge, inquiry, self-efficacy, curriculum, STEAM, and NGSS.

In summary, bibliometric studies centered around science teaching indicate a burgeoning interest in this area [30, 32]. Numerous articles are being published, deriving mostly from the USA, the UK, Australia, Canada, Turkey, and Germany [29, 31]. The authors of these articles predominantly hail from universities [1, 29]. The focal points that dominate the interest of the authors revolve around the dimensions of teaching science, as evinced by frequently used keywords such as curriculum, teaching strategies, teacher education, pedagogical content knowledge, and NGSS. Further, there is a substantial emphasis on relevant technology, wider social issues, STEAM, the nature of science, and socio-scientific issues [30–32].

3. Methodology

3.1 Scope of study

Common themes have emerged from bibliometric studies around teacher training and science education. Both fields have grabbed the interest of researchers, as indicated by the growing number of publications, especially after the first decade of 2000 [24, 26, 30, 32]. A majority of these publications were submitted by authors working in universities, more specifically in areas related to education and social studies but also to humanities, environmental studies, science, and engineering [1, 28, 31]. The countries that have the most publications in both fields are the USA, Australia, the UK, Canada, China, Turkey, Germany, and Spain [24, 25, 29, 31].

Additionally, there are similarities in the topics that researchers in both fields prioritize. There seems to be an emphasis on teacher education, teacher knowledge, and pedagogical content knowledge [25, 28, 30, 32]. This is in line with the theoretical perspective that teacher training must aim to equip future educators with a robust body of knowledge, either general or specific, about the subjects they will teach [2, 4, 9, 17].

Furthermore, there is a notable focus on the content and context that teachers will deliver to their future learners, particularly in relation to the curriculum, teaching practices, inquiry-based learning, the nature of science, and socio-scientific matters [1, 24, 25, 32]. This aligns with the theoretical viewpoint that teachers need to be familiar with effective strategies and practices; teacher training must facilitate this familiarity, along with providing practical experience in actual school contexts [5, 11, 13, 17].

Technology is also a common topic in both teacher training and science education. Various dimensions surrounding the role of technology in education and learning have been explored [25, 28–30]. This aligns with the theoretical points emphasizing the significance of technology and computers, especially in issues such as Technological Pedagogical Content Knowledge [12] and the introduction of STEAM education [22, 23].

Moreover, the role and significance of higher education is underscored in both fields [24, 27, 31, 32]. This falls in line with the theoretical viewpoint regarding the importance of universities in offering teacher training programs, often in collaboration with other institutions [27].

In summation, the common topics identified by bibliometricians in publications on teacher training and science teaching revolve around the content of teacher training, qualities and competencies that teachers need to acquire, role of technology, and importance of higher education. These topics are also considered significant in literature [2, 6, 17].

There appears to be a shortage of bibliometric studies that specifically examine the trends in teacher training and science education. This study aims to bridge this gap by providing valuable insights into the characteristics and themes of publications that focus on the education and preparation of teachers to effectively instruct science subjects in the future. Bibliometric approaches are particularly suitable for this type of study. In this study, the data was collected using the Scopus platform. A crucial step in this research is to determine the appropriate query or the set of words that will be used to retrieve the desired papers from the platform [7].

3.2 Research questions

In this particular study, the set of words used should include terms such as "teacher training" [2], as well as terms relevant to science education, science teaching, and literacy [17]. With this in mind, the query was defined as follows:

(TITLE-ABS-KEY (teacher AND training) AND TITLE-ABS-KEY (science AND education OR science AND learning)). There was no restriction regarding the years of publication.

Once the search was executed and the articles were collected, four research questions were addressed.

1. What is the research output regarding teacher training in science teaching?

2. What are the affiliations and countries with most contributions?

3. In which fields of study is there interest around this topic?

4. What are the main themes examined by researchers?

For the first three research questions, the analysis was conducted with the help of the Scopus platform, which was easily accessible and has been used in relevant studies in teacher training [7, 26] and science teaching [30, 32]. For the fourth question, the VOSviewer program was employed, which is specifically designed for keyword analysis and clustering, making it a valuable asset for studies of this nature [7, 33].

4. Findings

4.1 1st research question: research output

With regard to the first research question, a total of 4532 articles were collected after executing the query on the Scopus platform. However, after a thorough review, this number was reduced to 3695, as it was discovered that some of the initially collected articles were not particularly relevant to the study's topic. The representation of the publication progress over the years is presented in **Figure 1**. The range of publication years extends as far back as 1967. However, until 1980, the number of publications was relatively low. It was mainly after the late 1990s when the publication rate exceeded 20 articles per year. Since then, the number has steadily increased, indicating significant research output.

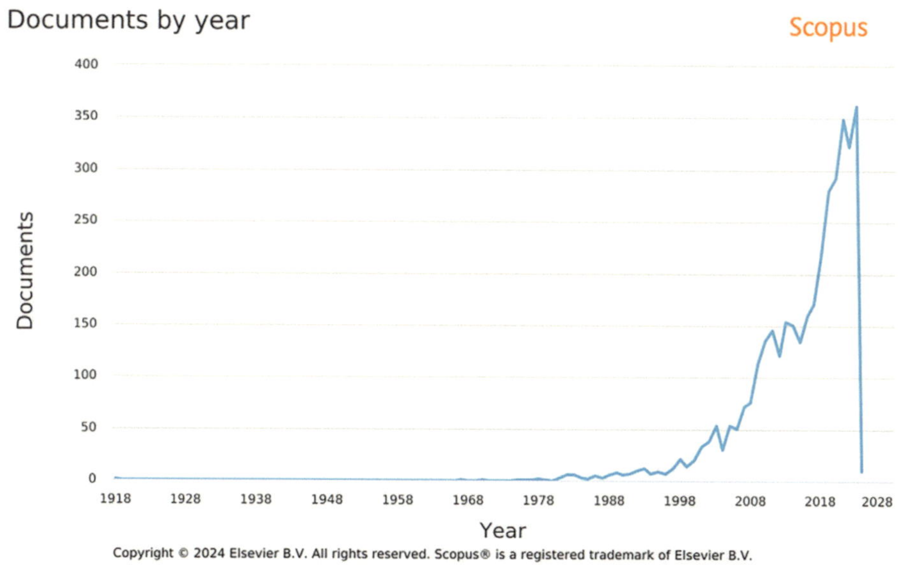

Figure 1.
Number of publications per year.

The research landscape concerning teacher training in science subjects reflects a notable interest among scholars, mirroring the attention dedicated to teacher training and science teaching independently. Examining the pace of publications in both domains, as well as their intersection, reveals a synchronous focus [24, 26, 30, 32]. Scholars are evidently invested in understanding how teacher training can effectively prepare educators for enhanced science teaching practices.

This collective interest underscores the broader significance of the topic. The convergence of attention from researchers aligns with the broader discourse in literature [2, 4, 6]. Delving into the specifics, scholars are not merely exploring teacher training as a standalone theme but are intricately examining its nuanced relationship with science teaching. This nuanced approach demonstrates a holistic understanding of the interconnectedness between effective teacher preparation and successful science education.

The findings suggest that the academic community recognizes the pivotal role teacher training plays in shaping the quality of science instruction. Consequently, research in this realm contributes not only to advancing knowledge on teacher training but also to the overall improvement of science education. The convergence of attention from various scholarly quarters emphasizes the multifaceted nature of this discourse, further justifying the continued exploration and examination of teacher training in science subjects as a crucial area within educational research [2, 4–6].

4.2 2nd research questions: countries and affiliations

Regarding the second research question, **Figure 2** illustrates the countries with the highest number of publications, namely the USA, Spain, the UK, China, Russia, Germany, Brazil, Turkey, Indonesia, and Australia.

These publications primarily involve universities, as depicted in **Figure 3**.

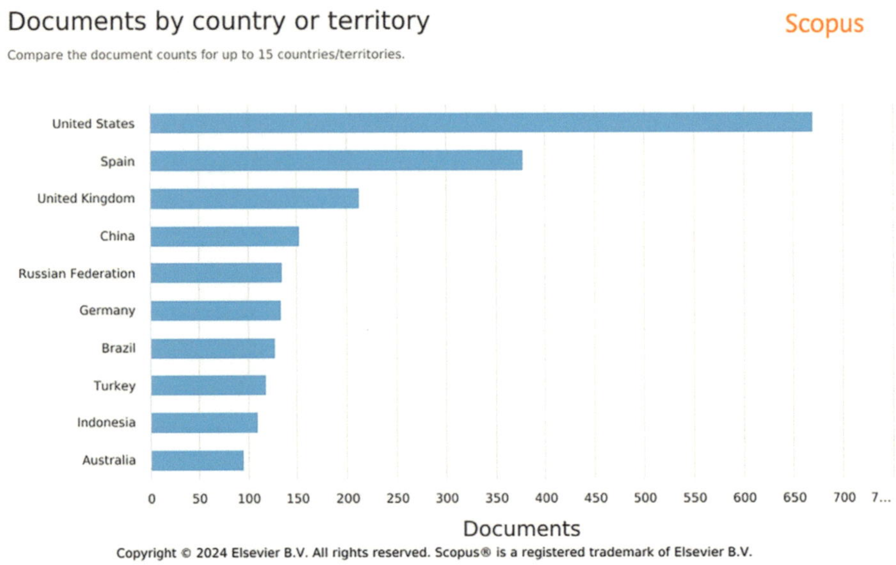

Figure 2.
Number of documents published per country or territory.

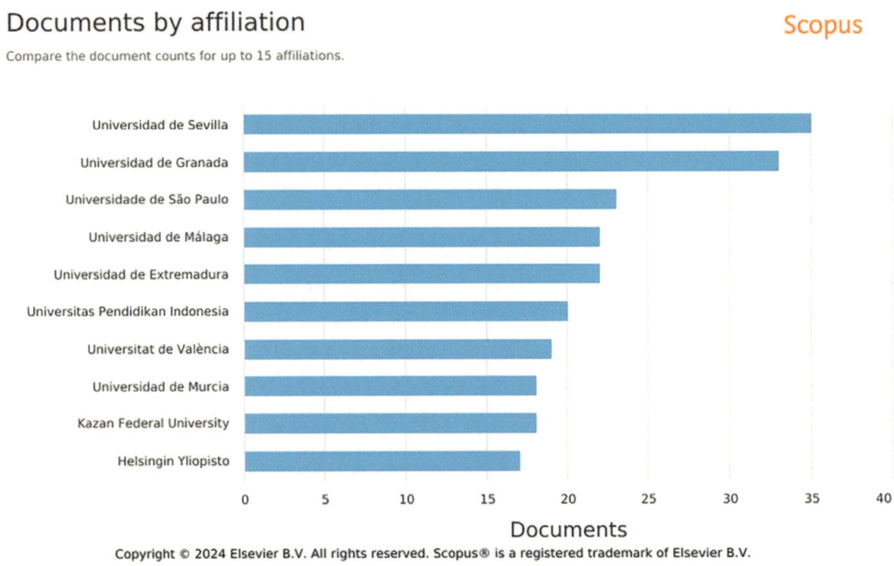

Figure 3.
Number of published documents by affiliation.

The funding for this research chiefly stems from national organizations, agencies, ministries, or institutions in the USA or Europe (where most publications come from), as seen in **Figure 4**.

Interestingly, publications funded by the National Foundation, ranking first on the list, exceed those funded by the European Commission by more than double.

These findings align with previous research on teacher training [24, 25] and science teaching [29, 31], highlighting the role of universities in preparing future

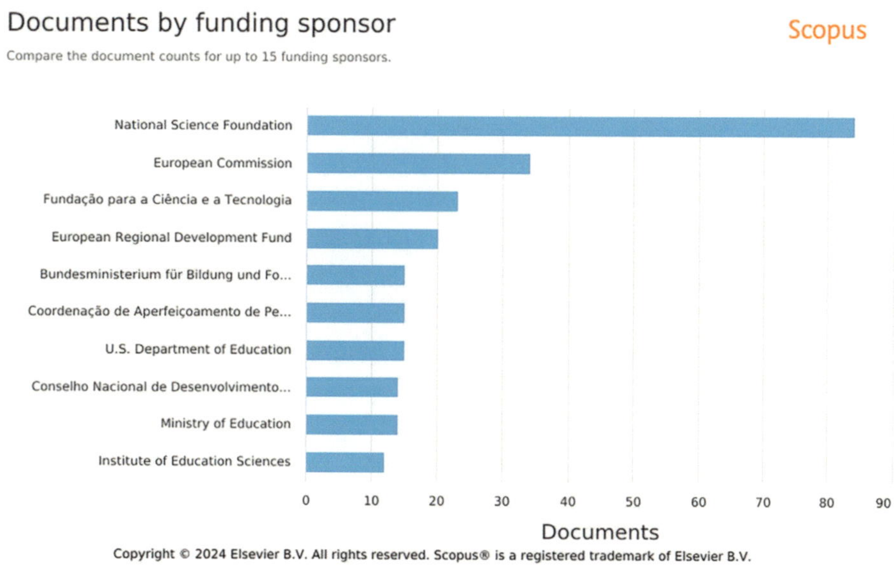

Figure 4.
Number of published documents by funding sponsor.

teachers for science education. Additionally, collaboration among institutions, as seen in previous studies, is also evident [27, 29]. Moreover, the fact that governmental and formal public organizations provide funding for this research underscores the connection and collaboration of universities to achieve optimal outcomes. These conditions are essential for ensuring effective teacher training, as universities demonstrate a commitment to offering relevant courses and prioritizing funding and research. This, in turn, nurtures evaluation and improvement in teacher training [2, 14].

4.3 3rd research question: fields of study

Delving into the third research question, as illustrated in **Figure 5**, a substantial portion of the compiled articles stems from the realm of social sciences. Impressively, this category encompasses a noteworthy 2470 articles, constituting a substantial 43.7% of the overall corpus. Surprisingly, this surpasses the combined total of articles from the second-highest field, Computer Science, which comprises less than half of the social sciences' contribution. Beyond these domains, the research landscape expands into fields pertinent to STEAM subjects, embracing contributions from disciplines like engineering, mathematics, physics and astronomy, environmental sciences, as well as earth and planetary science. Furthermore, the scholarly discourse on the topic extends its reach into the territories of arts, humanities, and decision sciences. Researchers from these diverse domains actively contribute to the growing body of knowledge surrounding the subject under investigation. This interdisciplinary collaboration highlights the multifaceted nature of the research, drawing upon insights and methodologies from a broad spectrum of academic disciplines.

In addition to these substantial contributions, a discernible presence is noted from researchers engaged in health studies. Notwithstanding its comparatively smaller footprint, this sector encompasses fields such as medicine, dentistry, biochemistry, nursing, and psychology. The inclusion of these health-related perspectives further

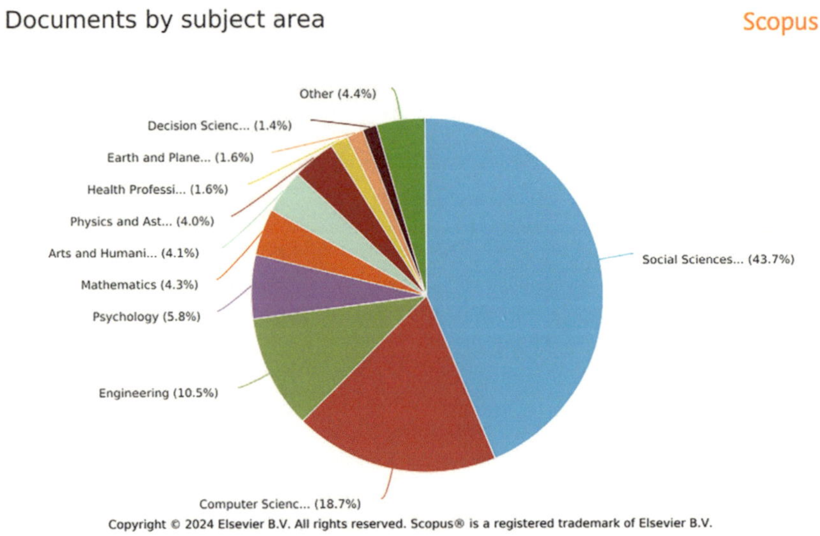

Figure 5.
Number of published documents by subject area.

enriches the comprehensive understanding of the subject matter, offering a holistic view that incorporates insights from both the social sciences and health sciences.

The varied composition of contributors underscores the interdisciplinary nature of the study, emphasizing the interconnectedness of different academic domains in exploring and addressing the research question at hand. As the amalgamation of perspectives continues to broaden, the resulting discourse contributes to a more nuanced and comprehensive understanding of the intricate facets associated with the overarching research inquiry.

In summary, the overall findings align seamlessly with those derived from independent studies specifically focused on teacher training and science instruction. The congruence in outcomes not only reaffirms the validity of the current research but also highlights the consistency and reliability of the observed patterns and trends across a broader spectrum of educational investigations. This coherence enhances the robustness of the conclusions drawn, providing a comprehensive and cohesive understanding of the intricate dynamics associated with teacher preparation and the effective imparting of scientific knowledge in educational settings [26, 27, 30–32]. The dominant representation of researchers from fields of STEAM, social studies, arts, and humanities substantiates the crucial correlation these disciplines share with training teachers for science subjects, as elucidated in the existing literature. This dominance underscores the acknowledged importance of a multidisciplinary approach in shaping effective science education. The collective expertise from diverse academic realms enriches teacher training initiatives, emphasizing the interconnectedness of science education with broader educational, social, and humanistic perspectives. The defined framework of the literature aptly recognizes and validates the pivotal role played by researchers from these varied fields in fostering a holistic and well-rounded approach to science teacher preparation [19, 21, 30, 32].

4.4 4th research question: themes

Regarding the fourth research question, the keywords that emerged most frequently were grouped in the VOSviewer into four clusters, as presented in **Figure 6**. The first cluster includes keywords that are focused on teaching and learning along with relevant sub-topics and dimensions. Among them, the keywords with the highest occurrences are teaching, cognition, and exercise. Other keywords in this cluster are education, learning, curriculum, review, feedback, science teaching, teacher, training, student, assessment, evaluation, human, problem-based learning, and practices. The second cluster includes keywords that are focused on the actual context wherein contemporary science teaching and learning occur, along with associated functions. The keywords that emerged most frequently in this cluster are classroom management, student learning outcome, and learning analytics. Other keywords in this cluster are classroom environment, curriculum, subject-specific teaching, and education computing. The third cluster centers around higher education, science, and technology teaching. The primary keywords are teacher education, STEM education, and education technology. Additionally, this cluster includes other keywords like teacher training, pedagogical content knowledge, STEAM, education innovation, and didactics. Finally, the fourth cluster entails keywords concerning the professional aspects of teaching and teacher training. The keywords that dominate this cluster are personnel training, job analysis, and assessment. Other important keywords in this cluster are behavior science, motivation, teacher professional development, and perception. In summary, the research findings indicate that researchers are particularly interested in various aspects of teaching and learning, including the content and context of teacher preparation and competencies, education technologies, contemporary approaches, and professional aspects related to teachers' preparation.

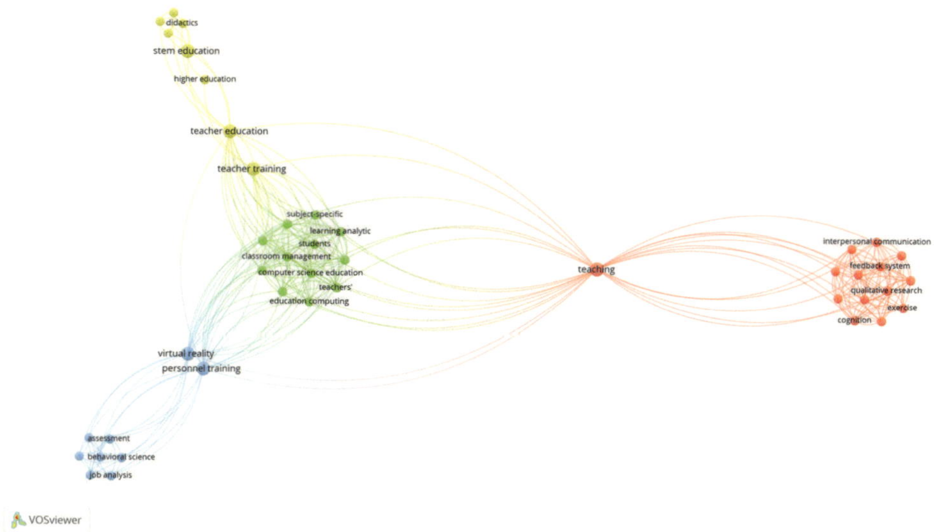

Figure 6.
Keywords and clusters.

One major finding is that the topics covered in this study align with those that attract researchers who focus solely on teacher training or science teaching 24, 25, 32, 34]. There is a clear interest in what constitutes effective education, both in general and specifically in the field of science. This includes identifying appropriate practices, acquiring knowledge about pedagogy and content, and becoming familiar with the working environment of schools. These qualities are important for contemporary teachers [6, 11, 13, 17]. The existence of the term Technological Pedagogical Content Knowledge is also of great significance as it is considered essential for teachers [12].

Another noteworthy finding is the emphasis placed on teachers' relationship with technology, which has a dual aspect. First, technology is approached as a subject of education that is relevant to science. This aligns with the findings of current theory teaching [11, 13] and science teaching in particular [5, 17]. This also relates to the emphasis observed on STEAM subjects, which is an emerging trend in education [20 22, 23]. Second, technology is approached as a perspective for teachers, providing new means, opportunities, and modes for knowledge delivery. This is a point that is also emphasized in educational theory and teacher training [2, 3].

Finally, there is a notable interest in the teaching profession, including its traits and conditions. Researchers seem willing to examine how teachers appreciate their work, how it is evaluated, and how it can be improved. They pay attention to the way training is delivered through universities, in cooperation with schools, other institutions, or organizations. There is concern among researchers about professional development and ways in which teachers can enhance their performance and improve learning outcomes within the school organization environment. These aspects are essential for teacher education [2, 9, 11, 17].

5. Conclusions

This research aimed to provide substantial information on the research trends in teacher training for science education. To achieve this, a bibliometric approach was implemented, which was deemed appropriate for the scope of this study. While there have been a considerable number of bibliometric studies conducted separately on teacher training [24–28] and science teaching [1, 29–32], there appears to be a limited number of studies that combine these two areas. The data for this research were collected from articles through the Scopus platform by executing a relevant search command. The research trends were derived from the analysis of these articles. Specifically, the analysis aimed to identify various aspects, including research output, researchers' countries and affiliations, their fields of study, and the themes they focused on. These findings provide significant information regarding the current research trends [7, 33].

By executing an appropriate query on a platform, a total of 3695 articles were collected, published between the years 1967 and 2024. The number of papers has been steadily increasing, particularly after 2000, when the annual publication rates of articles experienced a drastic surge. The majority of publications originate from researchers based in countries such as the USA, Spain, the UK, China, Russia, Germany, Brazil, Turkey, Indonesia, and Australia. These researchers primarily work at universities and higher education institutes, often collaborating with governmental bodies and organizations for funding and support. The fields of study encompass a wide range, with a predominant focus on social sciences. However, researchers also work in fields such as engineering, computing, science, mathematics, health studies, arts, and humanities. The specific topics that they examine are relevant to teaching and learning, the structure of the training program, science and technology issues, and professional aspects of teachers' work.

This demonstrates that researchers and theorists have been investigating the topic of teacher training in science with growing significance. There exists evident interest in assisting science teachers in acquiring the knowledge and competencies necessary for effective teaching and science teaching approaches, as outlined in theory and literature [6, 17]. Additionally, there is a focus on helping them appreciate the role of technology in science teaching through different dimensions [4, 6]. This also extends to equipping trainee teachers with crucial terms such as Technological Pedagogical Content knowledge [12] and STEAM education [22, 23].

Universities play a significant role in establishing and maintaining courses around teacher training, both in general and specifically for science subjects. In doing so, they attempt to establish collaborations with other organizations. These organizations can include central administrative bodies that provide funding [2, 9], as well as educational institutions that offer opportunities for future teachers to gain experience and bridge the gap between theory and practice [11, 13]. These conditions contribute to the development of well-structured, well-managed, and well-supported teacher training courses at universities [14].

Acknowledgements

I would like to express my gratitude to the people I work with, along with my colleagues and partners from the University of the Aegean, for their invaluable assistance and support throughout this study.

Conflict of interest

The authors declare no conflict of interest.

Author details

Konstantinos Karampelas
University of the Aegean, Rhodes, Greece

*Address all correspondence to: kkarampelas@aegean.gr

References

[1] Dogan OK. Trends and issues in science education in the new millennium: A bibliometric analysis of the JRST. Science Insights Education Frontiers. 2023;**16**(1):2375-2407. DOI: 10.15354/sief.23.or249

[2] Harris DN, Sass TR. Teacher training, teacher quality and student achievement. Journal of Public Economics. 2011;**95**(7-8, 798):-812. DOI: 10.1016/j.jpubeco.2010.11.009

[3] Ome A, Menendez A, Elise Le H. Improving teaching quality through training: Evidence from the Caucasus. Economics of Education Review. 2017;**61**:1-8. DOI: 10.1016/j.econedurev.2017.09.003

[4] Laugksch RC. Scientific literacy: A conceptual overview. Science Education. 2000;**84**(1):71-94. DOI: 10.1002/(sici)1098-237x(200001)84:1<71::aid-sce6>3.0.co;2-c

[5] National Research Council. Next Generation Science Standards: For States, by States. Washington, DC: National Academies Press; 2013 10.17226/18290

[6] National Research Council. A Framework for K-12 Science Education: Practices, Crosscutting Concepts, and Core Ideas. Washington, DC: The National Academies; 2012. DOI: 10.17226/13165

[7] Donthu N, Kumar S, Mukherjee D, Pandey N, Lim WM. How to conduct a bibliometric analysis: An overview and guidelines. Journal of Business Research. 2021;**133**:285-296. DOI: 10.1016/j.jbusres.2021.04.070

[8] Aaronson D, Barrow L, Sander W. Teachers and student achievement in the Chicago public high schools. Journal of Labor Economics. 2007;**25**(1):95-135. DOI: 10.1086/508733

[9] Betts JR, Zau AC, Lorien A. Determinants of Student Achievement: New Evidence from San Diego. San Diego: Public Policy Institute of California; 2003

[10] Nye B, Konstantopoulos S, Hedges LV. How large are teacher effects? Educational Evaluation and Policy Analysis. 2004;**26**(3):237-257. DOI: 10.3102/01623737026003237

[11] Teo T, Unwin S, Scherer R, Gardiner V. Initial teacher training for twenty-first century skills in the Fourth Industrial Revolution (IR 4.0): A scoping review. Computers & Education. 2021;**170**:104223. DOI: 10.1016/j.compedu.2021.104223

[12] Koehler M, Mishra P. What is technological pedagogical content knowledge (TPACK)? Contemporary Issues in Technology and Teacher Education. 2009;**9**(1):60-70. Available from: https://www.learntechlib.org/primary/p/29544/

[13] van Laar E, van Deursen AJAM, van Dijk JAGM, de Haan J. The relation between 21st-century skills and digital skills: A systematic literature review. Computers in Human Behavior. 2017;**72**:577-588. DOI: 10.1016/j.chb.2017.03.010

[14] Le Cornu R. Key Components of Effective Professional Experience in Initial Teacher Education in Australia. Melbourne: Australian Institute for Teaching and School Leadership; 2015. Available from: https://www.aitsl.edu.au/docs/default-source/

default-document-library/aitsl_key-components-of-effective-professional-experience.pdf

[15] Summers M, Childs A, Corney G. Education for sustainable development in initial teacher training: Issues for interdisciplinary collaboration. Environmental Education Research. 2005;**11**(5):623-647. DOI: 10.1080/13504620500169841

[16] Rubba PA, Anderson HO. Development of an instrument to assess secondary schoolstudents' understanding of the nature of scientific knowledge. Science Education. 1978;**62**(4):449-458

[17] OECD. PISA 2025 Science Framework. Organisation for Economic Co-operation and Development OECD. Paris: OECD Publications; 2023. Available from: https://pisa-framework.oecd.org/science-2025/assets/docs/PISA_2025_Science_Framework.pdf

[18] Adebusuyi OF, Bamidele EF, Adebusuyi AS. The role of knowledge and epistemological beliefs in chemistry teachers STEM professional development and instructional practices: Examination of STEM-integrated classrooms. European Journal of Science and Mathematics Education. 2022;**10**(2):243-255. DOI: 10.30935/scimath/11799

[19] Allina B. The development of STEAM educational policy to promote student creativity and social empowerment. Arts Education Policy Review. 2018;**119**(2):77-87. DOI: 10.1080/10632913.2017.1296392

[20] Perignat E, Katz-Buonincontro J. STEAM in practice and research: An integrative literature review. Thinking Skills and Creativity. 2019;**31**:31-43. DOI: 10.1016/j.tsc.2018.10.002

[21] Shatunova O, Anisimova T, Sabirova F, Kalimullina O. STEAM as an innovative educational technology. Journal of Social Studies Education Research. 2019;**10**(2):131-144

[22] Pérez Torres M, Couso Lagarón D, Marquez Bargalló C. Evaluation of STEAM project-based learning (STEAM PBL) instructional designs from the STEM practices perspective. Education in Science. 2023;**14**(1):53. DOI: 10.3390/educsci14010053

[23] Quigley CF, Herro D. "finding the joy in the unknown": Implementation of STEAM teaching practices in middle school science and math classrooms. Journal of Science Education and Technology. 2016;**25**(3):410-426. DOI: 10.1007/s10956-016-9602-z

[24] Zhang Y, Wang P. Twenty years' development of teacher identity research: A bibliometric analysis. Frontiers in Psychology. 2022;**12**. DOI: 10.3389/fpsyg.2021.783913

[25] Hursen C. Examination of studies on critical thinking in teacher education: A bibliometric analysis. Revista Romaneasca Pentru Educatie Multidimensionala. 2023;**15**(3):288-311. DOI: 10.18662/rrem/15.3/767

[26] Hallinger P, Kulophas D. The evolving knowledge base on leadership and teacher professional learning: A bibliometric analysis of the literature, 1960-2018. Professional Development in Education. 2020;**46**(4):521-540. DOI: 10.1080/19415257.2019.1623287

[27] Cretu DM, Morandau F. Initial teacher education for inclusive education: A bibliometric analysis of educational research. Sustainability. 2020;**12**(12):4923. DOI: 10.3390/su12124923

[28] Gavinolla MR, Livina A, Swain SK. State of the research on teacher education

and sustainability: A bibliometrics analysis. Journal of Teacher Education for Sustainability. 2022;**24**(2):147-165. DOI: 10.2478/jtes-2022-0022

[29] Wang S, Chen Y, Lv X, Xu J. Hot topics and frontier evolution of science education research: A bibliometric mapping from 2001 to 2020. Science & Education. 2023;**32**(3):845-869. DOI: 10.1007/s11191-022-00337-z

[30] Effendi DN, Irwandani A, Jatmiko A, Rahmayanti H, Ichsan IZ, Mehadi Rahman M. Bibliometric analysis of scientific literacy using VOS viewer: Analysis of science education. Journal of Physics Conference Series. 2021;**1796**(1):012096. DOI: 10.1088/1742-6596/1796/1/012096

[31] Maryanti R, Bayu A, Nandiyanto D, Hufad A, Sunardi S, Novia D, et al. A computational bibliometric analysis of science education research using vosviewer. Journal of Engineering Science and Technology. 2023;**18**(1):301-309. Available from: https://jestec.taylors.edu.my/Vol%2018%20Issue%201%20February%20%202023/18_1_20.pdf

[32] Pham HT, Vu TC, Nguyen LT, Vu N-TT, Nguyen TC, Pham H-HT, et al. Professional development for science teachers: A bibliometric analysis from 2001 to 2021. Eurasia Journal of Mathematics Science and Technology Education. 2023;**19**(5):em2260. DOI: 10.29333/ejmste/13153

[33] Van Eck NJ, Waltman L. Visualizing bibliometric networks. In: Measuring Scholarly Impact. London: Springer; 2014. pp. 285-320

[34] Dee TS. Teachers, race, and student achievement in a randomized experiment. The Review of Economics and Statistics. 2004;**86**(1):195-210. DOI: 10.1162/003465304323023750

Chapter 6

Publication Pattern and Research Assessment of Cyber Security: A Bibliometric Study

Suhaib Ali and Muzamil Mushtaq

Abstract

In today's digital age, where technology shapes our lives, the importance of cyber security cannot be overstated. As technology advances, the need for cyber security becomes crucial to ensure the integrity, confidentiality, and availability of sensitive data. The study conducted a bibliometric analysis to examine cyber security literature from 2013 to 2022 published in the Scopus database, indexing 5600 documents. Employing tables, graphs, and charts, the analysis reveals key findings: Lingfeng Wang from the University of Wisconsin-Milwaukee is the most prolific author, followed by Taha Selim Ustun and Kim-Kwang Raymond Choo. IEEE Access leads in the journal analysis, followed by "Computers and Security" and "Sensors." The peak publication year is 2022, with 2013 as the least productive. The USA is the most prolific country, followed by China, UK, and India. Top affiliations include the King Abdulaziz University, Deakin University, and Norwegian University of Science and Technology. The study also reveals the open-access availability of literature in different categories. Overall, analysis provides a comprehensive understanding of the evolving landscape of cyber security literature, emphasizing key authors, journals, affiliations, countries, years, literature availability in open access, and publication trends.

Keywords: cyber security, bibliometric analysis, scopus, cyber threats, publication trends, research assessment

1. Introduction

Nowadays, sending and receiving data is very simple; we can send and receive any type of data with just a press of a key. But can we consider the data we share or receive secure and safe from being leaked or stolen by cybercriminals? In order to overcome this problem, we need cyber security, and it works as a safeguard of our computer systems, networks, and programs from unauthorized access and loss. As we know, the Internet is currently the fastest-rising infrastructure in the modern era. In today's digital age, numerous emerging technologies are reshaping human beings, and because of these new technologies, we are failing to save our valuable data and information from the attacks of cyber criminals, which is leading to the growth of cybercrimes day by day, which is not a good sign [1]. Any action that could result in the loss of information, software, or data, processing incompatibilities, or hardware damage poses a threat to computer protection. In our increasingly digital landscape, protecting sensitive information and systems through effective cybersecurity measures is crucial. As technological advancements continue to shape our world, ensuring the integrity and confidentiality of data has become an essential safeguard against potential threats and vulnerabilities. The primary goal of cybersecurity is to safeguard our computer systems, networks, and programs from unauthorized access and loss. By preventing data loss, theft of identities, and digital attacks, cyber security measures play a crucial role in supporting risk management initiatives. Organizations may successfully avoid and handle these risks with the help of a solid network security framework and an effective crisis management strategy [2]. Furthermore, the use of cybersecurity technologies promotes a secure digital environment by safeguarding sensitive data while also improving stakeholder confidence and trust in general.

Like in the field of cyber security, the growth in literature is enormously increasing day by day in every field of study, and because of this, it is very difficult to retrieve reliable information from documents. To overcome this problem, we need to analyze the documents published on any specific subject or topic. Amid this exponential growth of literature, employing data analysis is crucial to distil valuable insights from the abundance of information available. The process of data analysis can be done through the "bibliometric analysis." It is an important tool used to evaluate the trends in the pattern of expansion of the journal, including its execution. It is used to describe a piece of literature by highlighting the work he published, such as the regularity of the publication, coverage of the topic, structure of the authorship, and reference allocation [3]. This technique can be useful in finding out new research trends as well as knowledge sharing in the journal's specialized subject. It is one of the most widely used techniques for data analysis by research scholars and subject specialists in order to provide a better understanding of the literature.

2. Statement of the problem

The study was conducted to ascertain the progression of scholarly communication in the field of "cyber security" published during the recent decade, as well as the sources of publication, well-known authors, important journals, most productive affiliations and countries, and year-wise production. To conduct such aspects, the study employs bibliometric analysis to reveal key insights in the area of cyber security.

3. Aims and objectives

The objectives of this study outline the specific goals and aims that drive the research forward. It provides a structured approach to comprehensively explore cyber security literature. The primary goals of the investigation encompass the following objectives:

- To determine the distribution of research publications and identify the most prolific journals in the domain of cybersecurity.

- To recognize the authors and their contributions to the field.

- To ascertain the countries that contribute most significantly to the cybersecurity field.

- To create a list of institutions accountable for generating literature related to cybersecurity.
- To examine the open-access availability of literature on cybersecurity.

4. Limitations of the study

This study, focusing on cyber security literature through bibliometric analysis, acknowledges its inherent limitations that may impact the extent of generalization and interpretation of findings. The following are the limitations that should be acknowledged within the scope of this study:

- The current analysis covers a decade from 2013 to 2022, both years included. The records during the study period have been retrieved from Scopus databases.
- The temporal scope of the study could result in overlooking significant trends that occurred before 2013 or after 2022.
- The analysis may be limited to publications in specific languages present in the selected database, possibly excluding relevant contributions in other languages.
- While bibliometrics offers quantitative insights, they may not accurately reflect the quality or significance of research contributions.
- Choosing an alternative database like Web of Science can introduce potential limitations. It can influence the scope of the study by having different results compared to the previously obtained results.

5. Review of related literature

There are several studies in the field of cyber security that contributed in improving our understanding of the topic. Lu et al. [4] conducted a bibliometric study from 1974 to 2006 to explore the progression on computer crimes and cyber-crime studies. Shukla & Gochhait [5] extended the timeframe by analyzing the data from 1998 to 2020 and analyzing the evaluation of cyber security with the help of bibliometric study. Kyrdoda et al. [6] also investigated the cyber security technology developments from 2011 to 2021 through bibliometric technique. They examined significant journals, writers, nations, and widely referenced works across the domain of cyber security system. On the other hand, Altarturi et al. [7] highlighted the topic of cyber parental control by analyzing it through bibliometric technique. They reveal the growth patterns, countries, subject areas, and documents type within specific field. Meanwhile, Makawana & Jhaveri [8] conducted a bibliometric study to explored the field of the machine learning for cyber security, highlighting its contributions, while Arora & Jain [9] extending this topic by focusing on the threads of and their solutions with the help of deep learning techniques with the help of bibliometric analysis. Bringing these studies together via their common goal of enhancing our knowledge of cyber security amid the changing landscape of technology and digital threats.

The role of cyber security also has a big impact across the multiple areas, and several studies shows its importance through various point of views. Garg et al. [10] conducted a bibliometric study on cloud computing security, determining the emerging trends and pointing out China and India's significant contributions. Bolbot et al. [11] expanded the scope by focusing on maritime cyber security in the context of the emergence of Industry 4.0 by conducting a systematic evaluation of the literature as well as bibliometric evaluation. On the other hand, Fernandez de Arroyabe et al. [12] focused on the automobile sector. With the help of bibliometric analysis, this study highlights the necessity of cyber security in automobile sector. Also, in the healthcare industry, cyber security is a concern. Nair & Saha [13] conducted a bibliometric analysis to highlight the improvements in the healthcare information system and cyber security. These studies showed how important cybersecurity is for everyone and provided us with different viewpoints on how we can use cybersecurity in different fields.

Several studies focus on the intersection of cybersecurity and social media. Ismail & Saip [14] conducted a bibliometric study to investigate the trends in cyber security thread research on social media focusing on the challenges of security threats, and Zaimy et al. [15] conducted a bibliometric study that focused on cyber security risks in social media. The study reveals the changing pattern of publications over the last decade. On the other hand, Yumitro et al. [16] conducted a precise bibliometric analysis of international publication trends on the interaction of cyber security and terrorism between 2009 and 2022. These studies contribute to a better understanding on the complex relationship between cyber security and social media.

6. Research methodology

The methodology for this bibliometric study involved systematically searching the Scopus database for the term "cyber security" across all fields. We refined our search by applying specific filters. We focused on documents published between 2013 and 2022, related to the subjects of Engineering and Computer Science only, and restricted the documents originating from journals only. After applying these filters, we identified a dataset of 5600 relevant documents. This dataset was then exported in CSV format for further analysis. To further analyze the data, we used Microsoft Excel, creating tables and charts to extract valuable information. This approach allowed us to identify key trends in cyber security research, such as top authors, influential institutions, and leading countries, over the past decade.

7. Data analysis, interpretation, and discussion

This bibliometric study has been done to determine the growth of the literature on the topic "cybersecurity" from 2013 to 2022. The Scopus database, one of the most extensive and reliable databases, was utilized for this purpose.

The current study collected data from 5600 documents extracted from the Scopus database on the topic of "cybersecurity," covering the subjects of Engineering and Computer Science from a wide range of institutions throughout the world. The data was exported and subsequently subjected to analysis using MS Excel. The following sections represent the broader aspects of the study.

7.1 Ranking of authors

With the help of the current study, we have identified the most productive authors of a total of 5600 documents indexed in the Scopus database. This study shows the authors who were most productive and contributed the most documents.

Table 1 lists and ranks the 20 most productive authors. As reflected in the table, the most productive author is Lingfeng Wang of the University of Wisconsin-Milwaukee, USA. With 21 publications on the topic of cyber security, he is representing 0.38% of all documents. The most notable publications of Wang are in the IEEE Transactions on Smart Grid, published by IEEE, highlighting his expertise in the field. Taha Selim Ustun of the Japan's Fukushima Renewable Energy Institute, AIST (FREA). The most published works of Ustun are in Energies, published by the Multidisciplinary Digital Publishing Institute (MDPI), and IEEE Access, published by IEEE, indicating his prolific contributions to the field. Kim-Kwang Raymond Choo of the University of Texas at San Antonio, USA, who, respectively, produced 20 (0.36%) and 16 (0.29%), documents are next in author productivity. The publications of Choo are in these two journals, IEEE Internet of Things Journal (IEEE) and Computers and Security (Elsevier), showcasing his extensive work and expertise in the field of cyber security.

The analysis highlights the significant contributions of authors in the field of cyber security, particularly highlighting the prolific output of Lingfeng Wang, Taha Selim Ustun, Kim-Kwang Raymond Choo, Jawed Ahmad, Mamoun Alazab, etc. Their collective body of work constitutes a significant portion of the documents indexed

Sr. No.	Author	Affiliation	Country	Publications	Rank	% of 5600
1	Wang, Lingfeng	University of Wisconsin-Milwaukee	United States	21	1	0.38
2	Ustun, Taha Selim	Fukushima Renewable Energy Institute	Japan	20	2	0.36
3	Choo, Kim-Kwang Raymond	University of Texas at San Antonio	United States	16	3	0.29
4	Ahmad, Jawad	Edinburgh Napier University	United Kingdom	15	4	0.27
5	Alazab, Mamoun	Charles Darwin University	Australia	15	4	0.27
6	Jajodia, Sushil	George Mason University	United States	15	4	0.27
7	Lakhno, Valeriy	National University of Life and Environmental Sciences of Ukraine	Ukraine	15	4	0.27
8	Zeadally, Sherali	University of Kentucky	United States	15	4	0.27
9	Creese, Sadie	University of Oxford	United Kingdom	13	9	0.23
10	Ganesan, Rajesh	George Mason University	United States	13	9	0.23

Table 1.
Top 10 authors.

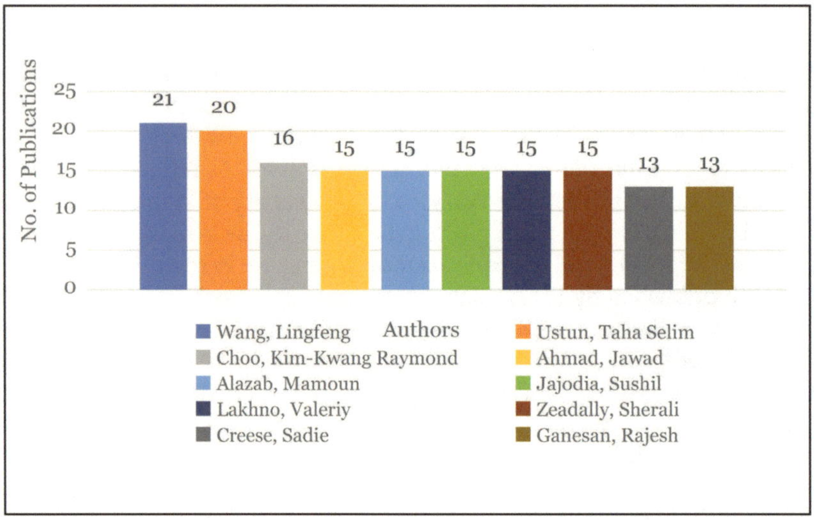

Figure 1.
Author-wise publications.

in the Scopus database, indicating their substantial impact and expertise in the field. These findings offer valuable insights for researchers and institutions engaged in cybersecurity research and development.

Figure 1 represents the publication profile of authors, and only the top 10 authors have been shown in the figure. The Wang, Lingfeng, with 21 publications and the Ganesan, Rajesh, with 13 publications, are clearly visible in the diagram.

7.2 Ranking of journals

A number of journals have produced documents on the topic of "cybersecurity" between 2013 and 2022. With the help of this study, we identified which journals are the most important and, hence, core journal collection publishing documents on the topic of cybersecurity in the area of Engineering and Computer Science.

IEEE Access produced 392 documents, constituting 7% of the total documents, and is ranked first in **Table 2** as the most prolific journal. It is published by one of the largest professional organizations in the United States, the Institute of Electrical and Electronics Engineers (IEEE), and most of its publications were from the affiliations of Deakin University, Australia. Its top author is Taha Selim Ustun from Fukushima Renewable Energy Institute, Koriyama, Japan. The *Journal Computers and Security*, which is published by Elsevier of the Netherlands, produced 182 documents, constituting 3.25 percent of the total. Its top affiliations include Deakin University, Australia; University of Melbourne, Australia; Norwegian University of Science and Technology, Norway; and the University of Texas at San Antonio, United States. Atif Ahmad from the School of Computing and Information Systems at the University of Melbourne, Australia, is the top author associated with this journal. Additionally, Sensors, which is published by the Multidisciplinary Digital Publishing Institute (MDPI), produced 157 documents, constituting 2.8% of the total. The top affiliations of the journal include King Abdulaziz University, Saudi Arabia; Edinburgh Napier University, Scotland, United Kingdom; Norwegian University of Science

Sr. No.	Journal	Publisher	Country	Publications	Rank	C.F.	% of 5600
1	IEEE Access	IEEE	United States	392	1	392	7.00
2	Computers and Security	Elsevier	Netherlands	182	2	574	3.25
3	Sensors	MDPI	Switzerland	157	3	731	2.80
4	IEEE Security and Privacy	IEEE	United States	150	4	881	2.68
5	Applied Sciences (Switzerland)	MDPI	Switzerland	130	5	1011	2.32
6	International Journal of Advanced Computer Science and Applications	Science and Information Organization	United Kingdom	103	6	1114	1.84
7	Electronics (Switzerland)	MDPI	Switzerland	90	7	1204	1.61
8	IEEE Transactions on Smart Grid	IEEE	United States	66	8	1270	1.18
9	IEEE Internet of Things Journal	IEEE	United States	61	9	1331	1.09
10	Security and Communication Networks	Hindawi Limited	United Kingdom	61	9	1392	1.09

C.F. = cumulative frequency.

Table 2.
Top 10 journals.

and Technology, Norway; and Deakin University, Australia. Among the top authors associated with this journal is Jawad Ahmad from University Hospital Coventry, Coventry, United Kingdom. These are the next two highly prolific journals. The table also demonstrates that both IEEE and MDPI each have published six journals, collectively accounting for 12 out of top 20 journals.

The analysis highlights key journals in the field of cyber security, with IEEE Access, Computers and Security, Sensors, IEEE Security and Privacy, and Applied Sciences being the most prolific. These journals play a crucial role in disseminating research in this area, serving as essential resources for researchers and professionals.

Figure 2 represents the journals that have been used for publication by the authors in the field of cyber security. Only top 10 journals have been listed in the figure, and it is found that IEEE as the publisher has been widely used by the researchers in the field for publishing their research output, with IEEE Access publishing 392 publications and Security and Communication Networks 61 publications.

7.3 Distribution of publications by years

The current study on the topic of "Cyber Security" shows the year-wise production of the publications from 2013 to 2022 in the Scopus database. With the help of this study, we found the most productive and the least productive year.

As indicated in **Table 3**, the most productive year is 2022, which is natural as being the most recent, while the least productive year is 2013. The majority of documents,

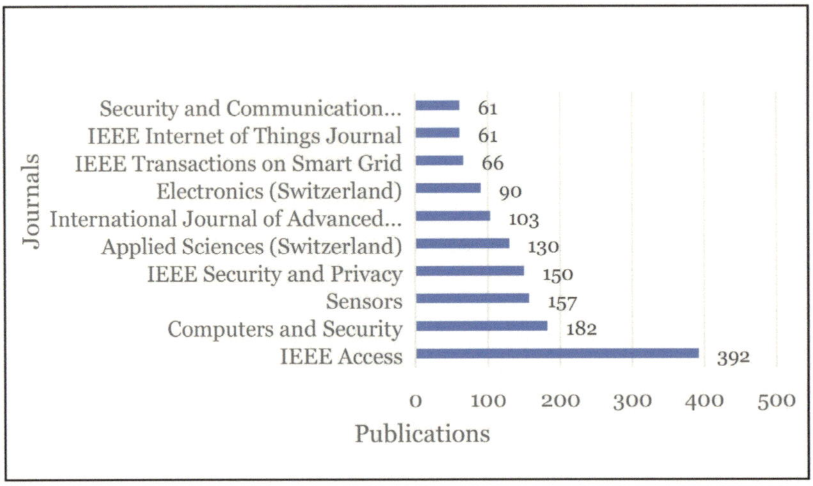

Figure 2.
Top 10 journals.

Sr. No.	Year	Publications	Cumulative Frequency	% of 5600	Growth Rate %
1	2022	2130	2130	38.04	78.39
2	2021	1194	3324	21.32	58.78
3	2020	752	4076	13.43	33.81
4	2019	562	4638	10.04	60.57
5	2018	350	4988	6.25	47.68
6	2017	237	5225	4.23	53.90
7	2016	154	5379	2.75	49.51
8	2015	103	5482	1.84	51.47
9	2014	68	5550	1.21	36.00
10	2013	50	5600	0.89	28.21
	Total	5600		100.00	

Table 3.
Distribution by years.

that is, 2130 (38.04%) of the total 5600, were published in 2022. This is followed by 2021, with 1194 (21.32%), and 2020, with 752 (13.43%) number of documents published. Only 50 (0.89%) documents were published in 2013, making it the least productive year. Besides, 2022 had the highest percentage growth rate. The increase in publications from 2021 to 2022 is about 78 percent in 2022, whereas the increment in 2013 is the least, increasing by only 28.21%.

The analysis indicates a notable upward trend in cyber security research output in recent years, highlighting a growing interest among researchers in this area. Keeping informed about these developments is crucial for effectively tackling the evolving challenges and complexities in cyber security. Furthermore, these trends suggest a significant evolution in the cyber security landscape, potentially reflecting the increasing importance of cyber security in the digital age. The rise in publications in recent years may indicate a response to the growing threat environment, with researchers and professionals working hard to develop innovative solutions to fight cyber threats. The data also highlights the dynamic nature of cyber security, highlighting the need for continuous research and adaptation to address emerging challenges effectively.

7.4 Distribution of publication by countries

This aspect of the study identifies the countries included in the publications of the documents on the topic of "cybersecurity" in the domain of Computer Science and Engineering during 2013–2023 and reveals countries that are more productive.

The United States, which produced 1572 documents, constituting 28.07% of the total 5600 documents, is the most productive country, as reflected in **Table 4**. The key publications from the United States include IEEE Security and Privacy, published by IEEE, and IEEE Access, also published by IEEE. Prominent affiliations in the United States include the University of Texas at San Antonio and Carnegie Mellon University. Notable authors from the United States include Lingfeng Wang from the College of Engineering & Applied Science in Milwaukee, Kim Kwang Raymond Choo from the University of Texas at San Antonio, and Sushil Jajodia from George Mason University in Fairfax. The USA is followed by China, which produced 647 (11.55%) documents in total. The key publications from China include IEEE Access by IEEE and Security and Communication Networks by Hindawi. Notable affiliations in China include the Chinese Academy of Sciences, the Ministry of Education of the People's Republic of China, and Huazhong University of Science and Technology. Key authors from China include Chunjie Zhou and Yuanqing Qin from Huazhong University of Science and Technology in Wuhan. The United Kingdom comes next with 469 documents, accounting for 8.36% of the total. Major publications from the United Kingdom include Computer and Security by Elsevier, IEEE Access by IEEE, Sensors by the Multidisciplinary Digital Publishing Institute (MDPI), and IEEE Security and Privacy by IEEE. Noteworthy affiliations in the United Kingdom include the University of Oxford and Edinburgh Napier University. Key authors from the United Kingdom include Jawad Ahmad from University Hospital Coventry in Coventry and Sadie J. Creese from Oxford Social Sciences Division in Oxford. It should also be noted that

Sr. No.	Country	Publications	Cumulative Frequency	% of 5600
1	United States	1572	1572	28.07
2	China	647	2219	11.55
3	United Kingdom	469	2688	8.38
4	India	454	3142	8.11
5	Saudi Arabia	375	3517	6.70
6	Australia	357	3874	6.38
7	Spain	235	4109	4.20
8	Italy	233	4342	4.16
9	Canada	214	4556	3.82
10	South Korea	214	4770	3.82

Table 4.
Top 10 countries.

many documents are the results of collaborative studies in which authors from different countries collaborate to write an article. That is the reason why the number of documents is showing more than the actual data, which is 5600.

The analysis highlights the United States' leading role in cyber security research, reflecting its strong focus and expertise in the field. Collaborative studies involving authors from various countries also contribute significantly to the global nature of cyber security research, highlighting the importance of international cooperation in addressing cyber security challenges.

Figure 3 represents the research contributions of the countries in the field of cybersecurity, which shows the USA as the leading country in the overall production of research in the field, followed by China. The figure reflects the number of publications of the countries based on the size and darkness of the color and reveals that the world's leading countries are at the forefront of cybersecurity research and development.

7.5 Distribution of publication by affiliations

In comparison to other institutions, some institutions are more involved in the study of a particular subject. It shows the institution's interest in the particular area of study. This aspect of the study reveals the most productive institutions from 2013 to 2022 on cyber security.

The top 10 institutions are listed in **Table 5**. Out of these institutions, King Abdulaziz University of Saudi Arabia produced 62 documents, constituting 1.11% of the total 5600 documents, which is the most productive institution on the list. The King Abdulaziz University has been published in prestigious journals such as IEEE Access, published by IEEE, and the International Journal of Advanced Computer Science and Application, published by the Science and Information Organization. The institution's top authors include Fawaz Alsolami and Mahmoud Ragab. Additionally, Mohammad Shahidehpour from the Illinois Institute of Technology, Chicago, United States, is also recognized as a top author in this field. It is followed by

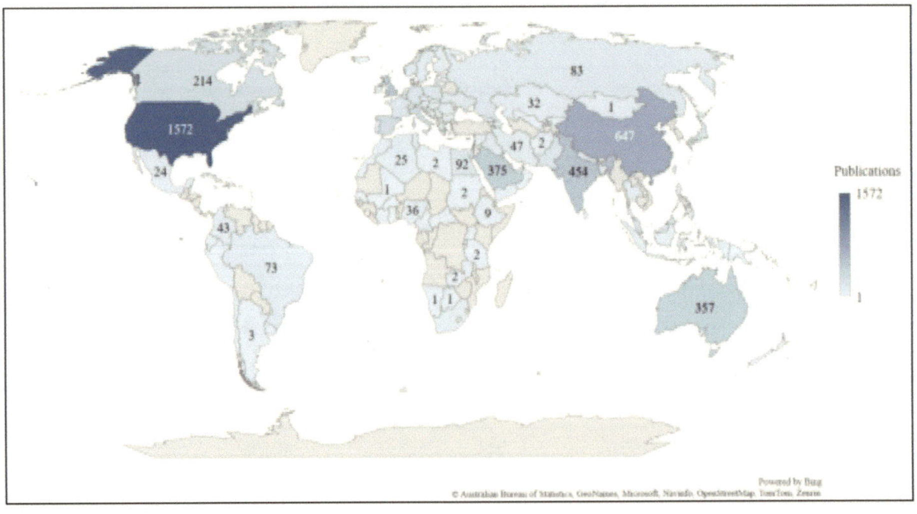

Figure 3.
Distribution by countries.

Sr. No.	Affiliation	Country	Publications	Cumulative Frequency	% of 5600
1	King Abdulaziz University	Saudi Arabia	62	62	1.11
2	Deakin University	Australia	54	116	0.96
3	Norwegian University of Science and Technology	Norway	44	160	0.79
4	The University of Texas at San Antonio	United States	43	203	0.77
5	Carnegie Mellon University	United States	41	244	0.73
6	King Saud University	Saudi Arabia	40	284	0.71
7	Chinese Academy of Sciences	China	38	322	0.68
8	Virginia Polytechnic Institute and State University	United States	36	358	0.64
9	Ministry of Education China	China	35	393	0.63
10	Taif University	Saudi Arabia	35	428	0.63

Table 5.
Top 10 affiliations.

Deakin University of Australia, producing 54 (0.96%). The Deakin University's publications included prestigious journals such as IEEE Access by IEEE, IEEE Computer and Security by Elsevier, and Sensors by the Multidisciplinary Digital Publishing Institute (MDPI). Noteworthy authors from Deakin University include Adnan Anwar and Zubair Baig. Furthermore, the Norwegian University of Science and Technology, which produced 44 (0.79%) number of publications. The institution's publications were featured in reputable journals such as Computer and Security by Elsevier, IEEE Access by IEEE, and the International Journal of Advanced Computer Science and Applications by the Science and Information Organization. Noteworthy authors from the Norwegian University of Science and Technology include Vasileios Gkioulos and Sokratis K. Katsikas.

The analysis underscores the active involvement and commitment of institutions like King Abdulaziz University of Saudi Arabia, Deakin University of Australia, the Norwegian University of Science and Technology, the University of Texas at San Antonio, Carnegie Mellon University, etc., in advancing cyber security research. This indicates a global interest and dedication to addressing cybersecurity challenges. The collaborative efforts among these and other institutions play a crucial role in driving innovation and knowledge dissemination in the field.

Figure 4 represents the productivity of the top 10 institutions in the field, with King Abdulaziz University with 62 publications leading the institutions and Taif University and Ministry of Education China with 35 publications, each occupying the last position in the list. It reflects the research interests and the area of specialization in the top institutes of the world.

7.6 Literature availability in open access

This aspect of the study shows the availability of open-access content in the published documents. It highlights the distribution of content across published literature and offers a comprehensive view of accessibility in the field of study.

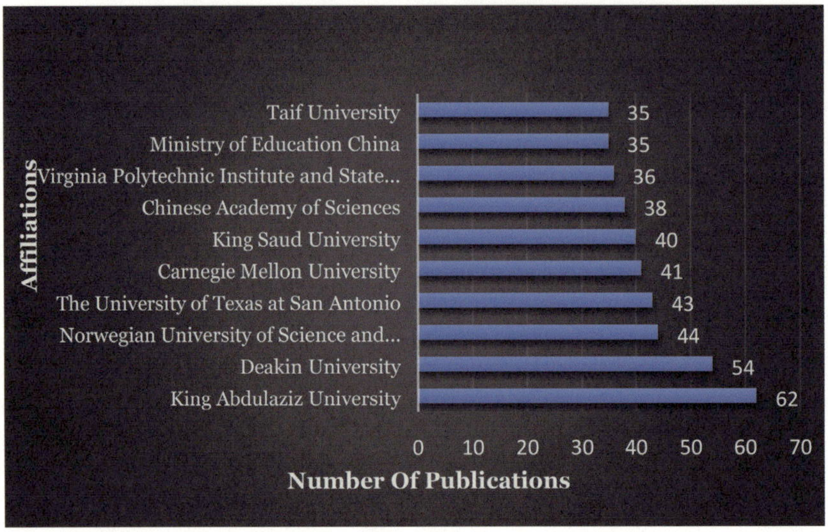

Figure 4.
Top 10 affiliations.

Sr. No.	Open Access	Publications	% of 5600
1	All open access	3139	56.05
2	Gold	1851	33.05
3	Green	1515	27.05
4	Bronze	543	9.70
5	Hybrid gold	286	5.11

Table 6.
Literature availability in open access.

Table 6 shows that 3139 (56.05%), the majority of documents out of 5600, have all open access status. 1851 (33.05%) documents have gold status, 1515 (27.05%) documents have Green status, 543 (9.7%) documents have bronze status, and 286 (5.11%) documents have hybrid gold status. It should be noted that many documents have multiple open access statuses, such as gold and all open access. That is why the total number of documents is higher than the data itself, which is 5600.

The large number of open-access documents in cyber security shows that people in this field are sharing knowledge. This helps researchers and academics get information more easily and makes the research community more informed. When researchers worldwide can access and use existing research, it encourages them to work together and come up with new ideas. This is good for the field because it helps it grow and develop in a more inclusive and dynamic way.

8. Major findings

The purpose of this study is to ascertain the expansion of literature on the topic of "Cybersecurity" between 2013 and 2022. For this, the data of 10 years has been taken for the analysis. A total of 5600 documents covering the areas of Engineering and Computer Science were taken from the Scopus database. The study found the most productive authors, top affiliations, journals, and countries in the field. It also finds the availability of the literature in open access.

The findings from the study reveal that Lingfeng Wang emerges as the most prolific author, hailing from the University of Wisconsin-Milwaukee, USA. Wang has authored 21 publications in the field of cyber security, constituting 0.38% of the total documents. Following Wang, Taha Selim Ustun from Japan's Fukushima Renewable Energy Institute, AIST (FREA), and Kim-Kwang Raymond Choo from the University of Texas at San Antonio, USA, are also prominent authors in the field, with 20 (0.36%) and 16 (0.29%) publications, respectively.

Focusing on the analysis of journals, the findings demonstrate that IEEE Access, published by IEEE in the USA, takes the lead, with 392 documents contributing to 7% of the total 5600 publications. Following closely is the *Journal of Computers and Security*, published by Elsevier in the Netherlands, responsible for 182 documents, accounting for 3.25% of the total publications. Additionally, Sensors, issued by the Multidisciplinary Digital Publishing Institute (MDPI), stands out with 157 documents, representing 2.8% of the total publications.

After analyzing journals, the study focuses on the year-wise production of the publication and examines the growth rate of the publications. The year 2022 witnessed the publication of a substantial number of documents, totaling 2130 (38.04%) of the overall count. The following are 2021 and 2020, with 1194 (21.32%) and 752 (13.43%) documents published, respectively. On the other hand, in 2013, there were only 50 documents, making it the year with the lowest productivity. Furthermore, the findings elucidate the annual growth percentage of publications during the last decade (2013–2022). Notably, the year 2022 experienced the highest annual growth rate of approximately 78%, marking a significant increase over the decade. In contrast, 2013 witnessed the lowest growth rate, standing at 28.21%, underscoring the variations in growth throughout the 10-year period.

Following the year-wise analysis of production, the study analyzed the countries and found the most productive countries. As a result, the United States emerges as the most productive nation, contributing 1572 documents that constitute 28.07% of the overall 5600 documents. Following closely is China, with a total of 647 (11.55%) documents; the United Kingdom, with 469 (8.36%) documents; India, with 454 (8.11%) documents; and Saudi Arabia, with 375 (6.70%) documents. These top five countries stand out for their notable contributions to the field.

This study also finds out the availability of the literature in open access published in different modes of open access, like all open access, green, bronze, gold, and hybrid gold. The findings reveal that 3139 (56.05%), the majority of documents out of 5600, have All Open Access status. (1851 33.05%) documents have gold status, 1515 (27.05%) documents have green status, 543 (9.7%) documents have bronze status, and 286 (5.11%) documents have hybrid gold status. It highlights the distribution of content across published literature and offers a comprehensive view of accessibility in the domain of the study.

With regard to prolific institutions, the King Abdulaziz University of Saudi Arabia emerges as the foremost contributor, producing 62 documents, equivalent to 1.11% of the total 5600 documents. Following closely is the Deakin University of Australia, producing 54 (0.96%) documents, and the Norwegian University of Science and Technology, which produced 44 (0.79%) documents. These findings underscore the distinctive contributions made by institutions in this field of study.

9. Conclusion

In this study, through a comprehensive bibliometric analysis, it has been attempted to examine the distribution of the literature on cybersecurity in the field of Engineering and Computer Science. The main objectives of the research encompassed analyzing the distribution of literature by year, authors, country, journals, affiliations, and literature availability in open access category. The findings of the study offer valuable insights into the growing field of cybersecurity research, highlighting key trends and contributions in this crucial field.

The study identified the most active authors, popular journals, and top institutions in this field, reflecting that cyber security is a global concern. The study also found that many research papers are available for free, which helps researchers share knowledge and work together across borders to fight cyber threats.

The findings show that people worldwide agree that cyber security is really important. The United States, China, the United Kingdom, and India are leading in cyber security research. This shows that many countries are working together to fight cyber threats, even though they are far apart. The study also found that many research papers are freely available to everyone. This helps people share knowledge and work together across the world. This teamwork is crucial for dealing with cyber threats that affect everyone and need a united global effort to tackle. The study not only identifies top authors and institutions but also gives insights into research trends. For example, by looking at the work of productive authors like Lingfeng Wang, Taha Selim Ustun, and Kim-Kwang Raymond Choo as they are leading figures in this field, and their work gives us valuable insights into the latest trends and advancements. These authors have contributed significantly to our understanding of cyber security challenges and solutions, shaping the direction of research and guiding the development of effective strategies to fight against cyber threats. This helps researchers understand where the field is heading and what to focus on in the future.

Furthermore, the ranking of journals serves as a compass for researchers navigating the huge amount of cyber security literature. Recognizing established journals like IEEE Access, Sensors, IEEE Security and Privacy, Computer and Security, and Applied Sciences (Switzerland) are considered the best for cybersecurity research. Researchers can aim to publish their work in these journals to make a bigger impact in the field. This keeps the field moving forward with new ideas and technologies to protect against cyber threats. Cybersecurity affects the whole world, and this study shows that research on the topic is happening everywhere. This highlights the need for global cooperation to tackle cyber threats that can affect everyone. With many papers being open access, anyone can access information on cyber security, which is important for both experienced researchers and newcomers looking to learn more. This helps create a more knowledgeable global community that is better prepared to deal with cybersecurity challenges.

The open-access nature of a significant portion of cybersecurity publications makes a strong argument for sharing knowledge in this important field. This not only empowers established researchers but also grants wider access to newcomers and professionals seeking to upskill themselves in the ever-evolving cybersecurity landscape. This helps create a more knowledgeable global community in cybersecurity, which is better prepared to deal with future challenges.

Finally, the top institutions, such as King Abdulaziz University, show a strong commitment to cybersecurity research. This is important for training skilled cybersecurity workers and creating new ways to protect against cyber threats. By

DOI: http://dx.doi.org/10.5772/intechopen.1005272

understanding the geographical distribution of research efforts, policymakers and educators can strategically allocate resources to strengthen cybersecurity education and training programs, ensuring a future generation well-equipped to safeguard our digital world.

The bibliometric study provides an interesting view of the cybersecurity research landscape, which is full of active research, global collaboration, and a growing focus on making knowledge freely accessible. As cyber threats continue to grow, the research findings from this study can be a guiding light for policymakers, researchers, and practitioners in their mission to protect our digital world. This study presents a multifaceted examination of cyber security research indexed in the Scopus database. We can ascertain the availability of literature on cyber security by authors, affiliations, countries, journals, and year. It helps to know the increasing number of cyber security publications, indicating the development and advancement in our technical world. Such a study is helpful in understanding the research on cybersecurity. As technology evolves continuously, data about cyber security and the quality of the research content is going to increase, which will be helpful for the future of cyber security research.

Author details

Suhaib Ali and Muzamil Mushtaq*
Department of Library and Information Science, Aligarh Muslim University, Aligarh, UP, India

*Address all correspondence to: naikoomuzamil@gmail.com

References

[1] Reddy GN, Reddy GJU. A study of cyber security challenges and its emerging trends on latest technologies. arXiv preprint arXiv:1402.1842. 2014;**4**(1):48-51. DOI: 10.485 5 0/ arXiv.1402.1842

[2] Seemma PS, Nandhini S, Sowmiya M. Overview of cyber security. International Journal of Advanced Research in Computer and Communication Engineering. 2018;**7**(11):125-128. DOI: 10.17148/IJARCCE.201 8.71127

[3] Chellappandi P, Vijayakumar CS. Bibliometrics, Scientometrics, webometrics / Cybermetrics, Informetrics and Altmetrics – An emerging field in library and information science research. Shanlax International Journal of Education. 2018;**7**(1):5-8. DOI: 10.5281/zenodo.2529398

[4] Lu C, Jen W, Chang W. Trends in computer crime and cybercrime research during the period 1974-2006: A bibliometric approach. In: Yang CC et al., editors. Intelligence and Security Informatics: Pacific Asia Workshop, PAISI 2007, Lecture Notes in Computer Science. Vol. 4430. Berlin, Heidelberg, Germany: Springer; 2007. pp. 244-250. DOI: 10.1007/978-3-540-71549-8_23

[5] Shukla G, Gochhait S. Cyber security trend analysis using web of science: A bibliometric analysis. European Journal of Molecular & Clinical Medicine. 2020;7(6):2567-2576. Available from: https://ejmcm.com/issue-content/cyber-security-trend-analysis-using-web-of-science-a-bibliometric-analysis-9881

[6] Kyrdoda Y, Marzi G, Dabić M, Daim TU. Cybersecurity technology: An analysis of the topic from 2011 to 2021. In: Cybersecurity. Cham: Springer; 2023. pp. 23-38. DOI: 10.1007/978-3-031-34843-3_2

[7] Altarturi HHM, Saadoon M, Badrul Anuar N. Cyber parental control: A bibliometric study. Children and Youth Services Review. 2020;**116**:105134. DOI: 10.1016/j.childyouth.202.105134

[8] Makawana PR, Jhaveri RH. A bibliometric analysis of recent research on machine learning for cyber security. Intelligent Communication and Computational Technologies: Proceedings of Internet of Things for Technological Development, IoT4TD 2017. 2018;**19**:213-226. DOI: 10.1007/978-981-10-5523-2_20

[9] Arora P, Jain A. Cyber security threats and their solutions through deep learning: A bibliometric analysis. In: 2021 3rd International Conference on Advances in Computing, Communication Control and Networking. Piscataway, NJ, USA: IEEE; 2021. pp. 1944-1949. DOI: 10.1109/ ICAC3N5 3548.2021.9725480

[10] Garg D, Sidhu J, Rani S. Emerging trends in cloud computing security: A bibliometric analyses. IET Software. 2019;**13**(3):223-231. DOI: 10.1049/ iet-sen.2018.5222

[11] Bolbot V, Kulkarni K, Brunou P, Banda OV, Musharraf M. Developments and research directions in maritime cybersecurity: A systematic literature review and bibliometric analysis. International Journal of Critical Infrastructure Protection. 2022;**39**:100571. DOI: 10.1016/j.ijc ip.202 2.100571

[12] Fernandez de Arroyabe I, Watson T, Angelopoulou O. Cybersecurity in the automotive industry: A systematic literature review (SLR).

Journal of Computer Information Systems. 2023;**63**(3):716-734. DOI: 10.1080/08874417.20 22.2103853

[13] Nair SV, Saha SK. Advancements in cyber security and information systems. In healthcare from 2004 to 2022: A bibliometric analysis. In: 2023 International Conference on Intelligent Systems, Advanced Computing and Communication (ISACC). Piscataway, NJ, USA: IEEE; 2023. pp. 1-6. DOI: 10.1109/ISA CC56298.2023.10084049

[14] Ismail NNS, Saip M. Trends in cyber security threat research on social media: A bibliometric analysis. Borneo International Journal. 2023;**6**(1):96-102. Available from: http://majmuah.com/journal/index.php/bij/article/view/350

[15] Zaimy N, Saip M, Fikri M. Cybersecurity threat in social media: A bibliometric analysis. Borneo International Journal. 2023;**6**(1):80-86. Available from: http://majmuah.com/journal/index.php/bij/article/view/348

[16] Yumitro G, Febriani R, Roziqin A, Indraningtyas A. Bibliometric analysis of international publication trends on social media and terrorism by using the Scopus database. Frontiers in Communication. 2023;**8**:1140461. DOI: 10.3389/fcomm.2023.1140 461

Chapter 7

Mapping the Global Research Landscape and Trends on Agricultural Value Chains: A Bibliometric Analysis

Kumbirai Takawira and Nyarai M. Mujuru

Abstract

Bibliometric research in value chain analysis has increased rapidly over the years. Focus has been placed on the multi-domain literature in analysing main trends in value chains. Nonetheless, there are no bibliometric studies to map out the global research landscape and trends in agricultural value chains. This chapter employed a title-specific algorithm to extract articles from Clarivate Analytics and Web of Science. The search was refined by limiting the results to only articles published in English from 2005 to the March 19, 2024. After applying the exclusion criteria, 600 documents were analysed using VOSviewer and R-Studio. The results showed that, from 2005 to 2016, there were few studies examining the agricultural value chains, with a significant increase in publications thereafter. Leading journals in total citations include Sustainability and Food Policy. Influential universities are primarily from Europe and the United States, with limited contributions from Africa. This study also offers a visual and schematic framework for pertinent research in agricultural value chains and the primary focus is on value chain development, value chain participation, and its impact on addressing global issues like food security. Therefore, there is an urgent need to promote research in the Global South and address new areas such as the role of artificial intelligence in agricultural value chains.

Keywords: agricultural value chain, supply chain, food value chain, science mapping, performance analysis, research trends

1. Introduction

The agricultural sector continues to play a significant role in supporting livelihoods and fostering innovations on a global scale. The sector remains fundamental to the social, economic, and environmental structure of societies worldwide. It, therefore, ensures the well-being of populations, promotes sustainable practices, addresses challenges such as climate change, and fosters rural development [1]. The emergence of the agricultural value chain concept resulted in an integrated approach to viewing the sequence of activities happening from the farm until the product reaches the final consumer. The transition towards value chain analysis indicates a deep understanding of the complex and dynamic interactions between production, processing, distribution, and consumption in the farming sector [2]. A value chain comprises a series of stages and activities designed to provide the product to the market [3]. The rising interest in agricultural value chain research underscores its efficacy in reducing hunger and poverty, and raising farm profits and household income [4–7]. However, this growth in academic literature lacks a comprehensive synthesis to map the research trend and suggest future research trajectories.

Bibliometrics refers to the statistical analysis of publications [8]. It has been a standard tool of science policy and research management over the last two decades [9]. Aria and Cuccurullo [10] further asserted that bibliometric analysis could establish an organised, open, and repeatable review procedure based on a statistical analysis of scientific activities. Researchers use bibliometrics for many reasons, such as unveiling emerging performance trends in journals and articles and collaborating among authors, institutions, and countries [11]. Data used in bibliometric analysis are voluminous and objective for thousands of publications with numerous citations, keyword occurrences, and topics [12]. Moreover, these data are interpreted subjectively and objectively using thematic and performance analysis [12].

Despite an extensive application of bibliometrics in academic research, there is a paucity of bibliometric reviews to map and analyse the growth in specific areas of agriculture such as value chains. Previous bibliometric studies focused on industrial clusters and global value chain (GVC) in the multi-domain literature [13]; the adoption of open innovation along the food value chain [14]; and labour in agricultural value chains [15]. The primary focus of this study is to map the global research landscape and trends in agricultural value chains. To achieve this, the study carried out citation, co-citation, and co-occurrence network analyses. In addition, the study also identifies the most relevant articles, authors, journals, and contributing institutions and nations on agricultural value chains. The citation data were retrieved from Clarivate Analytics of Web of Science (WoS) and analysed using R-Studio and VOSviewer.

According to Donthu et al. [12], the development of scientific databases such as Web of Science and Scopus has enhanced access to bibliometric data. Also, a wide array of bibliometric software has been developed over the years, including R for bibliometrics, VOSviewer, CiteSpace, Gephi, and Leximancer, inter alia. Consequently, bibliometric research rose significantly [12]. This study is divided into sections as follows: The introduction outlines an overview of research on agricultural value chains and the application of bibliometrics to research; a synopsis of the agricultural value chain articulates issues within the field; the methodology describes the data collection and analytical procedure; the data analysis section presents the findings on citation, co-citation, and co-occurrence analyses and others; finally, findings are discussed, and concluding remarks are presented.

2. A synopsis of agricultural value chains

There is a proliferation of numerous definitions regarding the concept of value chain emanating from different academic disciplines [16, 17]. Kaplinsky and Morris [3] and Hellin and Meijer [18] described a value chain as encompassing a comprehensive set of tasks necessary to take a product or service from its initial concept through various production stages. This process involves both physical changes and the incorporation of diverse producer services. Additionally, the value chain encompasses the delivery to end customers and the final disposal of the product after its use. The chain comprises actors such as input suppliers, producers, processors, and consumers, as well as various technical, business, and financial service providers that support them. These actors and supporting services create vertical and horizontal linkages that build and shape value at each stage of each product [19, 20].

As an analytical tool, Value Chain Analysis (VCA) monitors the movement of a specific product through various stages of product development [3]. It allows aggregation of important business units; hence, enterprises can identify crucial sources of competitive advantage [21]. Since its inception, the concept has been implemented and promoted in different sectors by various non-governmental organisations, government institutions, independent policy and action research organisations and international bodies [22]. For instance, the United Nations and World Bank have goals to eradicate poverty, promote inclusive growth, and foster sustainable development globally. Value chains enhance productivity, create job opportunities, and increase incomes for small producers [3]. By prioritising value chains, these global organisations can make considerable progress towards their objectives. An example of this effort is the United Nation's publication "Global Value Chains and Development: UNIDO's Support Towards Inclusive and Sustainable Development" which is geared towards supporting the industrialisation of developing countries.

As implemented by different practitioners, the primary focus of VCA was local, regional, and global value chain development with a particular interest on smallholder farmers [23]. Several VCA frameworks have been developed; however, they revolve around the work of [3]. Some frameworks emphasise specifically pro-poor growth [24, 25], on smallholders [26, 27], on gender [28], on local value chain promotion, or participatory approaches [26, 27]. Essentially, VCA revolves around four key aspects [3]: (1) understanding the structure of the value chains; (2) understanding value chain governance, which entails examining the degree of relationship and power among value chain actors [29]; (3) investigating the key leverage point—that is placed where minor changes trigger big transformation across the chains [4]; and (4) crafting interventions for upgrading the value chain. It is, therefore, apparent to investigate the academic research dynamics within global value chains.

3. Methodology

This section entails a detailed outline of the methods applied in conducting the research. These include the selection strategy, data extraction and conversion, sample description, and data analysis procedures.

3.1 Selection strategy

The process of selecting the database is the initial and most significant stage of bibliometric analysis [30]. Currently, the most frequently used databases include Scopus, Google Scholar, and Web of Science (WoS) [31]. These databases vary in terms of data values, quality, and functions. While WoS contains citation data dating back to the 1900s and encompasses 12,000 prominent journals globally, it has a lower number of publishers and journals compared to Scopus [30] with more than 30,000 peer-reviewed journals. It is ideal to combine data from two or more databases. However, the process becomes difficult if the study wants to analyse the data using two software, for example VOSviewer and R-Studio. However, the search string was initially run in both Web of Science and Scopus, and the results show that Scopus had fewer articles than Web of Science. Therefore, this study retrieved publications on agricultural value chains from WoS database following the Preferred Reporting Items for Systematic Reviews and Meta-Analysis (PRISMA) guideline [32]. The PRISMA approach is significant in enhancing the reporting of systematic reviews and meta-analyses. That is, the tool uses a guideline checklist recommendation that should be met to ensure the transparent and complete reporting of systematic literature reviews [33].

Bibliometric data were collected on 19th of March 2024 to identify all publications related to the field of agricultural value chains, and the search query was defined as follows: All fields ("value chain" OR "supply chain" OR "food value chain") AND agriculture) AND (LIMIT-TO, "Open access") AND (LIMIT-TO [LANGUAGE, "English"]) AND (LIMIT_TO [DOCTYPE, "article"]) AND (LIMIT-TO [TIMESPAN, "2000–2024")] AND (LIMIT-TO[Subject area, "Agriculture, Forestry, Business Economics, Food Science and Technology, Environmental Science and Ecology"]). The study followed a particular inclusion criterion of seven strategies reported in **Table 1**.

3.2 Software selection

Wang and Gu [30] stated that it is difficult to present citation, co-citation, and bibliometric coupling of multiple datasets from the Web of Science without the help of software. This paper used two software to present the results: VOSviewer and R-Studio. VOSviewer is a freely available application that is proficient in creating bibliometric maps showing intended networks within large dataset [30, 31]. VOSviewer, which has Java, generates diverse types of text maps [30, 34]. Additionally, the VOSviewer software generates a network map that includes specific items of interest (such as publications, authors, or keywords) and the connections (such as co-citations from the same publications, co-authorships, or co-occurrences) between them. However, VOSviewer has its limitations, which are covered by R-Studio, for example

Stage	Inclusion criteria	Documents retrieved from WoS
1	Select the Web of Science Core Collection Editions = A&HCI, BKCI-SSH, BKCI-S, CCR-EXPANDED, ESCI, IC, CPCI-SSH, CPCI-S, SCI-EXPANDED, SSCI	
2	Search and select all documents that contain the words (value chain, food value chain, supply chain) 'in the title (i.e. title algorithm search)	9426
3	Select only documents written in English	5234
4	Select the document type 'article'	4445
5	Select the time span 2000–2024	4443
6	Subject area (Research Areas: Forestry or Business Economics or Food Science Technology or Environmental Sciences Ecology or Agriculture or Agricultural Sciences or Agricultural Economics.)	3075
7	Reading the title and abstracts (Web of Science)	600

Table 1.
Search strategy and inclusion criteria.

linear data analysis [30, 34]. The study used the Biblioshiny, which is the subprogram to generate tables and images of the literature data from the selected data [30].

3.3 Data analysis

Bibliometric analysis is grouped into two categories: performance analysis and science mapping [12, 35]. Performance analysis is performed to examine the contributions of research elements in each field of research, and these include the number of publications, the number of citations for each author, and the average number of citations per year [12]. Science (bibliometric) mapping presents a visual representation of the intellectual structure and its evolution in the research field. Moreover, it shows the interaction between research elements and the strength of their relationships [12]. Science mapping involves five distinct analytical techniques: co-authorship, co-citation, co-occurrence, citation, and bibliographic coupling.

The bibliometric review employed both performance analysis and science mapping to investigate and interpret the cognitive and intellectual structure of agricultural value chains globally. Citation analysis was performed to identify the most prominent, effective, and valued publications about agricultural value chains. Also, citation analysis gave influential authors and affiliated universities. The co-citation analysis was conducted to visualise the network of authors that have leading publications for agricultural value chains. Finally, the co-occurrence analysis reveals notable keywords that would become the centre stage of research in agricultural value chains.

3.4 Sample description

The filtering process created a database that consists of 600 publications with the 2005–2024 timespan, by 2124 authors and published in 211 journals as depicted in **Table 2**. During this period, an annual growth rate of 13.97%, the average age of the document of 3.52, and an average citation per document of 15.04 were reported. Moreover, the contents of the documents included in this study had 1239 Keywords Plus (ID) and 2189 Author's Keywords (DE). Single-authored documents are 17, and the authors of multi-authored documents are 2112. In terms of author collaboration, an average of 4.11 co-authors per document was observed, with international co-authorship accounting for 40.83%.

4. Results

This section presents the findings from the bibliometric analysis of agricultural value chain research. Specifically, the section will present the descriptive statistics (mean, frequency) and data visualisation of citation, co-occurrence and co-citation analysis.

4.1 Annual scientific production

Figure 1 shows the overall trend in the number of publications in agricultural value chains over the period under investigation. Findings show that most of the publications (94%) relating to agricultural value chains were published between 2016 and 2024. From 2005 to 2015, the number of publications was below 10, and in 2006, there was no publication on agricultural value chains. The highest increase in the number of

Description	Results
Main information about data	
Timespan	2005:2024
Sources (Journals, Books, etc)	211
Documents	600
Annual Growth Rate %	13.97
Document Average Age	3.52
Average citations per doc	15.04
References	30,085
Document contents	
Keywords Plus (ID)	1239
Author's Keywords (DE)	2189
Authors	
Authors	2124
Authors of single-authored docs	17
Authors collaboration	
Single-authored docs	17
Co-authors per doc	4.11
International co-authorships %	40.83
Document types	
article	580
article; early access	16
article; proceedings paper	4

Table 2.
Main information about the data.

articles compared to the previous year occurred in 2021. Despite having fluctuations in the number of articles published, **Figure 1** shows an upward trend, depicting a general increase. Therefore, research on agricultural value chains has gained traction among scholars [30, 36].

4.2 Citation analysis with authors

Citation analysis was conducted to identify the most productive and effective authors in agricultural value chains. In VOSviewer, the minimum number of citations and articles was set at one; thus, 1854 out of 2297 authors met this threshold. Additionally, 582 authors with the highest total link strength and connections were used to create science mapping and performance analysis.

Table 3 shows the top 10 authors, sorted by the number of total citations. The most productive authors in the agricultural value chain are Butala, R, Choi, T, Dutta, P, and Somani, S with 436 citations from one article each. Soon, J.M has the least average citations (60.33). This result implies that these authors are publishing high-quality work receiving peer recognition.

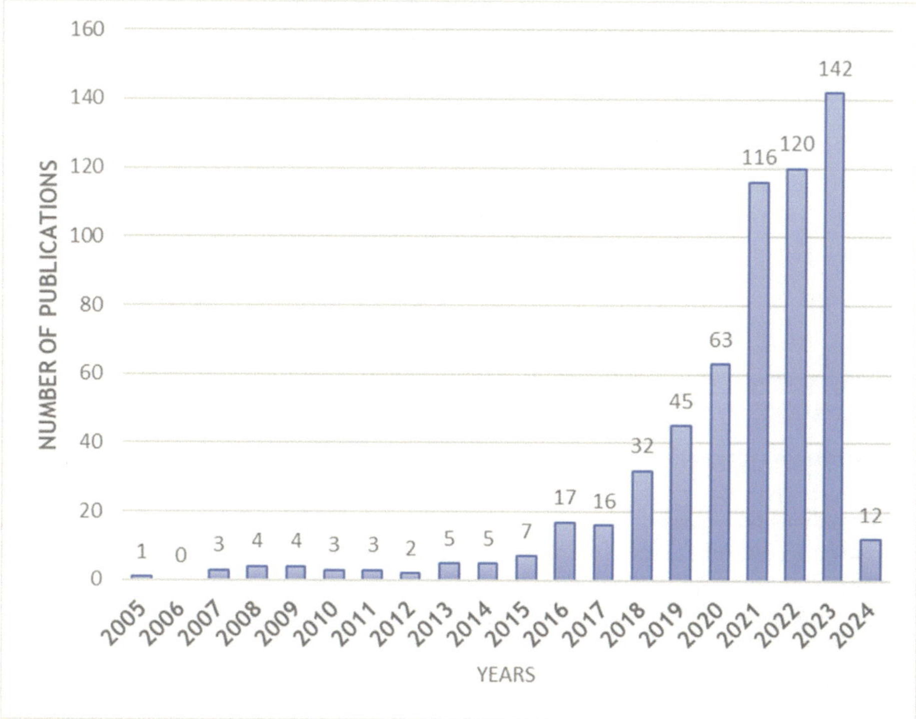

Figure 1.
The total number of publications.

Author	Documents	Citations	Average Citation
Butala, Richa	1	436	436
Choi, Tsan-ming	1	436	436
Dutta, Pankaj	1	436	436
Somani, Surabhi	1	436	436
Fonts, Agusti	1	412	412
Kamilaris, Andreas	1	412	412
Prenafeta-boldu, Francesc X.	1	412	412
Manos, B.	1	287	287
Manthou, V.	1	287	287
Matopoulos, A.	1	287	287

Table 3.
Twenty most cited authors.

Figure 2 displays the average normalised citations of the authors. The size of a node corresponds to the total number of citations an author has received, while the colour reflects the average normalised citation score. Essentially, the colours of the nodes signify the level of influence the authors hold in the field. Authors depicted in yellow are considered to have the highest influence, whereas those in blue are perceived to have less influence.

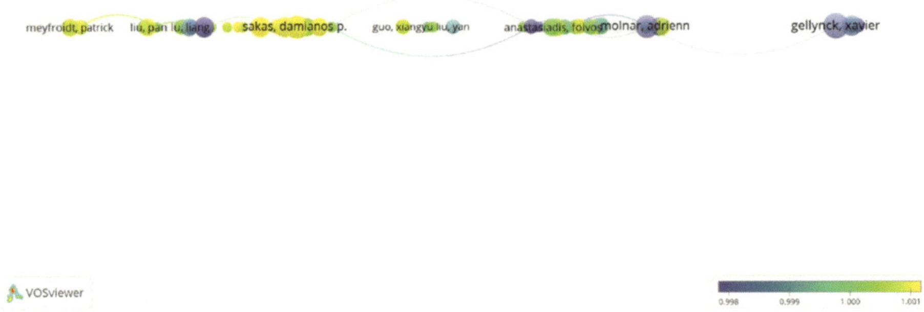

Figure 2.
Overlay visualisation of authors average citations.

4.3 Citation analysis with research institutions

The analysis was carried out on academic and non-academic research institutions that have contributed at least five articles, and 31 institutions satisfied this threshold, with the majority being institutions of higher learning. Consequently, 25 universities with the largest links were used for further analysis and science mapping. As seen in **Table 3**, in terms of the number of publications, Humboldt University of Berlin is the most productive university with 13 articles, followed by China Agricultural University and Agricultural University of Athens with 12 articles each. Considering the total citations, the top three most influential universities are Aristotle University of Thessaloniki (339), Cornell University (247), and Katholieke University Leuven (224). The average citation was calculated to ascertain the impact of the university. Results show that Cornell University, Aristotle University of Thessaloniki, and University of Sussex were in the top three with 49.4, 48,43, and 37.4 average citations, respectively. **Figure 3** shows the overlay visualisation of the most prolific research institutions in agricultural value chains in seven clusters. However, the results are inconsistent with **Table 4**. Institutions with the largest nodes include Humboldt University, China Agricultural University, the Swedish University of Agricultural Science, and the University of Queensland.

4.4 Citation analysis with journals

Citation analysis was conducted to identify the most productive and effective sources in agricultural value chains. In VOSviewer, journals with a minimum of one citation and article were chosen, resulting in 211 sources out of 175 meeting this criterion. From these selected journals, 83 authors with the highest total link strength were utilised for science mapping and performance analysis (**Figure 4**). **Table 5** shows the top 10 journals, sorted by the number of total citations. The most relevant journal concerning agricultural value chains is the Sustainability Journal with 1229 citations from 112 articles, followed by the Food Policy Journal with 741 citations from 10 articles and Transportation Research Part E-logistics and Transportation Review with 436 citations from one article. In terms of average citations, the top three journals with high average citations are Transportation Research Part E-logistics and Transportation Review (436), Scientia Agropecuaria (210), and Trends in Food Science and Technology (145). Additionally, the network of the most productive journals was presented using network visualisation as

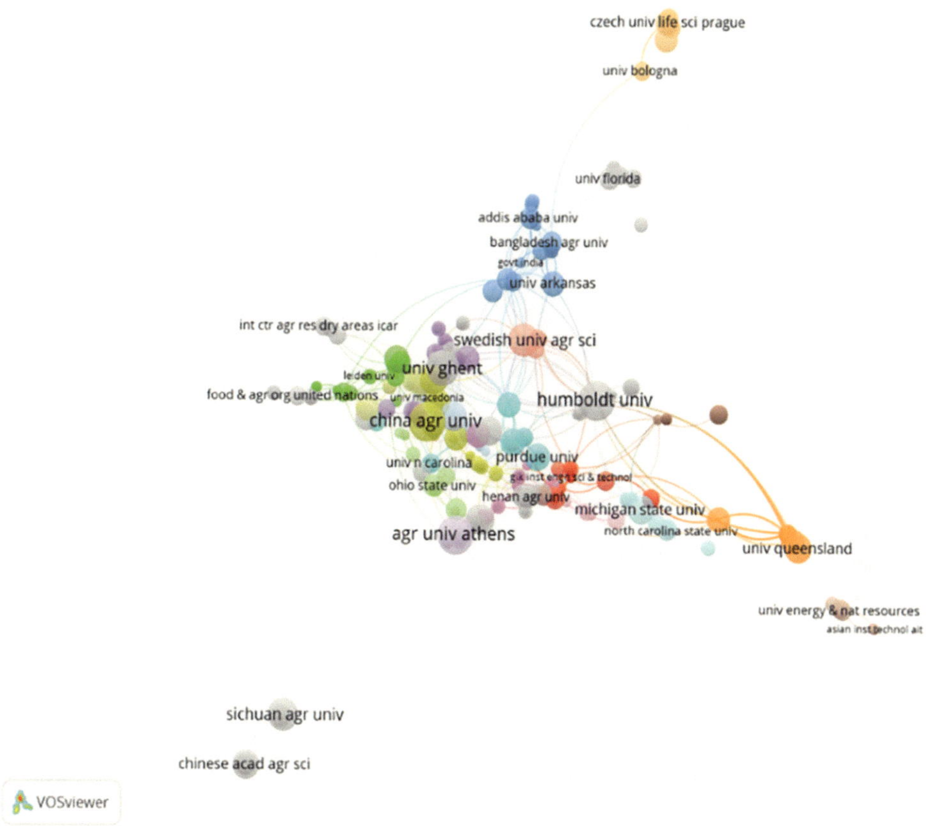

Figure 3.
Overlay visualisation of the universities.

Organisation	Documents	Citations	Average Citation
Aristotle University of Thessaloniki	7	339	48.43
Cornell University	5	247	49.40
Katholieke University Leuven	7	224	32.00
University of Sussex	5	187	37.40
Natational Institute of Technology	5	173	34.60
University of Ghent	10	172	17.20
International Food Policy Research Institute	5	167	33.40
Swedish University Agricultural Science	9	151	16.78
Iowa State University	5	149	29.80
Swiss Federal Institue of Technology	5	112	22.40

Table 4.
Most influential universities/organisations.

shown in **Figure 4**. It can be noted that journals with the largest nodes include the Sustainability Journal, Agriculture-Basel, International Food and Agribusiness, and Journal of Cleaner Production.

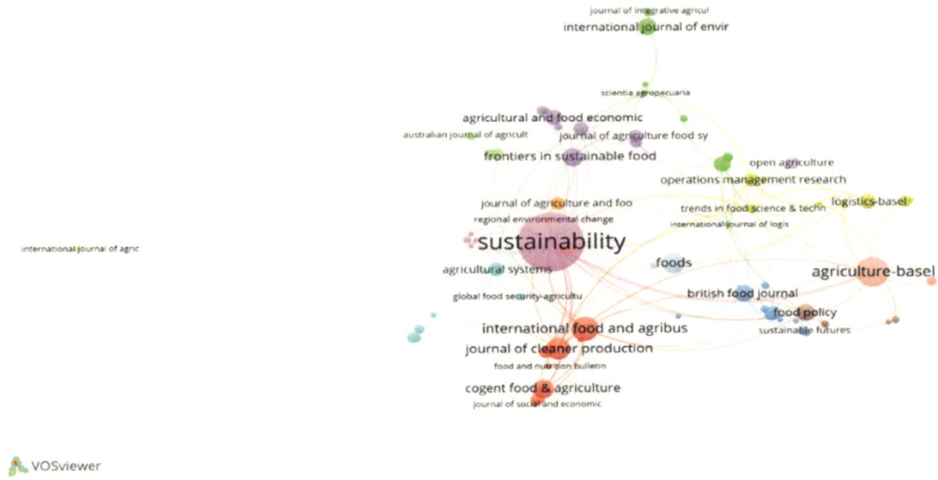

Figure 4.
Network visualisation of the journals.

Source	Documents	Citations	Average Citation
Sustainability	112	1229	10.97
Food Policy	10	741	74.10
Transportation Research Part E-logistics And Transportation Review	1	436	436.00
Trends In Food Science & Technology	3	435	145.00
Supply Chain Management-an International Journal	7	377	53.86
Applied Economic Perspectives and Policy	4	328	82.00
British Food Journal	9	297	33.00
Journal Of Cleaner Production	15	291	19.40
Agriculture-basel	29	247	8.52
Scientia Agropecuaria	1	210	210.00

Table 5.
Most influential journals.

4.5 Citation analysis with countries

In this section, we examine the most productive and influential countries in agricultural value chains. In VOSviewer, the minimum number of documents and citations per country was set at five, and of the 141 countries identified, 98 met the threshold. **Table 2** shows that the top five countries for publishing papers are the People's Republic of China, USA, England, Germany, and Italy. The United States is the most relevant and productive country in the field of agricultural value chains with 11,501 citations from 637 articles. However, emerging and developing countries such as China, India, and Kenya have been steadily contributing to the agricultural value chain discourse.

In general, most top countries that publish research in this field are developed nations. This is often so since developed countries have resources to support research on value chains. Also, papers from developing countries such as Kenya are cited across the globe, indicating the quality of research output from the global south. In terms of average citation, countries such as Spain, Scotland, Denmark, and Greece top the list. This study delves deep into the bibliographic coupling of countries to examine the relationship between countries and studies related to agricultural value chains. The results are shown in **Figure 5**. The network consists of 45 nodes, each representing a country. The links between the nodes show the degree of cooperation with other countries, and the number of cooperation is indicated by the size of the nodes. Countries with larger nodes collaborate more globally. The node's colour indicates the cluster created and the orientation of agricultural value chain research based on the strength of cooperative relationships.

Figure 5 shows that the United States of America, the People's Republic of China, England, and Germany have the largest nodes. Therefore, the research aggregation in agricultural value chains is the strongest in these countries. The USA and England have the most connections with other countries; hence, they influence the research trajectory of other countries. In Africa, a few countries such as South Africa, Kenya, and Ethiopia have made headway in AVC research, and they collaborate with many emerging and developing countries. This indicates Africa is still developing in research output in the AVC field. Sub-Saharan Africa is home to the largest number of smallholder farmers in the world, many of whom still live in extreme poverty. Investing in research and development in this area will benefit rural livelihoods in Africa. The other notable feature from **Figure 5** is the closeness of links between countries; for instance, Thailand, Ghana, and the Netherlands. They are in green clusters showing that they have similar research interests.

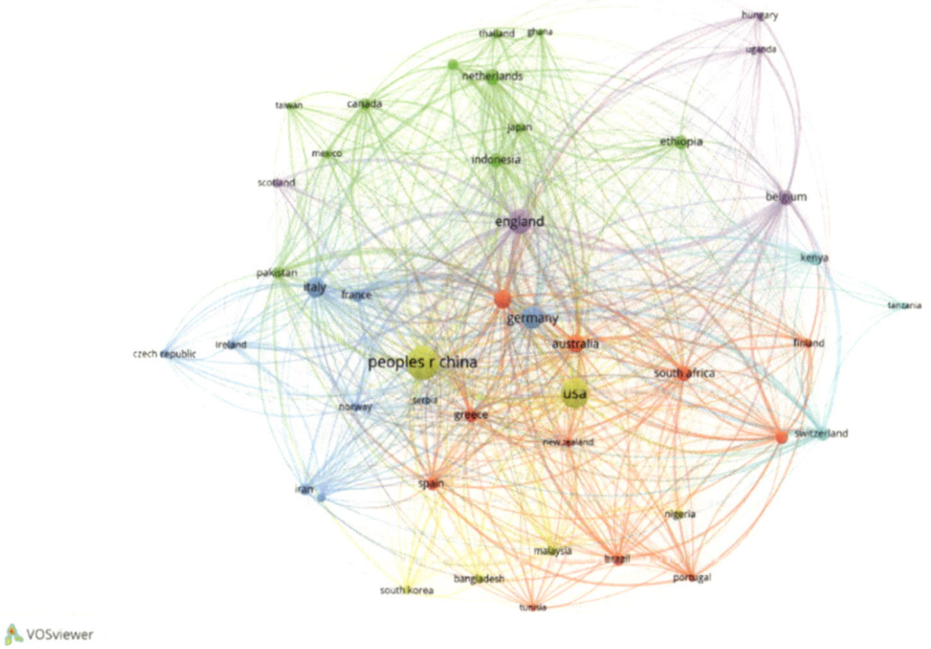

Figure 5.
Bibliographic coupling of most productive countries.

4.6 Co-occurrence analysis

The co-occurrence analysis highlights the most prominent and emphasised content, topics, or keywords within the agricultural value chains research domain. In VOSviewer, a keyword needed to appear at least five times to be considered, leading to 55 author keywords out of 2074 meeting this requirement. The findings in **Table 6** show that most of the studies were conducted on the agricultural supply chain, value chain, and food value chain. Other studies focused on management, value chain sustainability, and blockchain technology in agri-value chains.

Figure 6 illustrates the network of keywords commonly found in agricultural value chain research. Each node in the network represents one of the 55 keywords, with the node size reflecting the frequency of the keyword across various studies. Lines connecting nodes indicate co-occurrences of keywords in research studies, with the thickness of the line indicating the number of co-occurrences. The colours indicate the clusters to which the nodes belong, maintaining their significance [37]. From **Figure 6**, there are nine clusters for agricultural value chain research. The red cluster was the biggest with keywords that speak to the various aspects of the value chain, for example, value chains, global value chains, governance, and sustainable supply chain. The green cluster had words that focused on the utilisation of value chain analysis as an analytical tool in agriculture and the contribution of agri-value chains in reducing food waste and food security. Moreover, the blue cluster focused on technology adoption along the agri-value chains as indicated by keywords such as agri-food supply chain, blockchain, internet of things, traceability, and precision agriculture. The yellow cluster is like the blue cluster, however, with the addition of keywords such as innovation, big data, and e-commerce. The visualisation map in **Figure 6** shows areas of focus of past research in AVC and therefore determines future trajectory of research in this field.

4.7 Co-citation analysis

To identify and visualise the intellectual structure of agricultural value chains, the author co-citation analysis was performed. The fractional count was chosen in VOSviewer instead of full counting to enhance the impact of publications with long reference lists within the construction of the citation network. The minimum number of co-citations received by each author was set at 10. Out of the 22,479 authors, 159 met this threshold, and they were included in constructing the co-citation network. **Figure 7** shows that authors co-cited from the same publications were grouped into six different clusters. It is important to note that authors with more co-citations gravitate towards each other and four of the six clusters have bigger sizes than others.

It can be deduced from **Figure 7** that the blue cluster is the largest and it constitutes the most cited authors/institutions such as FAO, the European Commission, World Bank, and Gereffi, G. This cluster comprises the developer of the value chain concept (Poter, M), the modifier of Poter's work (Kaplinsky, R), and other that have led to the development of the global value chain concept and global value chain governance (Gereffi, G, Ponte, S). Moreover, authors such as Kaplinsky, R, Donovan, J and Bolwigs, S developed agricultural value chain analysis frameworks that work for smallholder farmers in developing countries.

The yellow cluster presents authors that worked on global food value chains (e.g., Reardon, T and Swinnen, J.F.M), general agricultural food value chains

Keyword	Occurrences
supply chain	93
value chain	64
agriculture	51
sustainability	51
food supply chain	37
covid-19	29
supply chain management	27
blockchain	24
value chain analysis	15
food security	14
food value chain	13
Ethiopia	12
food waste	12
climate change	11
food safety	11
governance	10
resilience	10
traceability	10
China	9
precision agriculture	9

Table 6.
Most relevant author's keywords.

(Barrett, C.B.), development of agricultural value chains in developing countries (Trienekens, J.H), and smallholder farmers' participation in these value chains and its benefits (Bellemare, M.F, Humphrey, J and Minten, B); and also agricultural value chain transformation (e.g., Sexton, R.J). Key researchers in the red clusters examined the rapid transformation currently taking place in the field of agricultural value chains (e.g., Kumar, A and Ivanov, D) and agri-value chain sustainability (Liu, Y) ensure through technology adoption (e.g., Kamble, S.S).

5. Discussion

This bibliometric review reinforced our understanding of global research trends in agricultural value chains. The study utilised performance analysis (citation analysis) and science mapping (co-citation and co-occurrence analysis). The data were analysed using VOSviewer and R-Studio. The initial task was to present the descriptive analysis of the articles included in this review, which was performed by presenting the production trend in **Figure 1**. Despite having restricted our search query to 2000–2024, our findings revealed that the first paper on agricultural value chains was published in 2005. The rapid increase in the number of publications from 2016

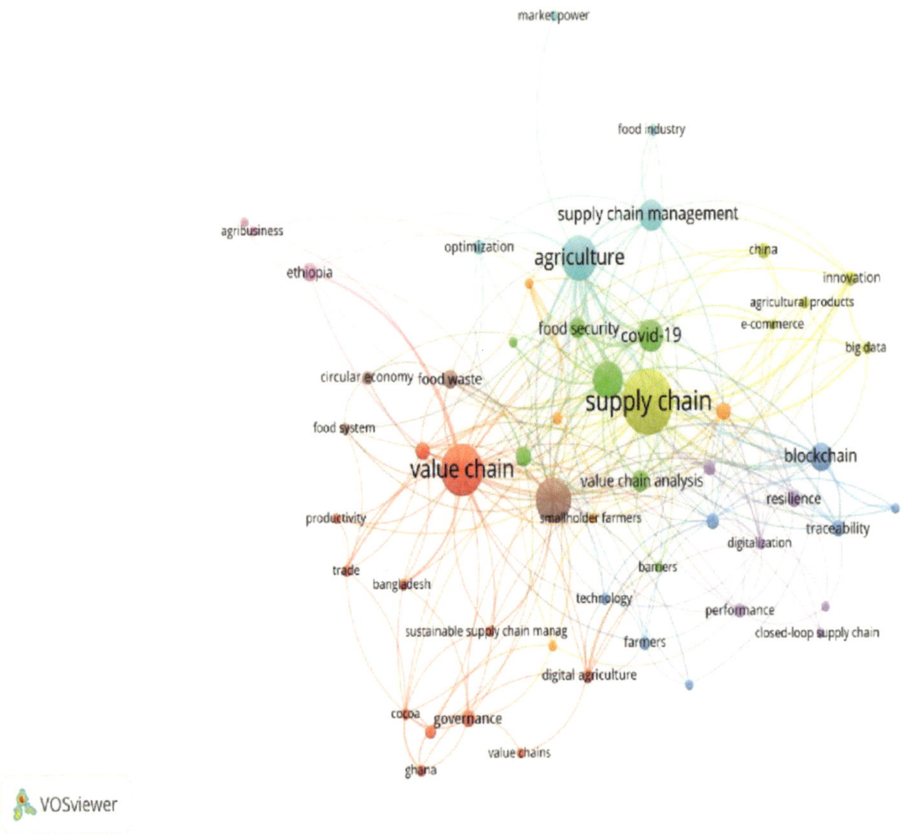

Figure 6.
Network visualisation of author's keywords.

to 2024 indicates a rising scholarly interest in agricultural value chains, underscoring their emerging significance in the agricultural landscape. This may be attributed to the transformation happening in the agricultural sector [7, 38]. Conventional farming systems have evolved into complex and dynamic agri-value chain systems, showing a paradigm shift towards integrated production, processing, and distribution networks [38]. This transformation in the agricultural sector is driven by factors such as rapid population growth, urbanisation, and rising consumer incomes [39]. The spike in the number of publications in 2021 can be attributed to global events such as COVID-19 that impacted global agricultural value chains, indicative of the fact real-world problems catalyses academic research. A bibliometric study [40] on the impact of COVID-19 on agricultural value chains revealed that most researchers focused on how the pandemic disrupted the value chains and how to increase their resilience. The absence of publications in 2006 and low publication numbers until 2016 point to the nascent stage of this research landscape. The upward trend in the research volumes shows a maturation of the field, with participation in agricultural value chains considered to improve household welfare [41, 42]. The results of this review concurred with the findings of Mensah et al. [38]. Their research mapped the field of value chains with a particular focus on the manufacturing industry. However, in mapping the global value chains Swinnen and Kuijpers [39] noted fluctuations in the number of publications.

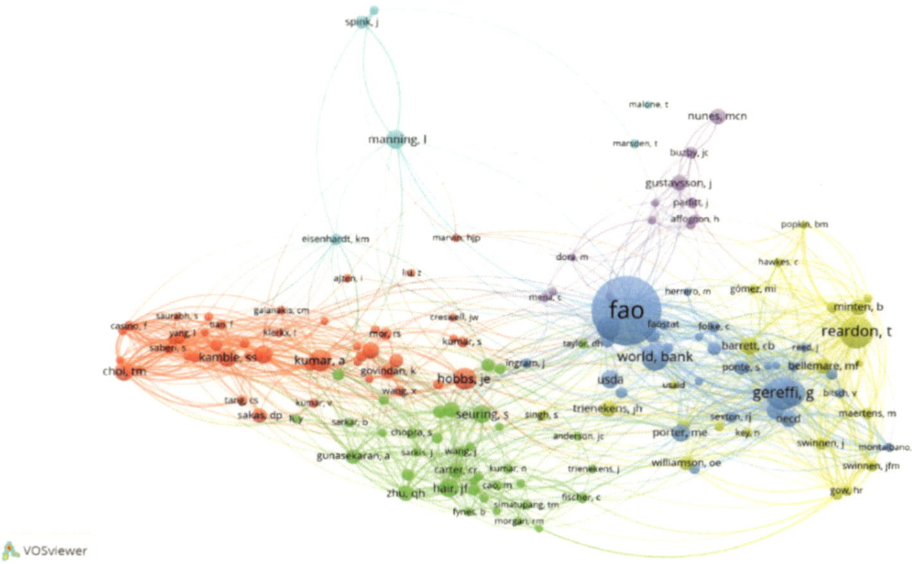

Figure 7.
Network visualisation for co-cited authors.

The study evaluated the contributions of authors, journals, and countries using citation analysis. **Table 3** indicates the influence of the most productive authors such as Butala, R., and Choi, T., whose work resonates significantly with the field of agricultural value chains, as testified by high citation counts from a single article. The disparities in mean citations, for example, the lower rate of authors such Soon, J.M., indicate the differing impact and the contribution on individual researchers in this research landscape. Ding et al. [43] stated scientific papers are the primary means through which scholars promote their findings. They garner attention through citations, which is peer recognition of their work. The essence of this task is not to only identify influential authors but to present a map for future emerging researchers to locate potential mentors and collaborators [30, 36]. An assessment of institutional impact (**Table 4**) shows varying outputs among universities and research institutions, with Humboldt University of Berlin in terms of the number of publications. On the contrary, using the citation impact the most influential institutions are Aristotle University of Thessaloniki, Cornell University, and Katholieke University Leuven. The disparities between the number of publications and total citations imply that while productivity is significant, the quality of the research and scholarly influence have a bearing on the ranking of the institution in this research field [44, 45].

The dominant positioning of journals such as the Sustainability Journal in **Figure 4** and **Table 5** indicates their crucial role in disseminating the research on agricultural value chain. The findings of this review, based on a wide range of citations across different journals, reveal that the field interact with multiple disciplines from logistics to food policy. This implies that agricultural value chains are complex, multifaceted, and dynamic in nature, hence requires diverse scholarly approaches to address complex real-world problems [46]. Additionally, using the citation analysis (**Table 7**) and bibliographic coupling (**Figure 5**), our results show geographic disparities in publication output. The dominance of developed

Country	Documents	Citations	Average Citation
USA	92	1826	19.85
Peoples R China	116	1448	12.48
England	62	1375	22.18
India	36	841	23.36
Germany	51	670	13.14
Spain	16	620	38.75
Greece	21	548	26.10
Italy	41	541	13.20
Belgium	24	507	21.13
Australia	32	370	11.56

Table 7.
Most productive countries.

countries such as the USA and England in terms of research output and total number of citations underscores inequality in resource distribution. However, the presence of emerging and developing countries such as China and Kenya indicates the importance of the inclusion of the Global South in crucial research pertinent to global development.

Finally, science mapping was performed using co-occurrence and co-citation analysis. The co-occurrence analysis sheds light on the thematic focal points in the field of agricultural value chains. The findings from co-occurrence analysis revealed that authors focused on various aspects of agricultural-value chains, for example analysing the smallholder farmers' participation in value chains, measuring the sustainability of the value chains, and incorporation of technology such as big-data analytics into agri-value chains. These results concur with the co-citation analysis with authors. **Figure 7** shows different clusters with authors that have focused on distinct aspects of agri-value chain, for instance, value chain development, value chain participation, and its impact in solving world problems such as food security.

6. Conclusion

This study presented a bibliometric review on global trends in agricultural value chain research. Bibliometric analysis provides an avenue for quantitative analysis of research output in this field. This was achieved through the utilisation of performance analysis (citation analysis, number of publications) and science mapping (co-citation analysis, co-occurrence analysis, and bibliographic coupling). The data used in this study were retrieved from the Web of Science and analysed using VOSviewer and R-Studio. Our findings revealed that the concept of agricultural value chains started gaining traction among researcher in the last decade. Most researchers focused on agricultural value chain analysis and value chain participation and its significance in raising the income, farm profits, and reducing poverty. Also, we noticed that most of the prolific authors, institutions, journals are from developed and emerging countries. Therefore, this study becomes vital to policymakers, researchers, and international organisations regarding current research trends, gaps, and most contributing authors. This study was limited to one database and two software for analysis. Therefore, future research should endeavour to utilise multiple databases and software for optimal results.

Conflict of interest

The authors declare no conflict of interest.

Author details

Kumbirai Takawira[1] and Nyarai M. Mujuru[2*]

1 Faculty of Agrisciences, Stellenbosch University, Stellenbosch, South Africa

2 Department of Agricultural Economics and Extension, University of Fort Hare, Alice, South Africa

*Address all correspondence to: nmujuru82@yahoo.co.uk

References

[1] Elawama A. The Influence of Natural and Human Factors on the Sustainability of Agriculture in Azzawia Libya. Penang, Malaysia: Universiti Sains Malaysia Penang; 2016

[2] Muflikh YN, Smith C, Aziz AA. A systematic review of the contribution of system dynamics to value chain analysis in agricultural development. Agricultural Systems. 1 Apr 2021;**189**:103044

[3] Kaplinsky R, Morris M. A Handbook for Value Chain Research. Brighton: University of Sussex, Institute of Development Studies Brighton; 6 Apr 2000

[4] Humphrey J, Navas-Alemán L. Value chains, donor interventions and poverty reduction: A review of donor practice. IDS Research Reports. 2010;**2010**(63):1-106

[5] Ma W, Abdulai A. The economic impacts of agricultural cooperatives on smallholder farmers in rural China. Agribusiness. 2017;**33**(4):537-551

[6] Maertens M, Velde KV. Contract-farming in staple food chains: The case of rice in Benin. World Development. 2017;**95**:73-87

[7] Singh H, Kumar S, Mittal S. Value chains of agricultural commodities and their role in food security and poverty alleviation–a synthesis. Agricultural Economics Research Review. 2011;**24**(1):169-181

[8] Ebrahim NA. Procedure to write a bibliometrics paper. Effective Use of Research and Publication Tools and Resources. 1 Mar 2016:1-48

[9] Tyagi S, Bharadwaj SN. Bibliometric analysis of papers published during 2016-2020 in 'Tulsi Prajna' research journal. Library Philosophy and Practice. 1 Mar 2021:1-18

[10] Aria M, Cuccurullo C. Bibliometrix: An R-tool for comprehensive science mapping analysis. Journal of Informetrics. 2017;**11**(4):959-975

[11] Verma S, Gustafsson A. Investigating the emerging COVID-19 research trends in the field of business and management: A bibliometric analysis approach. Journal of Business Research. 2020;**118**:253-261

[12] Donthu N, Kumar S, Mukherjee D, Pandey N, Lim WM. How to conduct a bibliometric analysis: An overview and guidelines. Journal of Business Research. 2021;**133**:285-296

[13] González-Torres T, Rodríguez-Sánchez J-L, Montero-Navarro A, Gallego-Losada R. Visualizing research on industrial clusters and global value chains: A bibliometric analysis. Frontiers in Psychology. 2020;**11**:565977

[14] Misra A, Mention A-L. Exploring the food value chain using open innovation: A bibliometric review of the literature. British Food Journal. 2022;**124**(6):1810-1837

[15] Malanski PD, Schiavi SM, Dedieu B, Damansceno JC. International research on labor in agri-food value chains: A bibliometric review from web of science. Frontiers in Sustainable Food Systems. 28 Oct 2022;**6**:852178

[16] Clay PM, Feeney R. Analyzing agribusiness value chains: A literature review. International Food and Agribusiness Management Review. 2019;**22**(1):31-46

[17] Gereffi G, Kaplinsky R. Introduction: Globalisation, value chains and development. IDS Bulletin. 2001;**32**(3):1-8

[18] Hellin J, Meijer M. Guidelines for Value Chain Analysis. Rome, Italy: Food and Agriculture Organization of the United Nations (FAO); 2006

[19] Donovan J, Franzel S, Cunha M, Gyau A, Mithöfer D. Guides for value chain development: A comparative review. Journal of Agribusiness in Developing and Emerging Economies. 2015;**5**(1):2-23

[20] Webber CM, Labaste P. Building Competitiveness in Africa's Agriculture: A Guide to Value Chain Concepts and Applications. World Bank Publications; 16 Dec 2009

[21] Llorente I, Baraibar-Diez E, Odriozola MD. Value chain analysis. In: Encyclopedia of Sustainable Management. Springer; 2022. pp. 1-8

[22] Rastuti U, Yunanto A, Jatmiko DP. Increasing the additional value of coffee cultivation results in Brebes regency with a value chain analysis approach. Quality-Access to Success. 2022;**23**(188)

[23] Herr ML. Local Value Chain Development. Colombo, Sri Lanka: International Labour Organization Enterprise for Pro-poor Growth (Enter-Growth); 2007

[24] GIZ. Valuelinks manual the methodology of value chain promotion. 2008. Available from: https://star-www.giz.de/dokumente/bib/07-0674.pdf

[25] M4P. Making Value Chains Work Better for the Poor. A Toolbook for Practitioners of Value Chain Analysis. Making Markets Work for Better for the Poor (M4P), UK Department for International Development (DFID). Phnom Penh, Cambodia: Agricultural Development International; 2008

[26] Lundy M, Amrein A, Hurtado Bermudez JJ, Becx G, Zamierowski N, Rodríguez F, et al. LINK methodology: A participatory guide to business models that link smallholders to markets. Version 2.0. 2014

[27] Riisgaard L, Bolwig S, Matose F, Ponte S, Du Toit A, Halberg N. A Strategic Framework and Toolbox for Action Research with Small Producers in Value Chains: DIIS Working Paper; 2008. Available from: https://www.econstor.eu/bitstream/10419/44681/1/573597898.pdf

[28] Mayoux L, Mackie G. Making the strongest links. In: A Practical Guide to Mainstreaming Gender Analysis in Value Chain Analysis. 2007. Available from: https://www.oitcinterfor.org/sites/default/files/Value%20Chain%20Design%20low%20res2%201.pdf

[29] Humphrey J, Schmitz H. Governance in global value chains. IDS bulletin. 2001;**32**(3):19-29

[30] Wang S, Gu Z. Mapping the field of value chain: A bibliometric and visualization analysis. Sustainability. 2022;**14**(12):7063

[31] Vinkler P. Indicators are the essence of scientometrics and bibliometrics: Comments to the book entitled "Bibliometrics and citation analysis, from the science citation index to Cybermetrics" from Nicola De bellis. Scientometrics. 2010;**85**(3):861-866

[32] Page MJ, McKenzie JE, Bossuyt PM, Boutron I, Hoffmann TC, Mulrow CD, et al. Statement: An updated guideline for reporting systematic reviews. BMJ. 2020;**2021**:372

[33] Sarkis-Onofre R, Agostini BA. Knowledge synthesis: How to improve the use of evidence from clinical trials? International Journal of Paediatric Dentistry. 2020;**31**:66-74

[34] Gao P, Meng F, Mata MN, Martins JM, Iqbal S, Correia AB, et al. Trends and future research in electronic marketing: A bibliometric analysis of twenty years. Journal of Theoretical and Applied Electronic Commerce Research. 2021;**16**(5):1667-1679

[35] Zupic I, Čater T. Bibliometric methods in management and organization. Organizational research Methods. 2015;**18**(3):429-472

[36] Farrukh M, Meng F, Wu Y, Nawaz K. Twenty-eight years of business strategy and the environment research: A bibliometric analysis. Business Strategy and the Environment. 2020;**29**(6):2572-2582

[37] Dede E, Ozdemir E. Mapping and performance evaluation of mathematics education research in Turkey: A bibliometric analysis from 2005 to 2021. Journal of Pedagogical Research. 2022;**6**(4):1-19

[38] Mensah JT, Adu G, Amoah A, Abrokwa KK, Adu J. What drives structural transformation in sub-Saharan Africa? African Development Review. 2016;**28**(2):157-169

[39] Swinnen J, Kuijpers R. Value chain innovations for technology transfer in developing and emerging economies: Conceptual issues, typology, and policy implications. Food Policy. 2019;**83**:298-309

[40] Das NK, Roy A. COVID-19 and Agri-food value chain: A systematic review and bibliometric mapping. Journal of Agribusiness in Developing and Emerging Economies. 2022;**12**(3):442-462

[41] Asfaw S, Lipper L, Dalton TJ, Audi P. Market participation, on-farm crop diversity and household welfare: Micro-evidence from Kenya. Environment and Development Economics. 2012;**17**(5):579-601

[42] Ngwako G, Mthenge M, Gido E, Kgosikoma K. Effect of market participation on household welfare among smallholder goat farmers in Botswana. Journal of Agribusiness and Rural Development. 2021;**60**(2):151-160

[43] Ding Y, Zhang G, Chambers T, Song M, Wang X, Zhai C. Content-based citation analysis: The next generation of citation analysis. Journal of the Association for Information Science and Technology. 2014;**65**(9):1820-1833

[44] Kinney A. National scientific facilities and their science impact on nonbiomedical research. National Academy of Sciences of the United States of America. 2007;**104**(46):17943-17947

[45] Moed HF, Moed HF. A comparative study of five world university rankings. Applied Evaluative Informetrics. 2017:261-285

[46] Muflikh YN, Smith C, Aziz AA. A systematic review of the contribution of system dynamics to value chain analysis in agricultural development. Agricultural Systems. 2021;**189**:103044

Chapter 8

An Overview of the European Research in Tourism, Leisure and Hospitality since the First Indexed Publication

Aitor Martinez-Garcia, Berta Ferrer-Rosell, Patricia Horrach-Rosselló and Carles Mulet-Forteza

Abstract

This document constitutes an overview of the research performed by authors whose main affiliation is in a European research institution, in the field of 'tourism, leisure and hospitality', since the first indexed publication in 1969. The method used includes measures, such as the most productive authors, institutions and countries, as well as relational techniques which depict results and allow for the analysis of the scientific and intellectual structure of the field, especially regarding the main topics addressed. Results show that Dimitrios Buhalis is the most productive author, authors from UK institutions are the most influential, UK and Spain are the most productive countries in terms of published articles and that the main topics addressed in the last decade refer to social media and climate change. Among the major implications are that it offers a retrospective overview of tourism research, contributes to the literature on research advances and it serves to identify the main research areas in this study.

Keywords: bibliometrics, tourism, leisure and hospitality, research productivity in Europe, WoS, VOSviewer software

1. Introduction

Research has increased significantly in the 'tourism, leisure and hospitality' (TLH) field over the last decade [1]. In fact, research in this field has become fundamental, directly contributing to the development of our society and economy. There are many ways of evaluating the research contributions. One of them is related to bibliometrics methods.

Recently, bibliometric studies in the TLH field have increased significantly. **Table A1** (see appendix) summarises some of those studies published since 2018 indexed in the Web of Science (WoS), grouping them by topic analysed.

Given this significant increase in bibliometric works in TLH, the goal of this chapter is to assess what other researchers have provided to this field, thereby complementing previous studies such as that of Mulet-Forteza et al. [2]. Some previous articles have presented research on a global level offering an overview of the tourism research [1]; others have undertaken studies for certain regions, such as Turkey [3–5] or Southeast Asia [6]; as observed in **Table A1**, many others have analysed the research on specific topics, such as sustainable tourism, trust, quality service, ICT and social media and tourism education [7] some studies have focused on specific journals [8]; others have addressed analysis on the evolution of topics of research combining bibliometrics with others methodologies [9]. Finally, it is noteworthy to highlight some guides to undertake bibliometric studies such as that of Mulet et al. [10].

The efficacy of bibliometric investigations is contingent upon their capacity to quantify the prominence of scholarly output within a given discipline. In addition to elucidating research productivity and impact, bibliometrics and reviews serve to corroborate assertions regarding the extent of research coverage and to delineate patterns for a comprehensive comprehension of the social processes underpinning the advancement of a particular field [11].

Our study complements that of Mulet et al. [2]. That work analysed the most cited documents, the co-citation among journals, the geographic patterns of collaboration and the main topics addressed in research from 1969 to 2018 in Europe. The citation structure indicated that the number of annual publications saw significant growth only after 2007. The co-citations between different journals revealed connections primarily within the 'hospitality, leisure, sports and tourism' category, with additional links to business and management journals. The study identified the 50 most cited documents and explored the geographic patterns of collaboration. The analysis of bibliographic coupling suggested collaboration trends between culturally or geographically proximate countries. Lastly, it revealed a high prevalence of keywords related to sustainable development. Our analysis aims to complement the mentioned work, revising the main topics addressed until 2021, and adding an analysis of the most prolific authors, institutions and countries in the TLH research field in Europe. The objectives of the study are specified in the following research questions:

- RQ1: Who are the European authors most productive in the field of TLH and what is the co-citation structure between them?
- RQ2: What are the European most productive institutions in the field of TLH and what is their bibliographic coupling?
- RQ3: What are the most productive countries in the TLH field and what is their bibliographic coupling?
- RQ4: What are the most prominent research topics analysed by authors whose main affiliation is a European institution in the TLH field?

Regarding RQ1 and RQ2, in line with works such as those of Martínez-García et al. [12], McKercher [13], Vishwakarma and Mukherjee [14] and Zhao et al. [15], we have analysed who are the authors from European institutions that have published the most in the TLH field. With regards to RQ3, we have selected all countries in the continent of Europe, not only those of the EU. RQ4 is in line with works in different disciplines: Lu et al. [16], Su et al. [17], Zhang [18] and Serrano et al. [19], which studied key topics addressed.

The article is divided as follows: next section presents the methodology, following section presents the results and their discussion. Finally, the last section offers the conclusions, limitations and implications of the document.

2. Methodology

Web of Science (WoS) is the most important database by the scientific community [20], which is the reason why it is used to undertake our work. Specifically, we have taken into consideration the journals indexed in June 2022 in the category 'Hospitality, Leisure, Sports and Tourism' as a starting point for the work, eliminating only those journals focusing strictly on sport. Once the journals that are part of the database were selected, the following was to refine the information offered by the database only for those documents affiliated with European countries. After applying these filters, the search returned 7597 documents. Only those having passed a strict arbitration process were considered, following works such as that of Coll-Ramis et al. [7], which is a total of 6587 documents.

In order to evaluate pertinent literature for this study, we implemented the preferred reporting items for systematic reviews and meta-analysis (PRISMA) flow diagram, recommended by authoritative scholars, including Munn et al. [21] Martinez-Garcia et al. [20] and Page et al. [22]. Deviating from the conventional application of PRISMA, we customised the flow by introducing a final phase or section dedicated to bibliometrics. This additional step involved a meticulous examination aimed at rectifying errors identified in the indexing of publications [23]. The graphical representation of this process through PRISMA is illustrated in **Figure 1**.

Given that there is no consensus in academia on the most appropriate bibliometric method, in this study we have used different bibliometric techniques [10]. In this

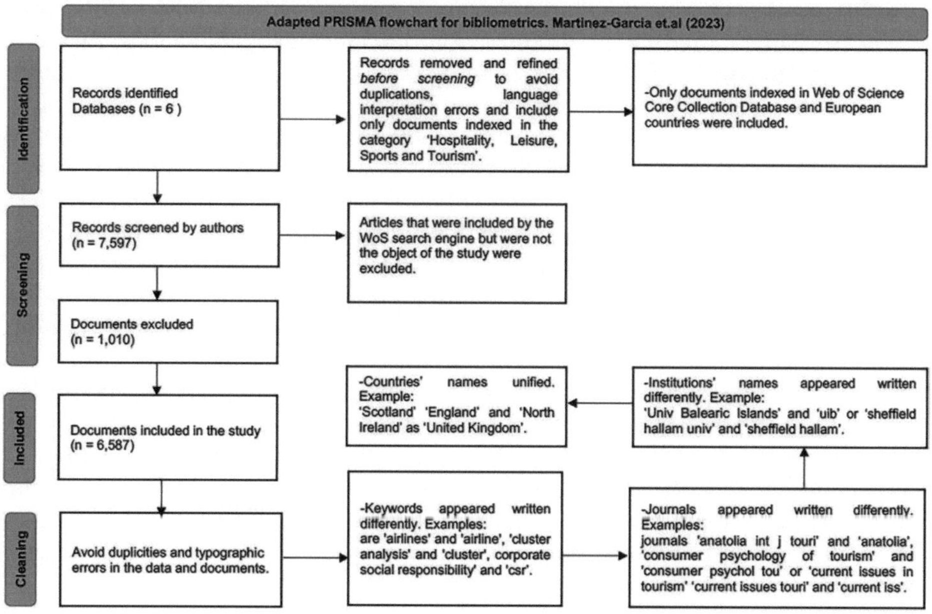

Figure 1.
Adapted PRISMA flowchart diagram applied.

regard, we use the number of publications and the number of citations, the *h*-index [24] and the volume of citations per document. These are indicators that combine both publications and citations in the same index. For that, *h*-index measures the number of documents that have obtained almost h citations, while the number of citations per document measures how influential each article is. Other measures included in this study are the authors, institutions and countries that have published the most; publications and citations per author from the most productive countries; general university classification such as 'Shanghai Ranking (ARWU)', and 'Quacquarelli Symonds (QS)'; publications per year; and most influential keywords. We have also depicted relational techniques [23] using the free software VOSviewer [25], such as co-authorship analysis, bibliographic couplings and author keyword co-occurrence. Co-authorship analysis refers to the production of a document by several authors; bibliographic coupling happens when two works cite a common third one in their reference lists indicating that there is a high probability that both works have addressed interconnected research topics [26]. Moreover, co-occurrence author key-words offer a map of the most frequent keywords used in the documents under analysis [23].

3. Results

First, we will analyse the first research question.

3.1 Most productive authors

In this section, we will assess the 50 most productive European authors and their co-citation structure, to answer RQ1.

Dimitros Buhalis (Bournemouth University, UK) is the author who has published the largest number of papers and with the highest number of citations, *h*-index and citations per paper. Other highly productive authors include Stephen John Page (University of Hertfordshire, UK), Stefan Gossling (Western Norway Research Institute, Norway), Xavier Font (University of Surrey, UK) and Tom Baum (University of Strathclyde, UK), all with 32 papers. With respect to the author's influence, Dimitros Buhalis is followed by Bill Bramwell, Stefan Gossling and Stephen John Page. That said, the numbers for Gang Li (University of Surrey, UK), Richard Sharpley (University of Central Lancashire, UK) and Annette Pritchard (Cardiff Metropolitan University, UK) are also very noteworthy, as they are in positions 5, 6 and 7, respectively, despite a lower number of publications, if **Table 1** is ranked by the volume of citations.

As for the *h*-index, it is observed that all of the authors in **Table 1** obtain at least an *h*-index of 7, with 39 of the 50 authors obtaining a two-digit *h*-index. Only three authors, Dimitrios Buhalis, Stefan Gossling and Bill Bramwell (Sheffield Hallam University, UK) obtain an *h*-index of 20 or above. As for authors with papers receiving 100 or more citations, we observe how Dimitros Buhalis again leads the ranking, obtaining more than twice the number of his immediate pursuers. In this regard, only 29 authors have a paper with 100 or more citations, while 46 have papers with at least 50 citations. Finally, 17 authors managed to have all their documents cited at least once, while another 20 managed to have all their documents except one cited.

Concerning the institutions represented in **Table 1**, we observe that the authors are distributed among 36 universities. Surrey is the University with the highest representation, with a total of six authors, followed by Bournemouth University, with four. We

R	Author	Institution	Country	TP	TC	SC	H	C/P	≥100	≥50	≥25	≥10	≥5	≥1
1	Buhalis, D	Bournemouth University	United Kingdom	40	4437	70	24	110.93	11	14	23	31	34	39
2	Gossling, S	Western Norway Research Institute	Norway	32	1530	59	21	47.81	3	9	21	27	27	32
3	Page, SJ	University of Hertfordshire	United Kingdom	32	1471	37	19	45.97	5	6	15	23	28	31
4	Font, X	University of Surrey	United Kingdom	32	1036	61	18	32.38	2	5	14	23	24	29
5	Baum, T	University of Strathclyde	United Kingdom	32	825	40	16	25.78	1	4	11	23	28	31
6	Bramwell, B	Sheffield Hallam University	United Kingdom	27	1752	56	20	64.89	5	11	19	22	25	25
7	McCabe, S	Nottingham University Business School	United Kingdom	27	700	22	14	25.93	1	4	10	15	24	27
8	Airey, D	University of Surrey	United Kingdom	26	909	7	14	34.96	1	7	11	16	21	24
9	Altinay, L	Oxford Brookes University	United Kingdom	26	652	22	14	25.08	1	3	9	17	22	26
10	Nijkamp, P	University Adam Mickiewicz of Poznań	Poland	24	438	19	10	18.25	1	2	5	10	16	22
11	Correia, A	University of Algarve	Portugal	24	322	21	11	13.42	0	1	5	11	17	20
12	Li, G	University of Surrey	United Kingdom	23	1142	22	14	49.65	2	4	10	16	17	22
13	Thrane, C	Inland Norway University of Applied Sciences	Norway	23	397	33	11	17.26	0	2	6	14	15	22
14	O'Gorman, KD	Heriot-Watt University	United Kingdom	23	198	19	9	8.61	0	0	1	8	13	21
15	Morgan, N	University of Surrey	United Kingdom	22	824	30	12	37.45	3	7	9	14	17	20
16	Cohen, SA	University of Surrey	United Kingdom	21	841	34	14	40.05	1	7	11	16	19	21
17	Ladkin, A	Bournemouth University	United Kingdom	20	904	9	12	45.20	2	6	11	13	14	20
18	Falk, M	Austrian Institute of Economic Research	Austria	20	256	14	9	12.80	0	1	2	9	12	17
19	Pritchard, A	Cardiff Metropolitan University	United Kingdom	19	1051	32	13	55.32	5	9	11	14	16	18
20	Smeral, E	MODUL University Vienna	Austria	19	415	32	9	21.84	0	3	5	9	12	19
21	Zehrer, A	MCI Management Centre Innsbruck	Austria	19	359	6	10	18.89	0	2	4	11	13	19
22	Sharpley, R	University of Central Lancashire	United Kingdom	18	1181	9	13	65.61	5	5	8	15	15	16
23	Alegre, J	University of the Balearic Islands	Spain	18	867	26	14	48.17	4	4	10	14	15	18
24	Barros, CP	University of Lisboa	Portugal	18	801	13	12	44.50	2	5	9	14	16	17
25	Baggio, R	Tomsk Polytechnic University	Russia	18	624	38	10	34.67	2	5	7	10	14	17
26	Larsen, S	University in Bergen	Norway	18	530	26	11	29.44	1	2	7	12	17	18
27	Kastenholz, E	University of Aveiro	Portugal	18	411	26	10	22.83	0	1	6	10	14	17

R	Author	Institution	Country	TP	TC	SC	H	C/P	≥100	≥50	≥25	≥10	≥5	≥1
28	Brown, L	Bournemouth University	United Kingdom	18	400	12	18	22.22	1	4	5	7	9	15
29	Laesser, C	University of St. Gallen	Switzerland	18	374	9	10	20.78	0	2	5	10	13	17
30	Coles, T	University of Exeter Business School	United Kingdom	18	324	11	11	18.00	0	2	2	12	16	18
31	Del Chiappa, G	University of Sassari	Italy	18	299	11	10	16.61	0	2	4	10	12	17
32	Cvelbar, LK	University of Ljubljana	Slovenia	18	290	14	10	16.11	0	1	4	11	14	17
33	Cooper, CP	Oxford Brookes University	United Kingdom	17	666	6	12	39.18	2	5	8	13	14	15
34	Mihalic, T	University of Ljubljana	Slovenia	17	661	15	9	38.88	2	4	5	9	11	14
35	Josiassen, A	Copenhagen Business School	Denmark	17	371	16	11	21.82	0	2	5	11	15	16
36	Garrod, B	Swansea University	United Kingdom	16	805	11	11	50.31	1	7	8	11	12	15
37	Witt, SF	University of Surrey	United Kingdom	16	776	19	15	48.50	2	5	9	15	15	16
38	Jacobsen, JKS	University of Stavanger	Norway	16	659	13	9	41.19	2	5	8	9	13	15
39	Prebensen, NK	University College of South-East Norway	Norway	16	652	25	10	40.75	4	5	8	10	11	15
40	Sainaghi, R	IULM University	Italy	16	541	56	11	33.81	0	4	8	12	15	16
41	Nawijn, J	Breda University of Applied Sciences	Netherlands	16	442	30	11	27.63	0	3	7	12	15	16
42	Ogaard, T	University of Stavanger	Norway	16	290	12	7	18.13	0	2	4	7	10	16
43	Taheri, B	Heriot-Watt University	United Kingdom	16	244	26	7	15.25	0	0	5	6	11	12
44	Pechlaner, H	Catholic University of Eichstätt – Ingolstadt	Germany	16	214	14	8	13.38	0	1	3	8	11	16
45	Gueguen, N	University of Bretagne-Sud	France	16	165	7	7	10.31	0	0	3	5	9	15
46	Jacob, C	University of Bretagne-Sud	France	16	165	7	7	10.31	0	0	3	5	9	15
47	Blake, AT	Bournemouth University	United Kingdom	15	758	13	14	50.53	3	4	11	14	14	15
48	Andriotis, K	University of London	United Kingdom	15	425	19	10	28.33	0	3	5	11	14	14
49	Beritelli, P	University of St. Gallen	Switzerland	15	389	19	10	25.93	1	2	4	10	10	14
50	Peters, M	University of Innsbruck	Austria	15	284	12	8	18.93	0	2	5	8	11	15

Notes: R: ranking; TP: total papers; TC: total citations; SC: self-citations; H: h-index; C/P: citations per paper: ≥100, ≥50, ≥25, ≥10, ≥5, ≥1: number of documents with at least 100, 50, 25, 10, 5 and 1 citation(s). Source: Web of Science, June 2022.

Table 1.
Most productive European authors in 'tourism, leisure and hospitality' according to the WoS.

find another six institutions (Oxford Brookes, University, Heriot-Watt University, University of Ljubljana, University of Stavanger, University of St. Gallen and University of Bretagne-Sud) with two authors in the ranking. In terms of countries, only 14 are represented in the table. The United Kingdom clearly leads with 23 authors followed at some distance by Norway and Austria with six and four representatives, respectively.

Another interesting analysis involves graphically visualising the co-authorship relationships that occur among the most influential European authors, as well as between them and the most productive and influential authors around the world. **Figure 2** presents a depiction of the main 100 connections between authors, considering a threshold of at least 15 documents.

Figure 2 shows a depiction of co-authoring among the main influential European authors publishing in the TLH field. **Figure 2** shows 11 groups of authors working together, although there are also relationships between the groups. The group with the largest volume of authors (in red) has nine representatives, including Stefan Gossling, Scott Cohen and Xavier Font, as well as New Zealander C. Michael Hall, who appears among the authors who have published more documents in this field worldwide [1]. The second most important group (in green) has eight authors, focused on the figures of Haiyan Song Scott McCbe and Levent Altinay. The third group in terms of importance (in dark blue) also has eight authors, with Larry Dwyer standing out. The remaining eight clusters are smaller, although we can see that most are headed by prominent authors in the TLH field, such as Albert Assaf, Sara Dolnicar, Dimitros Buhalis, Juan Gabriel Brida and Richard W. Butler, Richard W. Butler and Stephen John Page. Thus, we find that the most prominent European authors work closely with

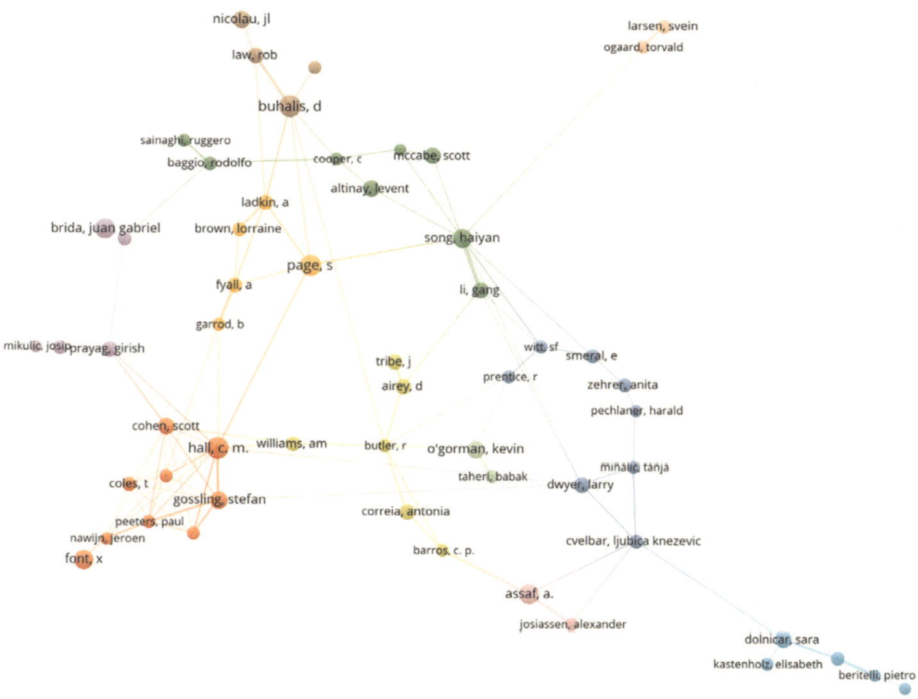

Figure 2.
Co-authorship with a citation threshold of 15 and the 100 most representative co-citation connections. Source: VOSviewer software.

the most prominent and influential authors in the field worldwide. Lastly, and with some exceptions, it can be observed (**Figure 2** and **Table 1**) that the results between the analysis performed considering fractional counting (VOSviewer software) and full counting (WoS) are similar.

3.2 Most productive institutions

The aim of this section is to determine the 50 European institutions that have published the most and their bibliographic coupling, together with their position in the ARWU (2021) and QS (2021). This analysis responds to RQ2.

Surrey and Bournemouth universities, both in the UK, are the most influential and productive institutions. In fact, six of the 50 most productive European authors are affiliated with the former institution, and four with the latter. Just seven institutions, five from the UK and the remaining two from Spain, have produced more than 100 documents. In terms of number of citations, the University of Balearic Islands (Spain) follows the two institutions mentioned above, although the citations obtained by the following institutions are also noteworthy: Sheffield Hallam University, University of Nottingham and University of Westminster of the United Kingdom and University of Valencia of Spain. Despite having a lower number of publications, they are placed in positions 4, 5, 7 and 8 if **Table 2** is ranked by number of citations.

As for the *h*-index, we observe that all the institutions in **Table 2** obtain at least an *h*-index of 10, although 20 of the 50 institutions obtain one of 20 or higher. As for those institutions with papers receiving 100 or more citations, we observe that the University of Surrey once again leads the way, with almost three times as many publications as its immediate pursuers. Concerning this, 40 institutions have at least one paper with 100 or more citations. These numbers improve if we count institutions with papers receiving 50 or more citations since in this case they all meet this criterion. Finally, only three institutions have had all of their papers cited at least once: the University of Canterbury, the University of Innsbruck and Edinburgh Napier University.

With regards to the countries represented in **Table 2**, we see that the 50 institutions are distributed among 11 European countries. The United Kingdom is the most represented country, with a total of 18 institutions, followed by Spain, with nine, and in third place the Netherlands, Portugal, and Sweden, with four institutions each.

As shown in **Table 2**, Edinburgh Napier University is the best institution ranked in the ARWU top 100, out of the 32 European institutions ranked in it. On the other hand, only three are ranked in the top 100 of the QS ranking, with Edinburgh Napier University also occupying the top position in this list (20). In total, 34 of these universities are represented in the QS ranking.

Another interesting analysis consists of graphically visualising the coupling bibliometric between main institutions. This is undertaken through the technique of bibliographic coupling. **Figure 3** presents a depiction of the main 100 connections between authors, considering a threshold of at least 25 documents.

Figure 3 contains three main nodes and two secondary nodes. The main node, in red, comprises 23 institutions, among which the University of Surrey and Bournemouth University stand out. We also observe that most of these institutions are in the United Kingdom. The second most important node, in green, is formed by 21 institutions, many of them belonging to northern European countries, such as Finland, Iceland and Sweden. The third node in importance, in blue, includes 20 institutions, most of them Spanish. The two secondary nodes are headed by the University of Ljubljana and the University of London, respectively. **Figure 2** shows how collaborations between institutions usually

R	Institution	Country	TP	TC	SC	H	C/P	≥100	≥50	≥25	≥10	≥5	≥1	ARWU 2019	QS 2020
1	University of Surrey	UK	273	11,187	343	58	40.98	30	71	119	179	216	257	301–400	274
2	Bournemouth University	UK	241	7189	231	41	29.83	12	34	75	143	173	222	—	701–750
3	University of Balearic Islands	Spain	117	3437	123	31	29.38	11	21	39	68	91	112	501–600	—
4	Leeds Beckett University	UK	111	2337	81	28	21.05	4	9	31	61	79	98	101–150	—
5	Oxford Brookes University	UK	107	2235	60	26	20.89	4	11	28	55	70	102	—	376
6	University of Strathclyde	UK	103	2667	93	32	25.89	2	14	38	67	82	100	501–600	296
7	University of Las Palmas de Gran Canaria	Spain	101	2263	102	25	22.41	3	17	25	42	70	92	—	—
8	University of Nottingham	UK	97	2909	64	31	29.99	7	20	36	60	75	93	101–150	96
9	University of Alicante	Spain	97	1859	64	25	19.16	1	11	25	46	68	88	801–900	701–750
10	University of Stavanger	Norway	81	1652	1595	21	20.40	3	8	16	38	62	79	—	—
11	University of Oulu	Finland	69	1779	87	23	25.78	2	8	22	40	53	68	501–600	374
12	Sheffield Hallam University	UK	68	2768	75	27	40.71	7	17	29	46	57	64	—	801–1000
13	University do Algarve	Portugal	68	907	51	18	13.34	0	2	12	32	46	58	—	—
14	University of London	UK	66	2004	28	24	30.36	3	12	24	41	52	64	—	—
15	Wageningen University Research	Netherlands	66	1173	41	17	17.77	2	4	12	37	46	53	101–150	125
16	University of Malaga	Spain	66	1051	42	18	15.92	1	6	12	33	44	64	801–900	—
17	Manchester Metropolitan University	UK	66	923	27	19	13.98	0	4	10	30	46	64	—	751–800
18	NHTV Breda University of Applied Sciences	Netherlands	63	1624	98	21	25.78	3	8	18	38	48	61	—	—
19	Free University of Bozen Bolzano	Italy	61	1062	66	18	17.41	2	5	13	31	41	58	701–800	—
20	University of Ljubljana	Slovenia	59	1710	44	17	28.98	5	8	13	25	38	53	401–500	591–600
21	University of Valencia	Spain	56	2413	22	19	43.09	5	9	15	25	44	55	401–500	581–590
22	Linnaeus University	Sweden	54	1654	59	21	30.63	4	8	17	33	36	49	—	—
23	University of Plymouth	UK	53	1232	17	19	23.25	3	4	11	32	40	46	801–900	651–700
24	University of Canterbury	UK	52	1876	52	24	36.08	4	10	24	36	41	52	401–500	227

R	Institution	Country	TP	TC	SC	H	C/P	≥100	≥50	≥25	≥10	≥5	≥1	ARWU 2019	QS 2020
25	University of Girona	Spain	52	913	29	18	17.56	0	4	11	28	39	47	—	—
26	University of Westminster	UK	50	2405	13	19	48.10	4	9	15	24	29	46	—	651–700
27	Middlesex University	UK	49	742	29	15	15.14	0	4	8	23	37	46	901–1000	801–1000
28	University of Innsbruck	Austria	48	1281	26	20	26.69	2	10	19	30	39	48	201–300	266
29	University of Lisboa	Portugal	48	1182	32	18	24.63	2	6	16	24	32	43	—	—
30	University of Eastern Finland	Finland	48	899	32	17	18.73	2	4	12	27	32	42	401–500	498
31	University of Barcelona	Spain	48	859	26	17	17.90	1	5	12	24	30	43	151–200	165
32	Lund University	Sweden	47	1595	38	22	33.94	2	9	21	34	35	46	101–150	92
33	The Arctic University of Norway	Norway	45	1045	43	17	23.22	4	7	11	24	30	40	—	389
34	University of Gothenburg	Sweden	45	956	23	15	21.24	3	8	11	23	28	39	101–150	256
35	University of Aveiro	Portugal	44	940	39	17	21.36	1	5	15	21	30	40	401–500	551–560
36	Cardiff Metropolitan University	UK	44	886	14	16	20.14	1	4	11	25	36	41	—	—
37	Mid Sweden University	Sweden	44	744	28	15	16.91	0	4	10	19	29	41	—	—
38	University of Exeter	UK	42	1452	22	16	34.57	5	8	14	28	34	40	151–200	163
39	University of Seville	Spain	42	595	15	14	14.17	0	2	9	18	30	39	501–600	601–650
40	Tilburg University	Netherlands	41	1690	14	21	41.22	5	12	18	23	28	37	501–600	371
41	University of Brighton	UK	41	1600	10	19	39.02	5	8	13	26	33	40	—	801–1000
42	Erasmus University Rotterdam	Netherlands	41	1588	4	20	38.73	4	13	20	31	37	39	79	183
43	University of Bologna	Italy	40	548	21	13	13.70	0	1	10	14	26	37	177	201–300
44	University of Sassari	Italy	38	656	15	15	17.26	0	4	10	20	24	35	801–900	—
45	Aalborg University	Denmark	38	522	14	14	13.74	0	1	5	21	27	35	201–300	324
46	University Institute of Lisbon	Portugal	38	408	15	10	10.74	0	1	4	13	25	36	151–200	338

R	Institution	Country	TP	TC	SC	H	C/P	≥100	≥50	≥25	≥10	≥5	≥1	ARWU 2019	QS 2020
47	University of Granada	Spain	37	570	25	15	15.41	1	2	6	17	24	35	201–300	511–520
48	Edinburgh Napier University	UK	36	755	30	14	20.97	1	3	5	18	30	36	32	20
49	Cardiff University	UK	36	717	12	16	19.92	1	5	8	20	27	29	101–150	154
50	Modul University Vienna	Austria	36	601	11	12	16.69	1	2	7	17	29	35	—	—

Notes: *R: ranking; TP: total papers; TC: total citations; SC: self-citations; H: h-index; C/P: citations per paper: ≥100, ≥50, ≥25, ≥10, ≥5, ≥1: number of documents with at least 100, 50, 25, 10, 5 and 1 citation(s); ARWU 2019: Academic Ranking of World Universities, 2011; QS 2021: Quacquarelli Symonds World University Ranking, 2020. Source: Web of Science, June 2022.*

Table 2.
Most productive European institutions in 'tourism, leisure and hospitality' according to the WoS.

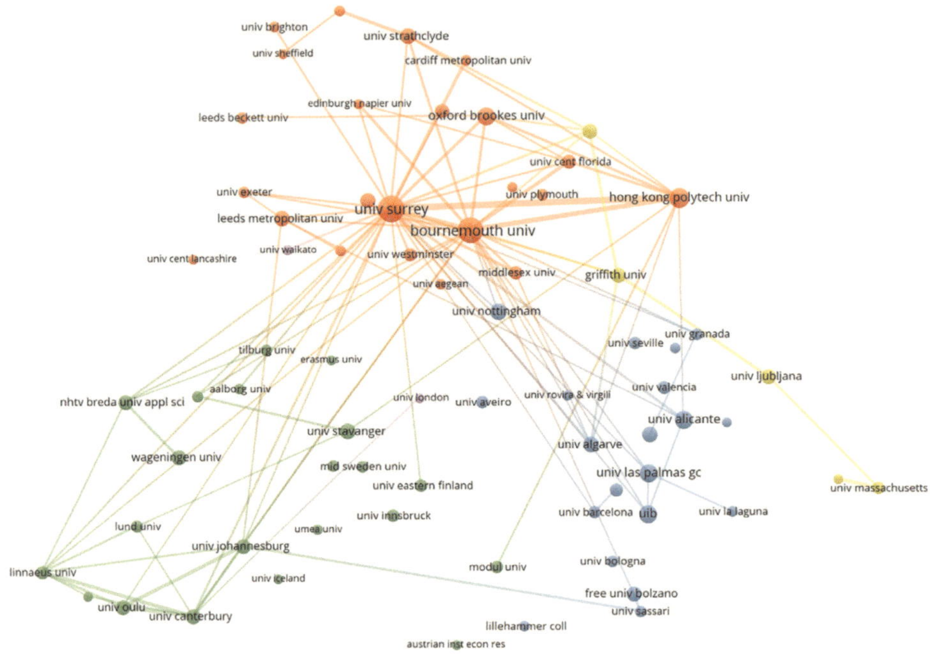

Figure 3.
Bibliographic coupling with a citation threshold of 25 and the 100 most representative co-citation connections. Source: VOSviewer software.

take place between areas that are geographically close to one another, although the two leading institutions, University of Surrey and Bournemouth University, maintain important connections with the rest of the nodes as well. Finally, and with some exceptions, it can be observed (**Figure 3** and **Table 2**) that the results between the analysis performed considering full counting and the fractional counting are similar.

3.3 Most productive countries

To address RQ3, in this section, we analyse the 30 European countries that have published the most and the bibliographic coupling between them.

The countries that have published the most and that have got the largest volume of citations, in the TLH field, are the UK and Spain, while only 14 countries have produced 100 documents or more. Analysing countries by number of citations, the top 10 ranking does not change substantially with respect to that referring to number of documents. The only difference is Finland being replaced in the top 10 by Denmark. Regarding the h-index, 23 countries in **Table 3** have a two-digit h-index, the UK being the only country with three digits.

As for those countries where institutions have had papers with at least 100 citations, we observe that the UK again leads the ranking, obtaining more than three times as many publications as its immediate pursuers. In this regard, 21 countries have at least one paper with 100 or more citations. These numbers increase if we analyse countries with papers that have received 50 or more citations, since 25 meet this criterion. Finally, only Bulgaria and Lithuania have had all their works cited.

If we analyse productivity per million inhabitants, we see that the ranking changes substantially, since in this case it is led by Iceland, Norway and Cyprus, both in terms

R	Country	TP	TC	S/C	H	C/P	≥100	≥50	≥25	≥10	≥5	≥1	Pop	TP/Pop	TC/Pop
1	UK	2298	66,354	5752	114	28.87	145	371	727	1314	1689	2151	66.04	34.80	1004.75
2	Spain	1065	25,240	2210	69	23.70	44	129	273	517	742	983	46.72	22.80	540.24
3	Italy	418	7465	560	45	17.86	8	40	93	194	276	386	60.59	6.90	123.21
4	Netherlands	356	9434	391	48	26.50	23	47	99	200	272	335	17.08	20.84	552.34
5	Norway	334	6945	432	43	20.79	14	33	72	167	239	323	5.26	63.52	1320.84
6	Sweden	275	5486	291	41	19.95	8	31	67	135	178	251	10.00	27.51	548.87
7	Portugal	270	4085	235	35	15.13	3	15	57	105	171	244	10.31	26.19	396.22
8	Austria	218	4224	190	37	19.38	3	22	55	122	164	210	8.77	24.85	481.48
9	Finland	203	3898	219	33	19.20	5	17	48	122	164	190	5.50	36.89	708.34
10	Germany	202	4223	85	38	20.91	4	19	57	113	149	191	82.79	2.44	51.01
11	France	198	3881	68	31	19.60	8	16	42	85	133	180	66.99	2.96	57.93
12	Switzerland	169	3072	73	29	18.18	3	14	38	87	121	158	8.42	20.07	364.85
13	Denmark	149	4275	104	34	28.69	8	20	45	93	118	142	5.75	25.92	743.61
14	Greece	138	3095	76	29	22.43	5	12	38	87	107	133	10.77	12.81	287.37
15	Poland	83	990	36	15	11.93	2	3	9	25	42	67	38.43	2.16	25.76
16	Slovenia	79	1997	56	20	25.28	5	9	18	33	50	71	2.07	38.24	966.60
17	Belgium	66	1669	18	20	25.29	5	10	18	38	48	63	11.35	5.81	147.05
18	Cyprus	54	1530	25	20	28.33	3	9	17	32	35	51	0.85	63.17	1789.89
19	Iceland	45	554	71	14	12.31	0	1	6	20	30	42	0.34	133.00	1637.36
20	Croatia	42	526	19	10	12.52	0	3	5	12	24	40	4.15	10.11	126.62
21	Serbia	39	286	12	10	7.33	0	0	3	11	20	33	7.02	5.55	40.73
22	Hungary	27	295	11	10	10.93	0	1	2	11	21	26	9.80	2.76	30.11
23	Russia	26	155	4	8	5.96	0	0	1	4	12	23	144.50	0.18	1.07

R	Country	TP	TC	S/C	H	C/P	≥100	≥50	≥25	≥10	≥5	≥1	Pop	TP/Pop	TC/Pop
24	Czech Republic	18	295	2	8	16.39	1	2	2	7	12	17	10.58	1.70	27.88
25	Estonia	17	356	7	10	20.94	1	2	3	10	14	16	1.32	12.92	270.52
26	Bulgaria	17	202	12	7	11.88	0	0	2	5	10	17	7.10	2.39	28.44
27	Romania	13	106	1	6	8.15	0	0	2	4	8	12	19.64	0.66	5.40
28	Slovakia	12	223	2	8	18.58	0	0	4	8	8	10	5.44	2.21	41.03
29	Lithuania	8	192	2	4	24.00	1	1	1	3	4	8	2.85	2.81	67.42
30	Malta	7	99	0	4	14.14	0	1	1	1	3	5	0.46	15.21	215.08

Notes: R: ranking; TP: total papers; TC: total citations; SC: self-citations; H: h-index; C/P: citations per paper: ≥100, ≥50, ≥25, ≥10, ≥5, ≥1: number of documents with at least 100, 50, 25, 10, 5 and 1 citation(s); Pop: population in millions of inhabitants; TP/Pop: documents by inhabitants, in millions; TC/Pop: citations per inhabitants, in millions. Source: Web of Science, June 2022.

Table 3.
Most productive European countries in 'tourism, leisure and hospitality' according to the WoS.

of number of citations and documents per million inhabitants, although in a different order. It is notable that the UK continues to hold a privileged position among the countries that receive the largest volume of citations per million inhabitants, despite being the fourth country with the highest number of inhabitants in the previous table.

3.4 Main research topics

Next, and responding to RQ4, in **Figure 4**, we have analysed a chronological evolution of the main research topics. **Figure 4** depicts the main 100 connections between authors, considering a threshold of 25 documents.

Figure 4 shows the main keywords that have been used in the TLH field since 2012. The most prominent keyword is 'tourism' (in green), and it seems that out of all documents considered in the analysis, those containing it have been published mainly between the years 2012 and 2013.

The next most dominant keyword is 'hotel' (in orange). And thus, out of all the documents included in the analysis, those containing 'hotel' have been published mainly in 2014. The same can be commented for the keyword 'leisure' (yellow). On the other hand, most keywords related to sustainable development started to garner interest after 2014. The figure shows how topics related to cultural tourism and

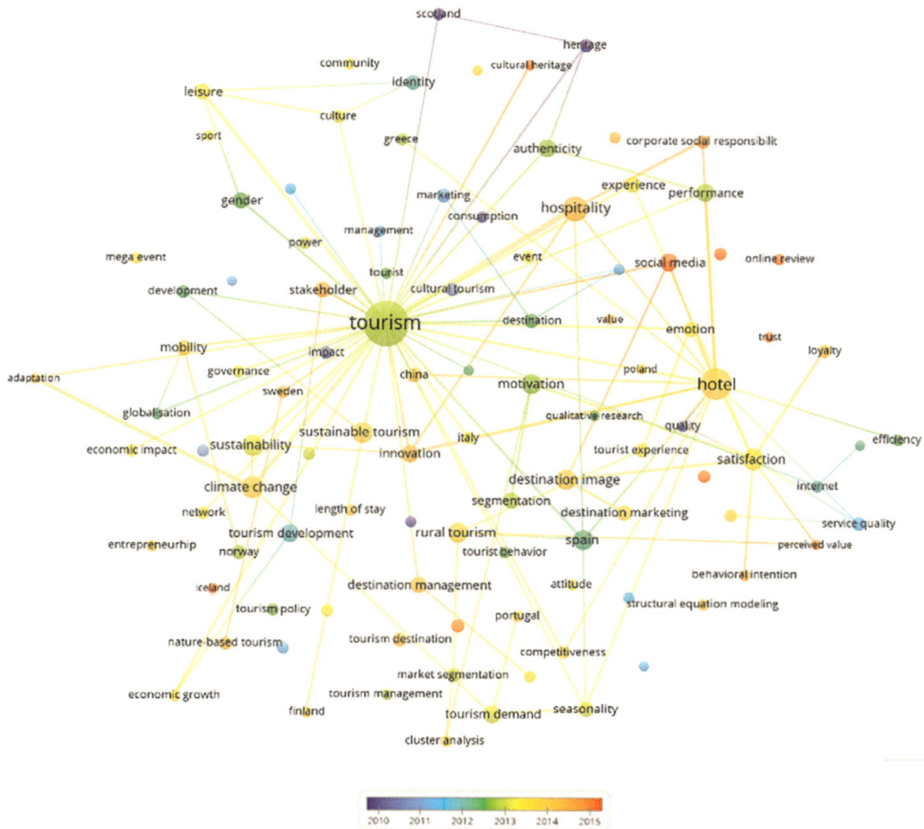

Figure 4.
Co-occurrence of author keywords with a citation threshold of 25 and the 100 most representative co-citation connections. Source: VOSviewer software.

tourism heritage were a trending topic prior to 2010. Topics related to gender studies, tourism development and its impacts, and other topics related to tourist behaviour stood out between 2011 and 2013. Finally, from 2014 onwards, the main topics addressed have been hospitality, corporate social responsibility, sustainability, social media, climate change and rural tourism. Therefore, the topics connected to social media, and the impacts of tourism on destinations, especially due to climate change and the problems of overtourism, will offer important opportunities in future [27].

4. Conclusions

This chapter undertakes a bibliometric analysis and endeavours to delineate the intellectual and conceptual framework of research in Europe pertaining to tourism and hospitality since 1969. Our study complements previous works such as those of Mulet et al. [2] and adopts a comprehensive approach utilising bibliometric methods to scrutinise the trajectory of research from 1969 to 2021. The employed methodology incorporates bibliometric techniques, including productivity measures and graphical mapping, to assess prominent authors, their co-authorship relationships, noteworthy institutions and countries and the evolution of research themes within this domain.

The study presented a bibliometric analysis in the TLH field, of researchers from European institutions. The objectives outlined have been achieved. Regarding the first research question, the 50 most productive authors have been analysed, as well as their citation structure. Dimitrios Buhalis is the most prominent author, holding the highest *h*-index, the major number of citations and citations per document. The second most productive author is Stefan Gossling. The main topics addressed by the most cited documents by the most productive authors coincide with the most used keywords. The number of authors affiliated with UK institutions is much higher than authors affiliated with other countries' institutions. Furthermore, the co-authorship analysis shows how the most prominent European authors in the TLH field closely collaborate with the most prominent and influential authors worldwide [1].

Productivity and relational measures (bibliometric techniques) have allowed us to determine the 50 most productive institutions, and together with their position in ARWU and QS rankings, RQ2 has been responded to. Out of the five most productive universities, 18 are based in the UK, while the rest are distributed among the other 10 countries. In fact, the two most productive universities are in the UK (Surrey and Bournemouth). Only 32 of the 50 most productive universities appear in the ARWU ranking, while 34 were in the QS ranking. The highest-rated institution in both rankings is Edinburgh Napier University.

Regarding the third research question (RQ3), the 30 most productive countries have been analysed. The UK is the top country, followed by Spain. Finally, as far as RQ4 is concerned, we have analysed the most prominent research topics in this field. Results show that social media and climate change will provide great potential opportunities for research.

As all studies, this also has limitations. The first limitation refers to the database used. WoS covers more than 75 million records in the main collection [28], while other databases, such as Google Scholar, cover more than 400 million records [29]. This lack of coverage of WoS causes a large part of the academic literature to be excluded from its records, especially that advocates the epistemologies and worldviews of the Global

South [30]. Another limitation of WoS database is that it collects the records based on the full counting method. To solve this limitation, it has also been considered fractional counting through VOSviewer software. The last limitation regards the analysed field cross, which means that some documents published in TLH were published in other research fields [20].

Still acknowledging the above-mentioned limitations, the study is sound and rigorous enough, and it offers a perspective of the state of the art of TLH research. This study increases the recent literature of documents that analyse the evolution of accomplishments, results and trends of research fields considering long periods of time. To identify the evolution of the main addressed topics helps to determine intellectual connections in the analysed field [31, 32]. In this respect, the depiction of intellectual connections helps to create new theories as well as further develop the existing ones, providing a new vision of what scientific research directions may take in the near future [33]. Secondly, the bibliometric overview presents a full picture of the TLH field allowing academics to focus on areas, providing new knowledge to the existing literature [34]. Thirdly, the results of the study help to identify those authors, institutions and countries offering major potential to share and develop research with them [35]. Fourthly, the study covers a long-time scope, which allows academics to get a full picture and its evolution of the addressed field. Finally, with the aim of providing knowledge about the evolution and research trends in the TLH field, the citation patterns have been analysed. This analysis offers a good starting point for new studies in other fields, also considering different bibliometric perspectives.

Appendix

Title	Topic	Author(s)	Journal/ conference	Year
Competitiveness in the tourism sector: a bibliometric analysis	Competitiveness	Estevao, C.; Costa, C.; Fernandes, C.	J. of Spatial and Organizational Dynamics	2019
Bibliometric visualisation: An application in tourism crisis and disaster management research	Crisis	Jiang, Y.W.; Ritchie, B.W. Benckendorff, P.	Current Issues in Tourism	2019
Tourism and its economic impact: A literature review using bibliometric tools	Economics	Comerio, N.; Strozzi, F.	Tourism Economics	2019
Food and gastronomy research in tourism and hospitality: A bibliometric analysis	Gastronomy	Okumus, B.; Koseoglu, M. A.; Ma, F.	International J. of Hospitality Management	2018
30 years of contemporary hospitality management uncovering the bibliometrics and topical trends	Hospitality Management	Ali, F.; Park, E.; Kwon, J.; Chae, B.	International J. of Contemporary Hospitality Management	2019
Forty-three years journey of tourism recreation research: A bibliometric analysis	Journal	Vishwakarma, P.; Mukherjee, S.	Tourism Recreation Research	2019

Title	Topic	Author(s)	Journal/ conference	Year
Twenty-five years of the journal of travel & tourism marketing: A bibliometric ranking	Journal	Mulet-Forteza, C.; Martorell-Cunill, O.; Merigó, J.M.; Genovart-Balaguer, J.; Mauleon-Mendez, E.	J. of Travel & Tourism Marketing	2018
Tourism research in the new millennium: A bibliometric review of literature in tourism and hospitality research	Journal	Strandberg, C.; Nath, A.; Hemmatdar, H.; Jahwash, M.	Tourism and Hospitality Research	2018
Thirty-fifth anniversary of the international journal of hospitality management: A bibliometric overview	Journal	Cunill, O.M.; Salva, A.S.; Gonzalez, L.O.; Mulet-Forteza, C.	International J. of Hospitality Management	2019
Twenty years of tourism geographies: A bibliometric overview	Journal	Merigó, J.M.; Mulet-Forteza, C.; Valencia, C.; Lew, A.A.	Tourism Geographies	2019
Religious tourism and pilgrimage: Bibliometric overview	Religious	Duran-Sanchez, A.; Alvarez-Garcia, J.; del Rio-Rama, M.D.; Oliveira, C.	Religions	2018
Quality in tourism literature: A bibliometric review	Research Quality	Garrigos-Simon, F.J.; Narangajavana-Kaosiri, Y.; Narangajavana, Y.	Sustainability	2019
A bibliometric analysis of knowledge development in smart tourism research	Social Media	Johnson, A.G.; Samakovlis, I.	J. of Hospitality and Tourism Technology	2019
A bibliometric analysis of social media in hospitality and tourism research	Social Media	Nusair, K.; Butt, I.; Nikhashemi, S.R.	International J. of Contemporary Hospitality Management	2019
A bibliometric analysis of trust in the field of hospitality and tourism	Trust	Palácios, H; de Almeida, MH; Sousa, MJ	International J. of Hospitality Management	2021
Mapping tourism and hospitality research on ICT: A bibliometric and scientific approach	ICT	Molina-Collado, A; Gómez-Rico, M; Sigala, M; Molina, MV; Aranda, E; Salinero, Y	Information Technology and Tourism	2022
Using bibliometric methods to shed light on the concept of sustainable tourism	Sustainable Tourism	Serrano, L.; Sianes, A.; Ariza-Montes, A.	Sustainability	2019
Sustainable tourism in the open innovation realm: A bibliometric analysis	Sustainable Tourism	Della Corte, V.; Del Gaudio, G.; Sepe, F.; Sciarelli, F.	Sustainability	2019
Tourism research on sustainability: A bibliometric analysis	Sustainable Tourism	Ninerola, A.; Sanchez-Rebull, M.V.; Hernandez-Lara, A.B.	Sustainability	2019
Sustainable tourism in sensitive areas: Bibliometric characterisation and content analysis of specialised literature	Sustainable Tourism	Sanchez-Canizares, S.M.; Castillo-Canalejo, A.M.; Cabeza-Ramirez, L.J.	Sustainability	2018

Title	Topic	Author(s)	Journal/ conference	Year
Sustainability and competitiveness in the tourism industry and tourist destinations: A bibliometric study	Sustainable Tourism	Segui-Amortegui, L.;Clemente-Almendros, J. A.; Medina, R.; Gala, M.G.	Sustainability	2019
Tourism and sustainability: A bibliometric and visualisation analysis	Sustainable Tourism	Garrigos-Simon, F.J.; Narangajavana-Kaosiri, Y.; Lengua-Lengua, I.	Sustainability	2018
A tri-method approach to a review of adventure tourism literature: Bibliometric analysis, content analysis and a quantitative systematic literature review	Tourism Research	Cheng, M.M.; Edwards, D.; Darcy, S.; Redfern, K.	J. of Hospitality & Tourism Research	2018
Cooperation and coauthorship pattern in the field of tourism: Bibliometric and social networks analysis in 14 Brazilian national scientific journals (1990–2016)	Tourism Research	Kohler, A.F.; Digiampietri, L.A.; de Almeida, G.S.	EM Questao	2019
Bibliometric analysis of bibliometric studies on tourism published in Turkey	Tourism Research	Yilmaz, I.	Anais Brasileiros de Estudos Turisticos-ABET	2019
#10yearschallenge: How co-creation permeated tourism research. A bibliometric analysis	Tourism Research	Tregua, M.; D'Auria, A.; Costin, H.	European J. of Tourism Research	2020
Bibliometric analysis of tourism research on the north coast of Honduras between 1988 and 2018	Tourism Research	Ramos-Zúniga, T.V.; Chávez-Dagostino, R.M.	LiminaR	2019
Bibliometric analysis of tourism research on the City of Girona	Tourism Research	Meneguel, C.R.D.; Rubio, S.P.; Mundet, L.	Rosa Dos Ventos-Turismo e Hospitalidade	2019
Tourism and photography: A bibliometric study of using image analysis methodologies in tourism research	Tourism Research	Godoy, K. E.; Leite, I.	LiminaR	2019
Bibliometric analysis of tourism research for the period 2007–2016	Tourism Research	Guzeller, C.O.; Celiker, N.	Advances in Hospitality and Tourism Research-AHTR	2018
Bibliometric analysis of the Minority Sports Tourism Research in Yunnan	Tourism Research	Zhou, Y.; Zhu, J.	Proceedings of ERSS	2018
A bibliometric research in the tourism, leisure and hospitality fields	Tourism Research	Mulet-Forteza, C.; Genovart-Balaguer, J.; Mauleon-Mendez, E.; Merigó, J.M.	J. of Business Research	2019

Title	Topic	Author(s)	Journal/ conference	Year
Research progress in tourism, leisure and hospitality in Europe (1969–2018)	Tourism Research	Mulet-Forteza, C., Lunn, E., Merigó, J. M., & Horrach-Rosselló, P.	International Journal of Contemporary Hospitality Management	2020
Relational bibliometrics for hospitality and tourism research: A best practice guide	Guides	Koseoglu, MA; Yick, MYY; King, B; Arici, HE	Journal of Hospitality and Tourism Marketing	2022
Bibliometric studies in the hospitality and tourism field: A guide for researchers	Guides	Mulet-Forteza, C.; Genovart-Balaguer, J.; Horrach-Rosselló, P.	Contemporary Research Methods in Hospitality and Tourism	2022

Source: Web of Science, January 2023.

Table A1.
Bibliometric documents published in the web of science. Years 2018–2022.

Author details

Aitor Martinez-Garcia[1*], Berta Ferrer-Rosell[2], Patricia Horrach-Rosselló[1] and Carles Mulet-Forteza[1]

1 Department of Business Economics, University of the Balearic Islands, Palma de Mallorca, Spain

2 Faculty of Law, Economics and Tourism, Lleida, Spain

*Address all correspondence to: aitor.martinez@uib.es

References

[1] Mulet-Forteza C, Genovart-Balaguer J, Mauleon-Mendez E, Merigó JM. A bibliometric research in the tourism, leisure and hospitality fields. Journal of Business Research. 2019;**101**:819-827

[2] Mulet-Forteza C, Lunn E, Merigó JM, Horrach P. Research progress in tourism, leisure and hospitality in Europe (1969–2018). International Journal of Contemporary Hospitality Management. 2020;**33**(1):48-74

[3] Köseoglu MA, Sehitoglu Y, Parnell JA. A bibliometric analysis of scholarly work in leading tourism and hospitality journals: The case of Turkey. Anatolia. 2015;**26**(3):359-371

[4] Yilmaz I. Bibliometric Analysis of Bibliometric Studies on Tourism Published in Turkey. ABET [Internet]. 2019;**9**(1, 2 e 3). Available from: https://periodicos.ufjf.br/index.php/abet/article/view/2711

[5] Evren S, Kozak N. Bibliometric analysis of tourism and hospitality related articles published in Turkey. Anatolia. 2014;**25**(1):61-80

[6] Naruetharadhol P, Gebsombut N. A bibliometric analysis of food tourism studies in Southeast Asia. Cogent Business & Management. 2020;**7**(1): 1733829

[7] Coll-Ramis MÀ, Horrach-Rosselló P, Genovart-Balaguer J, Martinez-Garcia A. Research progress on the role of education in tourism and hospitality. A bibliometric analysis. Journal of Hospitality & Tourism Education. 2023: 1-13. DOI: 10.1080/10963758.2023.2180377

[8] Cunill OM, Salva AS, Gonzalez LO, Mulet-Forteza C. Thirty-fifth anniversary of the International Journal of Hospitality Management: A bibliometric overview. International Journal of Hospitality Management. 2019;**78**:89-101

[9] Wang G, Wang H, Wang L. Research trends in tourism and hospitality from 1991 to 2020: An integrated approach of corpus linguistics and bibliometrics. Journal of Hospitality and Tourism Insights. 2023;**6**(2):509-529

[10] Mulet-Forteza C, Genovart-Balaguer J, Horrach-Rosselló P. Bibliometric studies in the hospitality and tourism field: A guide for researchers. In: Contemporary Research Methods in Hospitality and Tourism. Leeds: Emerald Publishing Limited; 2022. pp. 55-76 DOI: 10.1108/978-1-80117-546-320221005

[11] Mukherjee D, Lim WM, Kumar S, Donthu N. Guidelines for advancing theory and practice through bibliometric research. Journal of Business Research. 2022;**148**:101-115

[12] Martínez-García A, Horrach-Rosselló P, Valluzi C, Mulet-Forteza C. The impact of the European Accounting Review on accounting research (1992-2019). De Computis - Revista Española de Historia de la Contabilidad. 2021;**18**(2):98-142

[13] McKercher B. A citation analysis of tourism scholars. Tourism Management. 2008;**29**(6):1226-1232

[14] Vishwakarma P, Mukherjee S. Forty-three years journey of Tourism Recreation Research: A bibliometric analysis. Tourism Recreation Research. 2019;**44**(4):403-418

[15] Zhao W, Ritchie JB. An investigation of academic leadership in tourism

research: 1985–2004. Tourism Management. 2007;**28**(2):476-490

[16] Lu Y, Wang Y, Li B, Li J, Jiang H. Temporal and spatial variations in haze research: A bibliometric analysis. Environmental Reviews. 2020;**28**(1): 12-20

[17] Yanbing S, Ruifang Z, Chen W, Shifan H, Hua L, Zhiguang D. Bibliometric analysis of Journal of Nursing Management from 1993 to 2018. Journal of Nursing Management. 2020; **28**(2):317-331

[18] Zhang X. A bibliometric analysis of second language acquisition between 1997 and 2018. Studies in Second Language Acquisition. 2020;**42**(1): 199-222

[19] Serrano L, Sianes A, Ariza-Montes A. Using bibliometric methods to shed light on the concept of sustainable tourism. Sustainability. 2019;**11**(24):6964

[20] Martinez-Garcia A, Horrach-Rosselló P, Mulet-Forteza C. Mapping the intellectual and conceptual structure of research on CoDa in the 'Social Sciences' scientific domain. A bibliometric overview. Journal of Geochemical Exploration. 2023;**250**: 107273. DOI: 10.1016/j.gexplo.2023.107273

[21] Munn Z, Peters MD, Stern C, Tufanaru C, McArthur A, Aromataris E. Systematic review or scoping review? Guidance for authors when choosing between a systematic or scoping review approach. BMC Medical Research Methodology. 2018;**18**(1):1-7

[22] Page MJ, McKenzie JE, Bossuyt PM, Boutron I, Hoffmann TC, Mulrow CD, et al. The PRISMA 2020 statement: An updated guideline for reporting systematic reviews. International Journal of Surgery. 2021;**88**:105906

[23] Martinez-Garcia A, Horrach-Rosselló P, Mulet-Forteza C. Evolution and current state of research into E-learning. Heliyon. 2023;**9**(10):e21016

[24] Hirsch JE. An index to quantify an individual's scientific research output. Proceedings of the National academy of Sciences. 2005;**102**(46):16569-16572

[25] Van Eck N, Waltman L. Software survey: VOSviewer, a computer program for bibliometric mapping. Scientometrics. 2010;**84**(2):523-538

[26] Martyn J. Bibliographic coupling. Journal of Documentation. 1964;**20**(4): 236-236

[27] Mercadé-Melé P, Almeida-García F, Martinez-Garcia A, Coll-Ramis MA. Hotel Rooftops as a Space for Consumption in Historic Centres: The Case Study of Palma (Spain). Land. 2023;**12**(3):657. DOI: 10.3390/land12030657

[28] Birkle C, Pendlebury DA, Schnell J, Adams J. Web of Science as a data source for research on scientific and scholarly activity. Quantitative Science Studies. 2020;**1**(1):363-376

[29] Gusenbauer M. Google Scholar to overshadow them all? Comparing the sizes of 12 academic search engines and bibliographic databases. Scientometrics. 2019;**118**(1):177-214

[30] Corona BS. Flujos metodológicos desde el Sur latinoamericano. La Zona de la Comunicación y las Metodologías Horizontales. Comunicación y Sociedad. 2017;**30**:69-106

[31] Koseoglu MA, Mehraliyev F, Xiao H. Intellectual connections in tourism

studies. Annals of Tourism Research. 2019;**79**:102760

[32] Köseoglu MA, Okumus F, Dogan IC, Law R. Intellectual structure of strategic management research in the hospitality management field: A co-citation analysis. International Journal of Hospitality Management. 2019;**78**:234-250

[33] Köseoglu MA, Mehraliyev F, Aladag OF, King B. Origins, evolution and themes of scholarly hospitality sources: 1960–2019. International Journal of Hospitality Management. 2021;**94**:102817

[34] Ghorbani Z, Kargaran S, Saberi A, Haghighinasab M, Jamali SM, Ale EN. Trends and patterns in digital marketing research: Bibliometric analysis. Journal of Marketing Analytics. 2022;**10**:158-172. DOI: 10.1057/s41270-021-00116-9

[35] Law R, Chon K. Evaluating research performance in tourism and hospitality: The perspective of university program heads. Tourism Management. 2007; **28**(5):1203-1211